MARIE ANTOINETTE
STYLE

MARIE ANTOINETTE
STYLE

Edited by
SARAH GRANT

V&A PUBLISHING

Exhibition sponsored by

MANOLO BLAHNIK

With support from Kathryn Uhde

First published by V&A Publishing to accompany
the exhibition *Marie Antoinette Style*, on view from
20 September 2025 to 22 March 2026 at the
Victoria and Albert Museum, South Kensington,
London SW7 2RL – vam.ac.uk/publishing

This exhibition has been made possible by the
provision of insurance through the Government
Indemnity Scheme. The V&A would like to thank
HM Government for providing Government Indemnity
and the Department for Culture, Media & Sport and
Arts Council England for arranging the indemnity.

Inspirations: capturing Marie Antoinette
Text © Antonia Fraser

Distributed in North America by Abrams, an
imprint of ABRAMS.
V&A Publishing books are represented in the
UK and Europe by Abrams & Chronicle Books,
1 West Smithfield, London, EC1A 9JU, UK and
57 rue Gaston Tessier, 75166 Paris, France
abramsandchronicle.co.uk
info@abramsandchronicle.co.uk

The moral right of the authors has been asserted.

ISBN 9781 83851 054 1 (Hardback)
ISBN 9781 83851 066 4 (Paperback)

10 9 8 7 6 5 4 3 2
2029 2028 2027 2026 2025

A catalogue record for this book is available from
the British Library.

Front cover: detail of fig.68
p.2 detail of fig.50
p.5 detail of fig.165

Designer: Daniela Rocha
Copyeditor: Kate Bell
Indexer: Nic Nicholas
New V&A photography: Kieron Boyle

Reprographics by Dexter
Printed in Italy by Printer Trento

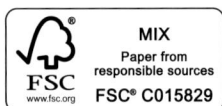

FSC
MIX
Paper from
responsible sources
FSC® C015829
www.fsc.org

V&A Publishing
The power of creativity

Discover more at vam.ac.uk

p.6
MARIE ANTOINETTE'S FOLLY **(DETAIL) BY
BETH KATLEMAN, 2025**
PORCELAIN, MIRROR AND WIRE.
PHOTOGRAPH BY ALAN WIENER

p.10
**'ANTONIETTA' SHOE DESIGNED BY MANOLO
BLAHNIK FOR THE 2006 *MARIE ANTOINETTE*
FILM, DIRECTED BY SOFIA COPPOLA**

CONTENTS

FOREWORD

Tristram Hunt
DIRECTOR, V&A

'Marie Antoinette', declared the British ambassador to the French court in 1784, 'is all graciousness but talks too much english Politicks'. The Queen of France was a devoted Anglophile with an intense interest in all that went on across the Channel. This fascination was returned – the British, too, avidly followed her every move, from her spectacular wedding to her terrible end. After Marie Antoinette's death, British collectors were instrumental in preserving and reviving her style, snapping up the queen's former collections that came to auction. Among them was John Jones, whose 1882 bequest to the then South Kensington Museum helped to make it one of the greatest collections of eighteenth-century French decorative arts in the world. One of his most prized pictures was a portrait of the 17-year-old dauphine in sumptuous court dress. So it is fitting that the first exhibition on Marie Antoinette ever to be held in Britain be staged here, at the Victoria and Albert Museum.

This exhibition would not have been possible without the blessing and generous support of the Musée national des châteaux de Versailles et de Trianon. I extend my gratitude to Christophe Leribault, President of the Établissement public du château, du musée et du domaine national de Versailles; Laurent Salomé, Director of the Musée national des châteaux de Versailles et de Trianon; Frédéric Lacaille, Conservateur général, en charge des peintures du XIXe siècle et des prêts aux expositions; and to Hélène Delalex, Conservatrice en chef du patrimoine Mobilier & Objets d'art.

Other French institutions have lent precious objects belonging to Marie Antoinette, some of which have never left Paris before: I particularly wish to acknowledge and thank Bruno Ricard, Director of the Archives nationales, Laurence des Cars, President-Director of the Musée du Louvre, and Valérie Guillaume, Director of the Musée Carnavalet.

We are grateful for Manolo Blahnik's generous sponsorship of the exhibition, and would also like to thank Kathryn Uhde for her continued support. We thank Richard Mansell-Jones for his support in the preparation of this book.

Our exhibition marks the 270th anniversary of Marie Antoinette's birth, and for the first time since the queen's death we have brought together some of her only very recently resurfaced jewels and reunited them with her personal jewellery box. The exhibition has also occasioned an opportunity to reassemble most of the surviving fragments of the queen's long-lost wardrobe – again, a moment of real historical significance.

To demonstrate the extraordinary legacy of Marie Antoinette's influence as an early modern style icon, we draw on the V&A's exceptional collections of historical dress and textiles, together with objects from other collections across the museum. By placing Marie Antoinette at the heart of her own story, we hope to draw out the complexities of this charismatic and very human figure, one whose presence, in the words of eighteenth-century English politician, Horace Walpole, 'effaced all the rest'.

FOREWORD

Kristina Blahnik
CEO, MANOLO BLAHNIK

We are thrilled to support the first exhibition dedicated to Marie Antoinette at the Victoria and Albert Museum, celebrating the enduring legacy of a figure whose style has shaped her timeless appeal and influence. This partnership is especially meaningful, as it reflects my uncle's admiration of the former Queen of France – not only her lasting charm but also the profound impact she has had on his designs.

The exhibition beautifully bridges past and present, fantasy and playfulness, echoing the unconventional, uncompromising spirit that defines us as well. It is an honour to contribute to this extraordinary showcase, furthering our commitment to supporting the arts and education.

FOREWORD

Manolo Blahnik

I have been obsessed with Marie Antoinette for as long as I can remember. My mother, who adored and revered her, read the Stefan Zweig biography to me as a child – skipping the horrific end at the guillotine, of course. I was instantly captivated by Zweig's account of the youngest daughter of the formidable Empress Maria Theresa of Austria, plucked away from her native country aged 14 and transplanted to the court of Versailles, where she would flourish, becoming the most talked about monarch in French history.

Since then, Marie Antoinette has been a constant in my life and in my work. How could she not be? A woman of such style, who broke away from the plethora of formalities dictated by court etiquette and revolutionized eighteenth-century women's court dress, shunning protocol to replace damasks, corsets and crinolines with a less structured and rigid form of dressing (albeit still sumptuous). Let us not forget that she was a Habsburg and had their innate taste of simplicity, although using the most exquisite materials and embroidery. Over the years, there has not been a book about her that I have not read, nor a film that I have not seen. I am to this day enraptured by everything about her and by the following that she posthumously created.

Marie Antoinette has been a recurrent source of inspiration in my work and her influence can be traced back to my earliest collections. Serendipitous moments with her followed. When I was asked by Milena Canonero to design the shoes for Sofia Coppola's 2006 film, it was, for me, a privilege. I made the shoes myself, by hand in England, using the most exquisite Lyon silks from Claremont and sumptuous English embroideries from Stephen Walters. Details like the rosettes on the shoes and the silks I frayed myself. I instinctively knew how they needed to be created. It was important for me to get them perfectly right, while Canonero's dictum to 'not be academic' rang in my ears. For our Palais Royal Paris store opening, I designed a collection evoking Marie Antoinette's style, using prints and silks from Valencia like the ones Rose Bertin would send to the French court. The queen knew what she wanted to wear and certainly had her very own view of it. Every woman in the court and beyond aspired to dress like her.

It is an honour for me to be part of such a momentous presentation at the V&A and to celebrate the first exhibition about Marie Antoinette in London.

MARIE-ANT.ᵀᴱ D'AUTRICHE,
Reine de France et de Navarre.

INTRODUCTION: MARIE ANTOINETTE STYLE

Sarah Grant

'All eyes will be on you.'
Maria Theresa, Empress of Austria,
to her daughter, Marie Antoinette, 1770[1]

In a letter written only a few hours after Marie Antoinette had departed Vienna for Versailles, Maria Theresa, Empress of Austria, set out in detail, to the child she had just farewelled and would never see again, a long series of instructions, or in modern parlance, a survival guide, for her daughter's new life in France. Maria Theresa had never visited Versailles but with her characteristic acuity she grasped the magnitude of the challenge that lay ahead for Marie Antoinette at this most famous of European courts, cautioning her: 'All eyes will be on you'.

As her mother foresaw, Marie Antoinette went on to become one of the most closely scrutinized queens in history. But what is it about Marie Antoinette that has continued to draw the gaze and interest of successive generations in the 232 years following her death? There is a unique alchemy in the personal characteristics of this young queen and the tumultuous circumstances in which she found herself that few have been indifferent to. She is a complex figure whose style, youth and notoriety have all contributed to her timeless appeal. The name Marie Antoinette continues to operate as a byword for frivolity and excess, but at the same time her tragic story is one that captivates: married at the age of 14, queen at 18 and guillotined at 37. And while it is usually the names of male monarchs that are attached to style epochs, it was unequivocally Marie Antoinette, and not Louis XVI, who was instrumental in creating a timeless style, which designers and the creative industries continue to embrace today.

In recent decades, curators and historians have overturned the longstanding view of the ill-fated queen as a vacuous profligate, but her considerable influence as an artistic patron and style icon is still being explored. This book considers the Marie Antoinette style: how Marie Antoinette, the person, shaped not just the fashion, design, interiors, gardens, fine and decorative arts of her own time but has continued to exert an influence over more than two and a half centuries of graphic and decorative arts, fashion, photography, film and performance.

In its time, the Marie Antoinette style marked a deliberate shift away from the heavily ornate formality and rigidity of the past. It was provocatively modern and, at times, controversial. The style is elegant, fresh and feminine, characterized by naturalistic floral patterns, a palette both pastel and bright, of embroidered silks, printed cottons, diaphanous muslins and blonde lace, white biscuit porcelain, white and gold panelling, real and silk flowers, and wood marquetry. Over time, elaborate p.12

1. PORTRAIT OF MARIE ANTOINETTE
(AGED 19), 1777
JEAN-FRANÇOIS JANINET (1752–1814),
AFTER JEAN-BAPTISTE ANDRÉ GAUTIER-
DAGOTY (1740–1786), COLOUR ETCHING AND
AQUATINT ON PAPER, 40.8 × 31.9 CM.
V&A: BRYAN BEQUEST E.422–1905

2. INTERIOR OF MARIE ANTOINETTE'S
FORMAL BEDCHAMBER
WITH A PORTRAIT BUST OF MARIE ANTOINETTE
BY FÉLIX LECOMTE (1737–1817) ON THE
CHIMNEYPIECE, CHÂTEAU DE VERSAILLES

3. BUST OF MARIE ANTOINETTE (AGED 26),
1788 (AFTER A MARBLE BUST OF 1781)
LOUIS SIMON BOIZOT (1743–1809), SÈVRES SOFT-
PASTE BISCUIT PORCELAIN, 40.7 × 26 × 15 CM.
V&A: C.367–1983

powdered coiffures and glittering parures gave way to more natural hair and simple jewels. Interiors and furniture became intimate in size and purpose. Fashions became increasingly streamlined and relaxed.

This style came at a cost, as the charge of gross expenditure with which the queen was confronted at her trial in 1793 made clear to her. Historians agree, however, that by the time Marie Antoinette arrived in 1770, France was already in dire financial straits and primed for a revolution, following decades of overspending by previous monarchs.[2] The cost of maintaining the court under the

reign of Louis XVI represented six per cent of the national budget, but it was a cost that was far more visible than the ruinous spending on wars. Marie Antoinette's predecessor, Marie Leszczyńska (1703–1768), also spent lavishly but had none of her conviviality, showed a slavish devotion to court etiquette and lived quietly and devoutly, giving birth to 10 children. As queen consort, with no political role, Marie Antoinette's purpose was one of soft power: she was expected to support the luxury-goods trade and French manufactories, patronizing artists and artisans in the centuries-old courtly tradition.

In many ways, Marie Antoinette proved modern and forward-thinking, particularly in her significant patronage of some of the first professional women artists and the influential female côterie she assembled at court. She showed her receptiveness to aspects of Enlightenment thought with her enthusiasm for Anglomania and by embracing new approaches to maternity, becoming the first French queen to nurse her own children. In 1784, the royal governess to Marie Antoinette's children, the duchesse de Polignac, gave their notoriously hard-living English friend, the Duchess of Devonshire, some frank advice that reflects the surprisingly advanced attitudes within the queen's circle, telling her,

> I fear that the life you lead is very much the opposite of that which is necessary to nurse. If you have the courage to rest, to go to bed early, I approve of your project very much. Without this precaution, allow me to tell you that not only would it be wrong for you to feed, but even for your child.[3]

Marie Antoinette's receptiveness to Enlightenment ideals is also reflected in her adoption of new thinking towards health, in particular the consumption of milk and dairy products, seen in the now famous *jatte téton/bol-sein* or 'breast cup' – one of four from the Sèvres Rambouillet dairy service delivered in 1787 – which has led to the persistent though erroneous belief that it was modelled on the queen's own breast, inspiring modern-day examples (fig.4). The cup was in fact copied directly from an antique source: a Greek drinking cup in the shape of a woman's breast known as a 'mastos'.

Marie Antoinette also supported new technologies such as copper-plate printed textiles and biscuit porcelain, and was particularly influential in her patronage of the fashion and textile industries. The woven silks and printed cottons she adopted in her wardrobe and interiors bolstered these and other trades while her likeness provided the template for the mannequins seen in many late eighteenth-century fashion plates.

4. *BOL-SEIN* (BREAST CUP) FROM A SERVICE MADE FOR MARIE ANTOINETTE'S DAIRY AT RAMBOUILLET, 1787
JEAN-JACQUES LAGRENÉE THE YOUNGER (1739–1821) AND LOUIS SIMON BOIZOT (1743–1809), SÈVRES SOFT- AND HARD-PASTE PORCELAIN, 16 × 12.2 × 13.4 CM. SÈVRES MUSÉE NATIONAL DE CÉRAMIQUE: INV. MNC 23400

Yet there is also an inherent tension between the queen's enlightened interests and the brutal realities of the *ancien régime*. Marie Antoinette's reign was also a period in which the spectre of European colonialism loomed darkly in a myriad of complicated ways, through precious materials extracted for use in the luxury trades, the appropriation of styles, such as chinoiserie and turquerie, fashions inspired by territories under colonial subjugation (such as the infamous *chemise à la reine*) and, in particular, the significant wealth brought to France and the French court by their involvement in the traffic of enslaved people and coerced labour.[4]

At Versailles, Marie Antoinette encountered both free and enslaved Africans and African Europeans, most famously the master-fencer and composer, Joseph Bologne, chevalier de Saint-George (1745–1799) – whom the American diplomat and later, president, John Adams, described as 'the most accomplished Man in Europe' – and

Painted by M.ʳ Brown. Engraved by W. Ward.

MONSIEUR DE S.ᵗ GEORGE.

From an Original Picture at M.ʳ H. Angelo's Academy.

Dans les armes jamais on ne vit Son Égal ;
Aucun n'a jamais eu Comparateur habile.
En page au Patin et la Chasse, à Cheval,
Tout s'exerce avec Lui Semble facile.
dans tous ce qu'on a un Ange Original.

Si sortir n'est talens autant de modestie
Fait le rare plus utile de l'Heureux Français ;
Si que l'on a un Esprit exempt de jalousie
Va trouve le Bonheur en cette Courte vie
que dans les vrais amis que l'on a cœurs Soient faits.

Publish'd April 4.ᵗ 1790 by Bowles in S.ᵗ Coventry Street.

probably also the Haitian-born French general, Thomas-Alexandre Dumas (1762–1806); both of whom would later join the revolutionary cause (fig.5).[5] There was also Jean Amilcar (c.1782–1796), the freed son of enslaved parents who was brought from Senegal to Versailles in 1787 by an officer of the African battalion at the request of the French governor, the comte de Boufflers, and 'presented' to the queen as part of an inhumane practice by Boufflers and others to ingratiate themselves at court.[6] Marie Antoinette adopted Amilcar and financed his education at a Saint-Cloud boarding school until her imprisonment and execution. Tragically, the 14-year-old boy fell ill and died three years later.

The presence of an African or African-descended servant in the queen's household is also indicated by their appearance in two of her equestrian portraits by Louis-Auguste Brun (1758–1815) from about 1783, though their identity and circumstances are still to be established.[7] At the same time, laws of racial exclusion were in operation such as Louis XVI's edict of 1777, the *Déclaration du roi pour la police des noirs*. The legacies of colonialism, particularly in a vibrant toile-de-Jouy revival, can be seen in the work of contemporary artists and designers such as Renée Green and Victor Glemaud (see Banić and Harpley in this volume, pp.127–30).

Outside the court structure, to the people of France, and with the monarchy's rapidly receding authority, Marie Antoinette's style symbolized unattainable and unimaginable luxury and for this reason it can be seen to have hastened her path to the guillotine. In the revolutionary years, her style and her own image were turned against her. Royal manufactories that she had supported, such as Sèvres and Christophe-Philippe Oberkampf's printed cotton factory at Jouy-en-Josas, now issued wares brandishing revolutionary symbols. In a particular stroke of irony, the toiles de Jouy – whose idealized bucolic aesthetic in furnishing and floral dress textiles had been so enthusiastically embraced by the queen, and with which her style is still inextricably linked – now featured a design showing a humbled king and queen pledging their allegiance to the new regime (see fig.89). In explicit satirical imagery the figure of the queen many subjects knew from portraits circulated in reproductive prints and other commemorative designs across the decorative arts, became a wicked, debauched and monstrous creature (see Slater in this volume). Influential even in death, the queen's execution drove a craze during the Terror for black clothing, a contemptuous form of mock mourning, red-ribbon chokers – symbolizing the mark of the guillotine blade – and the 'porcupine' hairstyle, which imitated the shorn hair of condemned women.[8]

Throughout the nineteenth century Marie Antoinette was memorialized by royalist sympathizers and her style was revived under Empress Eugénie (1826–1920), who was

responsible for the establishment of a Marie Antoinette 'cult', in which objects and fashions associated with the queen were fetishized (see McQueen in this volume). Eugénie invoked Marie Antoinette in the creation of her own imperial persona, choosing to be painted and photographed dressed as the queen and inaugurating the first exhibition on Marie Antoinette at the Petit Trianon, in which the queen's bedroom was the star exhibit (fig.6). This romanticized view took hold and spread to the general public, helped by the publication of a flurry of biographies. A phenomenal wave of interest continued throughout the century, peaking again in the 1880s and 1890s. Elements of Marie Antoinette's style became the 'French' or 'French Revival' in Britain for over 50 years, from 1835 to 1885. Her style attained a veneer of decorum and respectability. For the aspirational middle classes it lent a certain legitimacy and pedigree to their interiors. English collectors, like John Jones, whose 1882 bequest formed the basis of the V&A's collection of eighteenth-century French paintings and decorative arts, sought to acquire objects associated with the queen. The enigma and perceived allure of Marie Antoinette was an important factor in driving this taste.

By the close of the century, Marie Antoinette had become a key element of her own style; her bust was prominently displayed in collectors' drawing rooms and members of the aristocracy and middle classes alike donned Marie Antoinette costumes at fancy-dress balls and when sitting for studio portraits (see North in this volume). Paul César Helleu's drypoint of a fashionably appointed belle-époque salon depicts his wife examining herself in the mirror over the chimneypiece, on which rests a bust of Marie Antoinette by Louis-Simon Boizot (fig.7). The bust recurs in George Barbier's playful Art Deco fashion plate featuring the famous actress Mademoiselle Sorel paying homage to the eighteenth century (see fig.172).

The flame of interest in the queen was continually stoked, with each new wave triggered by some political, social or literary event: for example, the exhumation of Marie Antoinette's remains in 1815 and the erection of her expiatory chapel in 1826, or the publication of a new biography or of re-discovered correspondence. However, as the decades passed and audiences became more and more removed from the original historical events, the style ceded much of its political impetus. From the late nineteenth century the Marie Antoinette style entered a new phase of fantasy, magic and fairy tales. The queen's image came to embody escapism and beauty, as well as decadence and debauchery (see Grant and Slater in this volume).

The ripples of Marie Antoinette's style in popular culture can be surprisingly nuanced. Edith Head channelled the Queen of France for the future Princess of Monaco when she created the spectacular gold lamé ballgown for the film star Grace Kelly in Alfred Hitchcock's *To Catch a Thief* (1955). Kelly, like her inspiration, uses

9. *MARIE ANTOINETTE'S FOLLY* (DETAIL)
BY BETH KATLEMAN, 2025
PORCELAIN, MIRROR AND WIRE.
PHOTOGRAPH BY ALAN WIENER

the gown to make the ultimate entrance to a masquerade ball in the film's climactic scene. Similarly, after designing the costumes for the MGM film *Marie Antoinette* in 1938, the costumier Adrian (born Adrian Adolph Greenburg) went on the very next year to work on *The Wizard of Oz*, where he gave Billie Burke's Glinda the Good Witch of the North, who was vastly altered from the elderly character of the original novel, a glamorous and distinctly Marie-Antoinette-inspired panniered silhouette (fig.8). Clearly, Marie Antoinette was a personality who stayed with Adrian; for just a few years later, he inserted the studio replica of the diamond necklace he had created for *Marie Antoinette*, into a scene in *The Philadelphia Story* (1940).

10. *L'HIVER,* COVER DESIGN FOR *HARPER'S BAZAAR,* NOVEMBER 1928
ERTÉ (ROMAIN DE TIRTOFF, 1892–1990), GOUACHE DRAWING ON CARDBOARD, 38.8 × 28.8 CM. METROPOLITAN MUSEUM OF ART, NEW YORK: 67.762.104. THE MARTIN FOUNDATION INC. GIFT, 1967

11. *LADY GREY, VOGUE ITALIA,* MARCH 2010
CHARLES GUISLAIN, WEARING GIORGIO ARMANI, ALSO FEATURING ROYAL NATIONAL THEATRE, ANGELS COSTUMES, ERICKSON BEAMON, MAWI AND MALCOLM EDWARDS. PHOTOGRAPH BY TIM WALKER

In the modern era, the Marie Antoinette style is often used to denote classic luxury, sophistication and a feminine, whimsical frivolity, but it is also employed by designers to communicate a number of often contradictory messages to audiences and consumers: innocence vs sensuality; classic good taste vs hedonistic luxury; a heightened fairy-tale virtue vs a dark, gothic morbidity. While the style has its origins in France, it has become truly universal, resonating particularly with British, North American and Japanese audiences. One of the most extraordinary features of the modern iteration of the Marie Antoinette style is that the queen's likeness, her physical appearance drawn from portraits and prints, is endlessly used by designers and artists, be it as a repeating motif in a flocked wallpaper by the British fashion house Biba, on a Dior evening gown, or in a biscuit porcelain installation by American artist Beth Katleman (fig.9). The ship headdress and vertiginous wedding-cake hairstyles modelled by the queen, which were the fashions of mere moments, have, ironically, proved especially enduring and become a visual beacon of decadence (fig.10).

One of the defining moments in the historiography of Marie Antoinette and her modern interpretation, was Antonia Fraser's groundbreaking 2001 biography of the queen and the Oscar-winning 2006 film by Sofia Coppola that it inspired. These have helped to shape a growing public sympathy for the queen, whose personality and character are now better known through the publication and circulation of her letters, in particular those written during her imprisonment and her famous last letter to her sister-in-law, Madame Élisabeth. The queen's very last missive, a final note written before dawn on the morning of her execution, with its imploring, utterly wretched tone, now reads like a voice reaching from beyond the grave, in a manner that is as chilling as it is affecting (fig.12). In a similar vein, what Fraser and in turn Coppola highlighted, which most biographers and historians had previously failed to convey, were Marie Antoinette's very human qualities: her extreme youth and considerable charm. These traits were noted at the time, as a contemporary biographer recalled:

> She appeared with radiance in a court that was beginning to grow old; and her marriage, which gave rise to the hope of soon seeing the monarch's grandsons have young and amiable companions, brought pleasure to the French, for whom the court was a spectacle in which they loved to see brilliant characters.[9]

Both historian and director captured the sense of a young, teenaged royal family that suddenly found themselves the centre of the court following Louis XV's death. Marie Antoinette ascended the throne aged 18 and experienced her first decade as

from Vienna to Versailles on 7 May, she was greeted with her own cipher lit up in fireworks in an elaborate lights display set to music staged by the episcopal palace.[12] Once installed at Versailles, the queen applied her monogram, 'MA', with ubiquity and ever-greater sophistication to her private interiors, furniture and furnishings, and many of her intimate possessions such as her *nécessaire de voyage*, a travelling toilette case, where almost every one of the 94 items, from her eyebath to her bedwarmer, bears a beautifully delineated monogram (fig.16). In so doing, the queen made her mark visibly and indelibly on her physical environment, a highly successful form of early modern branding that has contributed to the monogram's continued association with luxury and refinement in the modern era.

In recent years, it is record-breaking auctions that have once again reignited interest in the queen. It is only in the past decade that Marie Antoinette's own jewels have resurfaced and come to market, for the first time since her death 232 years ago (see Meylan in this volume). The French Crown jewels were famously subject to a theft in 1792 and then sold off and dispersed by the French state in 1887 in what was regarded as the sale of the century. However, what became of Marie Antoinette's personal collection of jewels – which she smuggled out of the Tuileries in the greatest secrecy in 1791, and entrusted to the Austrian ambassador,

the comte de Mercy-Argenteau, before the royal family's attempt to flee France – was not known, even among jewellery specialists, until they sensationally came to light ahead of a Sotheby's auction in 2018 (see figs 77 and 78).[13] Then, in 2021, Marie Antoinette's pair of dazzling diamond bracelets commissioned in about 1776 also re-emerged (see fig.72).[14] Similarly, in 2022 an Etruscan-style chair from the last suite the queen ever commissioned in 1788 achieved just under one million euros at auction,[15] while a Georges Jacob chair made for the boudoir in her private apartments at Versailles sold for a record price of €2.58 million in 2023.[16]

The queen's continued relevance also comes from the way her treatment as a prominent woman in the public eye foreshadowed the glare of social media and paparazzi today. Scholars consider Marie Antoinette an early modern 'celebrity' whose perceived power over or 'domination' of the king, and 'feminization' of the court, were major contributing factors in the decline of her popularity and continued to tarnish her reputation in the nineteenth century. Historians considering gender and queenship have underscored the distinctive degree of agency and sorority at Marie Antoinette's court, within her female circle, which was unusual for the time and was used to undermine her. This has compelling parallels today with the popular press's treatment of women in political power or the public eye in what historian Pierre Saint-Amand has coined the 'Marie Antoinette syndrome', which he characterizes as a 'fear of women in power'.[17]

In contemporary fashion and performance, it is particularly the trope of Marie Antoinette as glamorous villainess that resonates with today's audiences (see Reed in this volume). In the lyrics to his song 'Smile' (2017), which refer to the subject of his mother's coming out, the artist Jay-Z (Shawn Carter) wrote 'I just wanna see you smile through all the hate. Marie Antoinette Baby, Let them eat cake', thereby encapsulating the idea that Marie Antoinette's so-called catch-phrase, redolent with a dismissive contempt, is one that also communicates a confident devil-may-care defiance, the riposte of one who grants no significance to the public's perception of her.

Marie Antoinette's story has been retold and repurposed by each successive generation to suit its own ends. When her mother warned her, 'All eyes will be on you', she followed it quickly with 'so do not therefore create a scandal'. Had Marie Antoinette paid greater heed to her mother's advice, had her life passed without incident and not resulted in both celebrity and ignominy, she would doubtless not be the figure of fascination she remains today nor would her style hold the same enduring cachet. The rare combination of glamour, spectacle and tragedy she presents remains as intoxicating today as it was in the eighteenth century.

PART ONE

MARIE ANTOINETTE: THE ORIGINS OF A STYLE ICON 1700–1800

THE QUEEN'S PRIVATE APARTMENTS AND THE PETIT TRIANON

Hélène Delalex

There is a door nearly two and a half metres high, located in the alcove of the queen's formal bedchamber at Versailles, to the left of the state bed. A door hidden among the peacock feathers and brocaded lilac bouquets of the rich summer wall hangings. It is the door through which Marie Antoinette fled from rioters to take refuge with the king, on the morning of 6 October 1789, the day that sealed her fate. This door led to the queen's private chambers, a multitude of small rooms whose existence it was impossible to discern from the formal apartments. This is what struck her page Félix d'Hézecques when, after the attack on and invasion of Versailles in October 1789, he entered the queen's private chambers, discovering a maze of unexpected rooms: 'I went this way and that through this labyrinth of unknown passages, many of which were padded. I thus entered a host of small apartments belonging to the queen, whose existence I had never even suspected.'[1] For Marie Antoinette, they represented a world apart, a refuge far from the constraints of court etiquette. In this palace open to all, access to these spaces was strictly controlled: *femmes de chambre* (chambermaids) would only admit the privileged few, for which they had a list. The queen therefore found herself alone there, with her children or a few favourites.

As she was restricted only to minor amendments in the décor of her formal apartments, Marie Antoinette was personally invested in the decoration of her private quarters. She was involved in every stage of the works: not a single portion of the decoration or furnishings was carried out without her first examining the designs and making repeated modifications before they were executed, and it is undeniable that in this regard she demonstrated conviction and remarkable taste. Creating, enlarging, furnishing, improving, decorating and embellishing: these were the queen's great passions. Over the course of her 19 years at Versailles she constantly extended and transformed her private spaces like no other queen before her. Today, these chambers, with their unprecedented refinement, are the best evidence of the queen's personal taste and the essence of 'Marie Antoinette style', as it is now known. They also embody the last splendours of absolute monarchy, a culmination of French taste and *savoir faire*, whose influence was unrivalled in Europe.

On 24 May 1774, a few days after his ascension to the throne, Louis XVI offered the Petit Trianon to Marie Antoinette. 'You love flowers,' he is said to have told her. 'I have a bouquet for you – the Petit Trianon.' With these words and a symbolic gesture he handed her the key to her new kingdom, a master key decorated with 531 diamonds. This chivalrous scene, recounted and embellished countless times, is pure fiction. In reality, Marie Antoinette, long drawn to the little building, made the request herself to the king, which is more in keeping with her character.[2] The building and gardens thus passed from the King's Household to the Queen's, which was a revolution in

p.36

18. *MARIE ANTOINETTE IN FRONT OF THE*
***TEMPLE OF LOVE* (AGED ABOUT 24), c.1780**
JEAN-BAPTISTE ANDRÉ GAUTIER-DAGOTY
(1740–1786), OIL ON CANVAS, 41 × 33.3 CM.
MUSÉE NATIONAL DES CHÂTEAUX DE
VERSAILLES ET DE TRIANON: INV. V.2015.38

**19. VIEW OF THE PETIT TRIANON AND THE
TEMPLE OF LOVE**
MUSÉE NATIONAL DES CHÂTEAUX DE
VERSAILLES ET DE TRIANON

itself. In France, a queen had never dared to claim the right to possess a building in her own name, equal to the king.

The Petit Trianon soon became the queen's exclusive domain and the instrument of her independence. During the summer months, she made frequent visits to her new Arcadia. This intimate haven allowed her to escape the rigours of the court and to live privately, to quite simply, be herself (fig.18). First and foremost, she turned all her attention to the gardens, which she intended to completely remodel. In the last third of the eighteenth century the whole of Europe was in the grip of Anglomania, and the queen wanted to create a garden in the latest taste, that is, in the Anglo-Chinese style. Work began in the autumn of 1774 under the direction of her architect Richard Mique (1728–1794). The queen – a veritable site manager – was personally involved in the design of her gardens, which were completed in 1782. The new estate was now unrecognizable, with its lake and waterways with countless detours, its 'Chinese ring game' carousel, its belvedere, the monumental rock sculpted from soft stone, the Alpine garden and its miniature mountains, its rustic waterfalls, the Temple of Love, built on an island, its romantic moss-lined grotto, cooled by a stream and furnished with a daybed, its lilac-scented groves full of nightingales (fig.19).

As for the interiors, Marie Antoinette left the layout largely unchanged, but redecorated the four main reception rooms on the first floor – the antechamber, the large and small dining rooms, the salon – and the three small mezzanine rooms that made up her private apartment. Situated at the heart of the building, the staircase vestibule is its most spectacular feature. The floor is tiled with veined white marble and green Campan marble, soft green being the predominant colour in this country château, reflecting the freshness of its gardens. On the superb wrought-iron and gilt-bronze banister, a masterpiece by metalworker François Brochois, the queen had inserted her monogram, 'MA', replacing that of Louis XV (fig.20). If some features of this banister are still in the rococo style, others are clearly neoclassical, such as the friezes and posts, which resemble waves, and the *cassolette* (perfume burner) at the bottom of the banister. In the salon, the queen retained from the previous reign Honoré Guibert's graceful, sculpted Greek-revival mouldings, comprising flowers

and baskets of fruit, whose lightness and floral features must have appealed to her. She was content to simply have them repainted a soft sea-green colour.

The most important work was, in 1776, the removal of the king's private staircase in order to create the famous cabinet of moveable mirrors (fig.21). Adjoining Marie Antoinette's bedroom, this astonishing boudoir comprised wood panelling fitted with mirrors that rose from the lower floor thanks to an ingenious mechanism, enabling the windows to be transformed into mirrors, thus separating the room from the outside world. In the evening, with candlelight reflecting in the mirrors, the room took on infinite dimensions. In 1787, Marie Antoinette commissioned a new décor for the room: panelling in an arabesque style, painted pastel blue picked out in white, in the style of English Wedgwood porcelain. These mouldings, some of the finest ever made, matched the furniture. The carved woodwork by cabinetmaker Georges Jacob was painted white and trimmed with blue *pou-de-soie* silk finished with white silk embroidery and lace.

At the same time, the queen commissioned a completely new set of furniture for her bedroom, the so-called 'wheat sheaf' or 'wheat ear' design: the uprights, in the form of sprigs of straw garlanded with honeysuckle, jasmine, lilies of the valley, wheat sheaves and basketwork motifs, surmounted with pinecones, were painted realistically in the 'colours of truth and nature'. The furniture was covered in white cotton bombazine embroidered with bouquets of roses, buttercups and

23. MARIE ANTOINETTE'S BEDCHAMBER,
PETIT TRIANON, VERSAILLES
MUSÉE NATIONAL DES CHÂTEAUX DE
VERSAILLES ET DE TRIANON

24. PLATE FROM MARIE ANTOINETTE'S *PERLES
ET BARBEAUX* (PEARLS AND CORNFLOWERS)
SERVICE, ORDERED 1781
SÈVRES PORCELAIN FACTORY, SOFT-PASTE
PORCELAIN, PAINTED IN ENAMELS AND GILT,
D. 24.2 CM. V&A: 2012B–1855

cornflowers, of infinite grace and lightness. This exceptional ensemble was truly one of a kind and perfectly embodied the spirit of the countryside the queen intended for Trianon.

In a perfect harmony between the 'exterior and the interior', these cornflowers, found in the surrounding gardens, recur on the decorative motifs of the furniture and the *objets d'art* delivered to the Petit Trianon, such as the famous 'Pearls and Cornflowers' service delivered to the queen from Sèvres, the royal porcelain manufactory, in 1782 (fig.24), or the fall-front writing desk delivered in 1783 by Jean-Henri Riesener for the boudoir next to her bedroom, decorated with superb gilt-bronze garlands of naturalistic flowers (see fig.132). In the summer of 1783, the construction of the *Hameau* (hamlet) was the culmination of this aristocratic ideal of a return to nature. On a plot of land to the north of the gardens of the Petit Trianon,

25. THE QUEEN'S HAMLET, PETIT TRIANON, VERSAILLES
MUSÉE NATIONAL DES CHÂTEAUX DE VERSAILLES ET DE TRIANON

26. MARIE ANTOINETTE'S LIBRARY IN HER PRIVATE APARTMENTS, CHÂTEAU DE VERSAILLES
MUSÉE NATIONAL DES CHÂTEAUX DE VERSAILLES ET DE TRIANON

Richard Mique, alongside the painter Hubert Robert, devised an ambitious complex of 11 Normandy-inspired houses set around an artificial lake (fig.25). At the time, the rustic village incarnated a golden age of humanity, a place sheltered from the corruption of society, where man's simple, innocent virtues could flourish. At the end of a winding path, the village would suddenly and unexpectedly appear, like a stage set. The skilfully rusticated appearance of the exterior walls were in spectacular contrast to the sumptuous rooms they concealed, hung with precious silks and decorated with *objets d'art* and mahogany furniture.

In 1779 the queen was already absorbed by a new building project: the general refurbishment of her inner chambers in the main palace. On the first floor, the work first involved modifying and enlarging her former library (fig.26). To ensure perfect harmony, the room's two doors were concealed by rows of false books complete with bindings. The shelves of the cupboards were fitted with racks and the handles on the drawers were in the shape of an imperial eagle, recalling the royal house of Austria.

In the spring of 1781, the queen was expecting her second child. After the birth of her daughter three years earlier, the entire kingdom hoped for a dauphin – a male heir. The excitement surrounding the future event was conducive to new furnishings. Marie Antoinette thus asked Mique to redesign her boudoir. This tiny room, barely 12 metres square, named the *Méridienne* room after the divan on which the queen came to rest at midday, is one of the most refined in the château (fig.27). The new octagonal floorplan ensured the room's privacy by allowing the chambermaids to pass directly from the formal bedroom to the library, without having to go via the boudoir and 'disturbing' the queen. 'Her Majesty desiring to be alone when she sees fit, without disturbing her staff nor being disturbed by them', confirmed a note from the King's Inspector of Buildings. The new chamfered doors were decorated with transparent glass and fitted with remarkable gilt-bronze escutcheons bearing the queen's monogram. On 13 April 1781, the divan nook was fitted with 'extraordinarily large' two-way mirrors, to reflect light. For the panelling, Marie Antoinette called upon the Rousseau brothers, who developed their 'arabesque style': the surface of the panel, left bare and simply painted 'blanc de Roi' (King's white; a very pale grey) was framed by finely sculpted and gilded garland mouldings, graceful intertwining motifs in keeping with the purpose of the room. The ornamental motifs thus celebrated conjugal bliss and the long-awaited birth of the heir to the kingdom: hearts pierced by arrows crossed by a royal sceptre decorated with *fleurs-de-lis*, expressing the love and protection of the king, flaming torches, climbing stems of rose bushes and wreaths of plaited roses, dolphins surrounded by lilies, Juno's peacock and Jupiter's eagle celebrating the union of the royal couple. Today, the room has been restored to the scheme of the very last textile delivered to the queen in 1786, a rich silk in lilac and four soft shades of green, a very fashionable colour scheme in the 1780s.

The queen then turned to the transformation of the main reception room of her private chambers on the first floor. In order to bring as much light as possible into this room, which, like all the others, looked out onto a small, dark courtyard, she had installed, facing the two French windows, a vast alcove lined with mirrors and a sofa. The old panelling was replaced by white satin brocade embroidered with arabesques, flowers and medallions, a true masterpiece created by the Lyon silk manufacturer Jean Charton, which alone cost the astronomical sum of 100,000 *livres*.

This tremendous brocaded and embroidered silk, comprising an extraordinary 34 colours, was delivered in December 1779, one of the most opulent ever created under the *ancien régime*. Yet, fewer than four years later, Marie Antoinette had it all removed, when she decided to redo everything in wood panelling. The vividly coloured palette of the floral wall hanging did not suit the harmonious gold and black of her

new collection of Japanese lacquer boxes, an exceptional collection bequeathed to her by her mother in 1780. The precious fabric hanging was moved in 1786 to the queen's salon on the second floor. In 1783, to replace the hanging, the Rousseau brothers created a neoclassical décor inspired by Etruscan styles and the emerging Egyptomania. This dazzling new panelling gave the room the name by which it would now be known – the *cabinet doré* (gold cabinet).[3]

From 1779, Marie Antoinette extended her private quarters to the second floor of the château, taking over rooms previously kept for the king's valets, her chambermaids and her lady-in-waiting. These new rooms, which included a dining room (fig.28) and a boudoir (fig.29) were this time decorated with a large and colourful printed white ground cotton of the highest quality known as *Perse*, produced by the royal manufactory at Jouy-en-Josas (purveyors of the famous toile de Jouy). Printed fabrics were then hugely popular, and Marie Antoinette, who always wanted the latest style, naturally subscribed to this fashion. The production of these printed cotton fabrics (the finest texture was used for the queen's furniture) was far less costly than the rich Lyon silks and above all quicker to produce. Spread by the fashion journals, the continuous flow of new designs made it possible to indulge in the taste of the moment, which at the time changed rapidly.

Despite their elegance, over the years the queen tired of the dreary views from her chambers, which were arranged around two small, dark courtyards. In 1782, on the death of Madame Sophie, one of Louis XV's daughters, the queen took over one of the most beautiful apartments in the château, located on the ground floor of the main building. Overlooking the marble courtyard from one side, and the grand vista of the gardens from the other, it was flooded with light. It became her *Petit appartement*, which meant that, unlike her private chambers, it had a bedroom. Works began once again and she ordered a thousand and one new designs for which there was no limit to the budget.

In the summer of 1788, this time moving out her son's first *valet de chambre*, she had a vast bathroom installed, almost 40 metres square, lined in beautiful black and white marble tiles (see fig.101). The Rousseau brothers got back to work and produced a new, extremely elegant, panelled décor: the sculpted motifs – crayfish, swans drinking from basins, reeds and rushes, grooming implements, branches of coral and scrolls embellished with shells – were painted white on a pastel-blue background, as with the the cabinet of moveable mirrors. A pair of gilt-bronze goosenecks supplied the bathtub with hot and cold water, thanks to pipework coming from the tank room located on a mezzanine just above.

The queen would not see the completion of this last project and it was only the French Revolution that put a stop to her frenzy of building works. These private spaces, whose

décor, partitions, doors, staircases and passages she modified endlessly, and whose access she insisted on controlling, provide a moving testimony to her desperate quest for privacy.

Marie Antoinette is the only queen to have left her personal mark on Versailles. And while we commonly refer to the Louis XVI style, it would be right to describe the style of the period as the Marie Antoinette style, because it embodies the quintessence of the late eighteenth century, which is so complex to grasp. Throughout Europe, her taste became the fashion and the interiors created for her, like the furniture and the *objets d'art* delivered to her, represent the unrivalled apex of French decorative arts. The style attributed to her is also associated with a way of life that, even today, inspires contemporary creators, decorators and designers.

If we had to define it, Marie Antoinette's style would be above all a taste for lightness. White interiors were perceived at the time as characteristic of the 'goût Grec' (Greek antiquity). The queen equally appreciated the soft-pastel, almost evanescent, tones that were then very fashionable. The famous 'Trianon' colour, nowadays referring to a pale grey, actually comes from the state of the woodwork dating from the nineteenth century. Recent restoration of the building revealed the original colour of the interior, a pale green shade that brings the freshness of the surrounding gardens inside. The style is also characterized by the pure, elegant lines inspired by antiquity, but always with the lightness of its own century. In the mid-1780s, the 'arabesque style' dominated, with its extremely fine swirls, its graceful garlands of *fleurs-de-lis*, its acanthus scrolls, pearls, rosettes, ribbons and vases of flowers, all arranged in perfect symmetry and with a virtuosity contained by the classicism typical of Versailles.

Another constant is the *goût tapissier* or taste for embellished fabrics, in which cabinetmakers recreated in bronze, with the same lightness of touch, imitation drapery, fringes and ribbons, as can be seen in the famous porcelain *serre-bijoux* (jewellery box) made by Martin Carlin (see fig.67).[4] The queen favoured a decorative repertory of feminine motifs: pearls, ribbon bows and medallions, mixed with an abundance of flowers. Natural-looking flowers were all the rage in the eighteenth century. They are everywhere in Marie Antoinette's décor: scattered profusely on the furniture and bronze furnishings, on silks and printed cottons, each flower is distinct from one another and all are vividly created by hand.

Trianon also has its own style. Even before the Revolution, the Petit Trianon embodied the queen's life of pleasure, and was widely fantasized about, as was revealed by the visit of the deputies at the time of the Estates-General in the spring of 1789. They were curious to see the famous Trianon they had heard so much about. Many believed the queen had spent a large part of France's fortune there. Their astonishment increased as they visited her apartments: led by the caretaker, they discovered rooms that were elegantly furnished and decorated, but nowhere very opulent. The deputies asked to see every single room, hoping to discover some of the specific details they had read about in the press, notably a room lined with diamonds with twisted columns of sapphires and rubies…[5] But they saw nothing pompous or sumptuous in this small, intimate château. As Pierre de Nolhac (1859–1936), the château's first conservator and biographer of the queen, remarked: 'Taste alone in the place of the luxury expected'. The 'Trianon style' is one of an exceptional sophistication that appears natural: extreme elegance rather than magnificence, the illusion of simplicity, even though each element is testament to an art of formal perfection and unparalleled refinement.

COCOONED: MARIE ANTOINETTE IN SILK

Lesley Ellis Miller

'Clad in a light gown of gauze or taffeta, she [Marie Antoinette] was compared to the Venus de Medici, to the Atalanta in the gardens at Marly.' Madame Campan, 1822[1]

Silk cocooned Marie Antoinette throughout her short life. It enveloped her body, from the tips of her shoes and stockings to the ribbons that bedecked her remarkable hairstyles and hats. It furnished the grandest interiors in which she lived and through which she passed, covering walls, upholstering furniture and curtaining windows (fig.30). Even in 1792, once she was imprisoned in the Temple, green damask-covered chairs and blue taffeta curtains from her old apartments at the Tuileries mitigated the austerity of her surroundings,[2] while in the following year, after the execution of her husband, plain black taffeta for a mourning gown allowed her to maintain her dignity as a royal widow.[3] Alone in the Conciergerie, she cherished a package from her sister-in-law containing, among some fine linen items, black silk stockings and ribbons.[4]

These accessories were meagre reminders of her experience of and expenditure on silk before 1791. As a child she was dressed to meet the demands of Austrian court etiquette.[5] At the French border at the time of her marriage, she was undressed and then clad in French-made silken attire, thus symbolically embracing her new identity and conforming to unrelenting French protocol.[6] Subsequently, she developed her own taste in French fashionable novelties.[7] As Queen of France, she set the tone for the French and many other European courts, and for the wealthy middling ranks. Protecting and promoting French industry were her and her husband's duty, as the silk manufacturing guild in Lyon reminded Louis XVI in 1774.[8] Five years later, according to the author of the *Mémoires secrets pour servir à l'histoire de la République des Lettres*, deputies of commerce arrived in Paris reinforcing the message through

representations on the decline of the [silk] manufactures since Their Majesties did not set an example by wearing rich clothing with gold and silver. The King took note; consequently, the Queen has forbidden that anyone appears before her in a polonaise and silks woven with gold and silver have been ordered for the Court. There is no doubt that this example will revive taste for this type of magnificence which simple, plain silks had replaced.[9]

Yet, there is little surviving material evidence of Marie Antoinette's consumption of silk: a book of silk samples for 1782 (figs 37 and 38) kept by her *dame d'atours* Madame la comtesse d'Ossun, inside which was a simple taffeta bodice (fig.51);[10] a few items that the heirs of French émigrés believed to have been hers, including

30. MARIE ANTOINETTE'S BEDCHAMBER IN
THE QUEEN'S FORMAL APARTMENT,
CHÂTEAU DE VERSAILLES
MODERN REPLICA BROCADED SILK WALL
COVERING, REWOVEN 1946–75 BY PRELLE,
TASSINARI & CHANTEL, LYON, TO A DESIGN
ATTRIBUTED TO JEAN-FRANÇOIS BONY
(1754–1825), AND WOVEN BY DESFARGES
FRÈRES ET CIE IN 1786–7. MUSÉE NATIONAL
DES CHÂTEAUX DE VERSAILLES ET DE TRIANON

31. ARCHDUCHESS MARIE ANTOINETTE
(AGED 7), 1762
JEAN-ETIENNE LIOTARD (1702–1789),
SANGUINE, BLACK CHALK, GRAPHITE,
WATERCOLOUR AND PASTEL ON PAPER,
31.1 × 24.9 CM. MUSÉE D'ART ET D'HISTOIRE,
GENEVA: 1947–42. DEPOSIT OF THE SWISS
CONFEDERATION, FEDERAL OFFICE OF
CULTURE, GOTTFRIED KELLER FOUNDATION

two lavishly embroidered panels from formal gowns (see Grant in this volume);[11] silk-covered shoes collected as relics (see Cox in this volume);[12] and a few pieces of furnishings from the royal palaces.[13] Missing are the rather more ephemeral artificial flowers, blonde lace, gauze trimmings, *passementerie*, ribbons, sashes and stockings that formed such a significant part of her silken wardrobe. Portraits and fashion plates, financial accounts and inventories, memoirs and manufacturers' petitions fill in some of the gaps, providing a broader perspective on the diverse silk products that surrounded her, how fashions in woven silks changed, and how her choices impacted on her silk-manufacturing suppliers.[14]

By the mid-eighteenth century, silk had long been a luxury commodity valued for its lustre, strength, versatility and relative rarity.[15] From the late seventeenth century, Lyon in south-east France had been the premier silk-weaving centre in Europe. Vienna, too, boasted a flourishing silk industry that received state support under Marie Antoinette's mother, Empress Maria Theresa (1717–1780) and subsequently her brother Joseph II (1741–1790).[16] Viennese production apparently owed some of its progress to immigrant craftspeople and designers as well as to the importation of designs, samples and fabrics from France.[17]

Prior to 1770, therefore, Marie Antoinette may have worn Austrian and French silks and she was surely well aware of the dominance of French taste.[18] After her marriage, she was obliged to dress *à la française*. Her silks fell into the categories described in a report prepared in 1751 for the French economist Vincent de Gournay (1712–1759),[19] as did those of Louis XV's two fashion-leading mistresses, Jeanne Antoinette Poisson, marquise de Pompadour (1721–1764) and Jeanne Bécu, comtesse du Barry (1743–1793).[20] This report reveals just how little of the cost of a woven silk lay in the actual weaving and how much in the raw materials and the time-consuming and labour-intensive technical processes that went into preparing yarns and setting up basic and more complex looms for plain and figured silks respectively. The merchants' and retailers' mark-ups were also significant.

At the top end of the hierarchy were silks woven with gold (silver gilt) and silver threads; below them fell figured and plain velvets; then came figured all-silk fabrics (without pile); and finally plain (unpatterned) silks.[21] The guild-regulated categories did not change after 1744 although a variety of new fabrics were recognized from 1779 onwards, as long as they were appropriately labelled.[22] They reflected changes in taste and fashion, as was clear from the number of weavers and looms working in each category. The production of figured silks decreased in the mid-1770s, around the time Marie Antoinette became queen.[23] Plain silks were not, of course, necessarily left unadorned, as they were a suitable foil for either embroidered decoration or the

32. ROBE À L'ANGLAISE, c.1787
PROBABLY EUROPE, PINK AND STONE STRIPED
SILK SATIN, LINED WITH SILK GAUZE. ULSTER
MUSEUM COLLECTION: BELUM.T2411

Overleaf

33. ROBE À LA FRANÇAISE, 1765–70
PROBABLY LYON, PURPLE SHOT SILK BROCADED
WITH FLOWERS AND LACE PATTERN, LENGTH
OF REPEAT 49 CM. V&A: T.708–1913

**34. BROCADED SILK DRESS FABRIC WITH
FLORAL, STRIPED AND LEOPARD SPOT
PATTERN, 1770–80**
PROBABLY LYON, 76.3 × 51.5 CM, LENGTH OF
REPEAT 25.2 CM. V&A: 1265–1877

excessive trimmings added to finished garments by *marchandes de modes* (fashion merchants/milliners) such as Rose Bertin (1747–1813).

The simplest silks were those without patterns and they were a staple not only of royal but also of more modest wardrobes and households – though the quantities and qualities acquired varied according to the purchaser's income and status.[24] Three main weave types appear in the records: tabby, satin and twill. The first is crisp and relatively matte, probably similar to what Marie Antoinette is wearing in a portrait of 1762 (fig.31) while the second is resolutely glossy, as epitomized by the gown in her portrait with the rose (fig.55) and the striped gown (fig.32), which is similar to that worn by her daughter in a portrait of 1784.[25] These staples were associated with different seasons, according to silk manufacturer Jean Paulet (1731–after 1794): taffeta with summer, satin with winter and twill with spring and autumn.[26] The density of the warp and weft and variations in their thickness or twist could create a range of fabrics from ribbed and robust to soft and diaphanous. The plain weaves grosgrain, *gros de tours*, *gros de naples* and paduasoy, for example, were heavier than taffeta and had a slightly ribbed appearance.[27] Shot silks changed colour according to the angle of viewing and source of light because the warp was a different colour from the weft, while stripes and checks offered striking options. The surface of such plain silks could be enhanced after they came off the loom, so certain taffetas were extra shiny because they were lustred, and certain *gros de tours* had a watered effect (*moiré*).[28]

Unpatterned silks were the cheapest to weave and to buy, while velvets and silks brocaded with metal threads were complex and slow to weave and therefore expensive.[29] Metal content contributed to the difficulty of weaving as well as to the cost. Such rich silks were largely limited to court and church use, and few survive because the metal was reclaimed when they wore out or fell from fashion.[30]

Until the 1770s figured silks indicated how fashionable garments were, as their patterns changed seasonally at a time when dress styles evolved much more slowly over several years. The ground of the fabric might be one of the weaves mentioned above, and the patterning tended to be floral, the aesthetic moving from the scrolling rococo style popular between 1750 and 1770 into the more rectilinear neoclassical style from the 1770s onwards. Typical of the former is the brocaded shot silk of the *robe à la française* (fig.33). Such meandering designs gradually became disciplined into straight stripes, often complemented by independent 'floating' bouquets (fig.34). By the 1780s the motifs were even simpler, commonly small sprigs and buds (see, for example, the silk sample at the bottom of fig.37). In other words, the repeat pattern became progressively shorter and the designs increasingly simple.[31] The silk of the waistcoat that complements Marie Antoinette's red riding habit (as seen in her portrait held at the Schönbrunn

35. FILM STILL OF *MARIE ANTOINETTE*,
DIRECTED BY SOFIA COPPOLA, 2006
KIRSTEN DUNST AS MARIE ANTOINETTE, IN A
COSTUME DESIGNED BY MILENA CANONERO,
AGAINST THE REPLICA SILK FURNISHINGS OF
THE QUEEN'S BEDCHAMBER, VERSAILLES

36. *ROBE À LA FRANÇAISE*, 1775–80
FRANCE, ALTERED IN ENGLAND, SILK, LINEN,
SILK THREAD, LINEN THREAD, METAL, WHALE-
BONE, RIBBON AND FRINGE, BOBBIN LACE.
V&A: T.180&A–1965. GIVEN BY MISS LOUISE BAND

Palace, Vienna) was probably a *cirsaka*, a silk defined by Paulet as having a metal stripe alternating with a tabby, twill or satin stripe, and innovatively since the late 1760s sometimes with a brocaded motif.[32] Madame du Barry acquired one ell in 'plum-colour and gold' in October 1783 for 60 *livres* – about the yardage required for the shorter waistcoats of that date and the equivalent to a quarter to a third of the annual wages of a drawgirl (the girl who helped to operate the drawloom) in the silk industry.[33]

Of course, furnishing textiles retained a more generous scale, their designs incorporating the ubiquitous flowers and foliage alongside classical sculpture, architectural and pastoral motifs, arabesques, and sometimes elements of chinoiserie, indiennerie and turquerie. Such was the blue and white damask, 'The Four Parts of the World', ordered by Marie Antoinette in 1784 for her Grand Cabinet at Rambouillet. Africa, America(s), Asia and Europe were all represented by a European notion of Indigenous peoples and associated animals, integrated among putti and baskets of flowers.[34]

Chiné silks were a cheaper and lighter-weight alternative to figured silks, their patterns painted on the warp threads before weaving rather than woven in using additional wefts. Their designs varied from simple V-shapes to elaborate garlands of flowers. An evolution from heavier to lighter patterns is evident between the 1760s and 1780s, as comparison of samples from the 1760s with those of the 1782 gazette

37. PAGE FROM THE 'GAZETTE DES ATOURS DE MARIE-ANTOINETTE', 1782
WITH SAMPLES OF EMBROIDERED, CHINÉ AND BROCADED SILKS TO MAKE GOWNS WORN OVER SMALL HOOPS ('ROBES SUR LE PETIT PANIER'), SUPPLIED BY THE PARISIAN MERCER LENORMAND, ALONGSIDE ONE USED BY ROSE BERTIN FOR TRIMMING A GOWN, SILK ON PAPER. ARCHIVES NATIONALES DE FRANCE, PARIS: INV. AE I 6 NO.3

38. PAGE FROM THE 'GAZETTE DES ATOURS DE MARIE-ANTOINETTE', 1782
WITH SAMPLES OF CHINÉ SILKS FOR 'GRANDS HABITS' (COURT GOWNS), SUPPLIED BY THE PARISIAN MERCERS LENORMAND AND BARBIER ABOVE A PLAIN SILK TO BE TRIMMED WITH CHINÉ. ARCHIVES NATIONALES DE FRANCE, PARIS: INV. AE I 6 NO.3

39. *ARCHDUCHESS MARIE ANTOINETTE (AGED 14)*, 1769
JOSEPH DUCREUX (1735–1802), PASTEL ON PARCHMENT, 64.8 × 49.5 CM. MUSÉE NATIONAL DES CHÂTEAUX DE VERSAILLES ET DE TRIANON: INV.DESS 1207

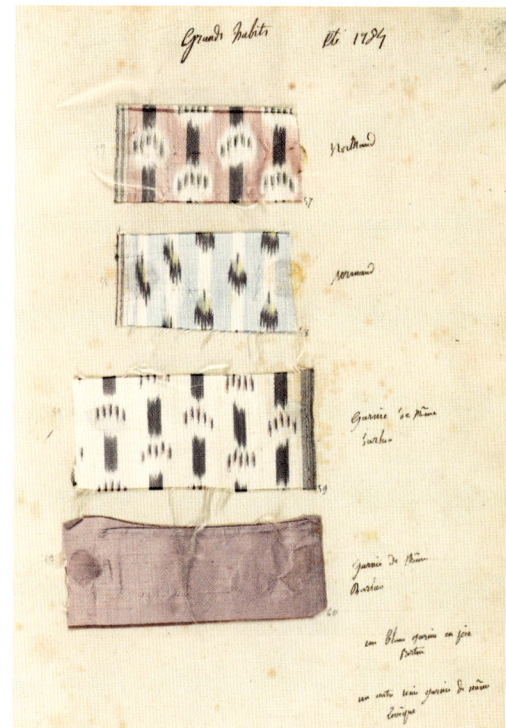

reveals (figs 37 and 38). Sometimes, a woven stripe in the background gave depth to the pattern.[35] Marie Antoinette already favoured chiné for her portrait of 1769 (fig.39), similar to a surviving gown of comparable style (fig.40). She apparently owned 19 gowns of chiné taffeta and one of chiné velvet in 1771, and ordered a chiné grosgrain to furnish her games room at Compiègne in 1786.[36] In 1783 Madame du Barry bought a chiné taffeta as well as a 'miniature zebra chiné taffeta', which may have borne some resemblance to Marie Antoinette's samples.

Some manufacturers considered that varying designs for chiné was more difficult than for figured silks because a limited range of flowers could be created this way.[37] Nonetheless, Antoine-Nicolas Joubert de l'Hiberderie (1729–before 1790) devoted a whole chapter to them in his 1765 manual, underlining the need for designers to understand the constraints under which *chineurs* worked in preparing the warps.[38]

Full-blown naturalism in flowers was only truly achieved through 'painting' on a plain silk – with a paintbrush or with a needle – services provided by specialist painters and embroiderers respectively. Many of them were women who constituted a cheap and plentiful workforce.[39] A white satin panel embroidered to shape for a court train reveals how sophisticated this work could be, yet easily replicable in

the hands of skilled craftspeople with access to the necessary materials: its edge is bordered with a row of chenille, applied velvet flowers and satin swathes, curly metal thread and swansdown (fig.41). Far more easily copied were the modest sprigs and buds favoured for fashionable gowns, like the sample at the top of the page of Madame d'Ossun's book (fig.37). Embroidery was also a genteel occupation, with Marie Antoinette herself labouring over a waistcoat for the king just after her arrival in France, for, of course, men of a certain rank wore silk suits, waistcoats and nightgowns (*robes de chambre*).[40]

Commercial directories reflected shifts in fashionable production and manufacturing specialisms. The 1788 edition of the *Almanach général du commerce, des marchands, négocians, armateurs etc.* listed 29 manufacturing partnerships that specialized in plain silks, 12 in brocaded and embroidered silks (as a single category), and seven in plushes and velvets.[41] These last had long been prestigious, costly because of the quantity of silk they required for the pile warp and the complexity of the weaving process.[42] Marie Antoinette owned three formal court gowns in different colours of cut velvet in 1771: white chiné, orange-red and black.[43] Subsequently, she donned the blue velvet mantle embroidered with gold *fleurs-de-lis* for her coronation, later immortalized in the 1775 portrait by Jean-Baptiste Gautier-Dagoty (1740–1786).[44] In the 1780s Élisabeth Vigée Le Brun (1755–1842) excelled in representing the queen's fashionable monochrome velvets. Notable was the red gown and matching petticoat trimmed with black fur (probably sable), possibly a tribute to her husband's grandmother Queen Marie Leszczyńska whom Jean-Marc Nattier (1685–1766) had painted in this colour, fabric and fur combination 40 years earlier.[45]

On a grander scale, the four partnerships that supplied the Royal Household from 1784 until the Revolution – Desfarges, Gros, Louis Reboul et Defontbrune, and Pernon – delivered both figured and embroidered furnishings for the queen and other members of the royal family, while Pernon also provided velvet for Marie Antoinette's sister-in-law Madame Victoire in 1785.[46] Outstanding was the suite of summer furnishings for Marie Antoinette's bedchamber in 1786–7 in which the brocaded panels and borders for the walls harmonized with the embroidered silk bed hangings, counterpane and chair backs (see fig.30).[47] The design of flowers, ribbons and peacock feathers is generally attributed to Jean-François Bony (1754–1825), and it was Desfarges frères et cie who had it woven in brocaded white *gros de tours* and embroidered white *gros de naples*. This suite replaced a blue brocaded and embroidered *gros de tours* acquired from Pernon just one year earlier in 1785: it differed in containing no metal thread. Its predecessor moved to the queen's bedchamber at Fontainebleau and was subsequently rewoven between 1900 and 1905.[48]

41. EMBROIDERED PANEL FOR A COURT TRAIN, c.1780–92
ATTRIBUTED TO JEAN-FRANÇOIS BONY (1754–1825), FRANCE, EMBROIDERED SILK SATIN WITH SILK VELVET APPLIQUÉ, CHENILLE, METAL PURL AND SWANSDOWN, 188.5 × 75 CM. V&A: T.89–1967

42. WEDDING *CORBEILLE* (WEDDING BASKET), c.1785
FRANCE, SILK TAFFETA EMBROIDERED IN COLOURED SILKS. V&A: T.42–2018

These two commissions for the same room and season at such a short interval are surprising, as Marie Antoinette had received only four deliveries for figured furnishings between 1771 and 1784 from Lyon. She had lived with her predecessor's winter bedchamber furnishings ordered in 1730, despite the old-fashioned rich colour and abundant metal threads.[49] Between 1785 and 1787, however, she commissioned a further four, surely an indication that the later orders were a response to Lyonnais pleas for support in the wake of the detrimental trade treaty with Great Britain in 1786.[50]

A luxurious wedding basket redolent of the floral opulence of the Desfarges commission, is a fitting finale to this overview (fig.42). Its extravagant embroidery and *passementerie* probably complemented a full suite of furnishings.[51] Such baskets, made to hold a bride's wedding presents, often served afterwards as containers for needlework tools. In this case, a matching handkerchief sachet protected delicate items to be presented ceremoniously to a noble or royal recipient, such as fine linen handkerchiefs trimmed with lace. This silken etiquette relied for its éclat on skilled designers, weavers and embroiderers as well as the trimmings makers who twisted silk threads round thick paper or parchment. These objects' form and use contrast poignantly with Marie Antoinette's gaoler's kind gift of a humble cardboard box to protect the last 'necessities' the queen received alone in the Conciergerie – fine linen handkerchiefs and shifts, nightcaps and a day dress, silk stockings and ribbons.[52]

MARIE ANTOINETTE'S WARDROBE

Sarah Grant

'I saw the Queen in her grandest dress; she was covered with diamonds, and as the brilliant sunshine fell upon her she seemed to me nothing short of dazzling.'
Élisabeth Vigée Le Brun, *Souvenirs de Madame Vigée Le Brun*, 1835–7[1]

For her proxy marriage in Vienna on 19 April 1770, the 14-year-old Marie Antoinette came down the aisle in a court gown of silver cloth so bright and reflective that it appeared white, a breathtaking display matched only by the glitter of the jewels of 'inestimable value' that covered her from head to toe, from the clusters in her hair to her shoe buckles.[2]

It was doubtless this same gown, the petticoat and long train trimmed with gold (silver-gilt) lace, that Marie Antoinette re-wore for her second marriage service, in the Royal Chapel at Versailles on 16 May 1770.[3] The gown, and her entire wedding trousseau, were paid for by her mother, Maria Theresa, Empress of Austria, but had been ordered from Paris, the centre of western European fashion and leader in court dress.

That afternoon the court packed the Royal Chapel, all dressed in their finest attire, a sea of gold and silver brocaded silk suits, gowns and jewels all set off in a scintillation of sparkle by the brilliant sunshine pouring in through the arched chapel windows.[4] The Duchess of Northumberland (Elizabeth Seymour Percy, 1716–1776), visiting from England, had managed to secure a coveted seat to watch the wedding of the century and recorded in her diary what is now the sole surviving first-hand description of the teenaged bride's appearance. As Marie Antoinette passed by her, the duchess observed: 'The Dauphine was very fine in Diamonds. She is very little & slender. I should not have taken her to be above 12 Years Old. She is fair and a little mark'd with the Smallpox'.[5]

The eagle-eyed duchess also noted of the bride's gown that 'the Corps of her Robe was too small & left quite a broad stripe of lacing & Shift quite visible, between 2 broader stripes of Diamonds w[hi]ch had a bad effect. She really had quite a Load of Jewells'.[6]

What the duchess believed to be a faux-pas – the visible chemise – may in fact have been the French fashion: at her court presentation some years later the marquise de La Tour du Pin displayed a deliberate gap in the lacings of her *corps* (stiffened bodice) to expose her chemise 'of the finest lawn'.[7] And at the tender age of 14, Marie Antoinette was of course still growing: her tutor, the abbé de Vermond, noted that she grew a foot (about 30 centimetres) between February and October in 1769, a few months before her wedding.[8]

p.68

43. MARIE ANTOINETTE IN COURT DRESS (DETAIL OF FIG.49)

44. FRENCH-STYLE *ROBE DE COUR*, WEDDING GOWN OF DUCHESS HEDVIG ELISABETH CHARLOTTA, LATER QUEEN OF SWEDEN (1759–1818), 1774
BROCADED SILK AND SILVER THREAD WOVEN IN A FLORAL, LACE AND DIAMOND-SHAPED PATTERN ON A TWILL GROUND, FRENCH SILK. LIVRUSTKAMMAREN, STOCKHOLM

Nevertheless, this was Marie Antoinette's dazzling entrance to French court society and the public debut of the woman who would become the most fashionable queen in history.[9] As queens of France were not crowned, Marie Antoinette's wedding gown was the most important item of clothing that she would ever wear. A French-style *robe de cour* wedding gown worn in 1774 by the future Queen of Sweden is very close to the gown Marie Antoinette would have worn, in fact it was a copy of the gown worn by Marie Antoinette's sister-in-law, the comtesse d'Artois, to her wedding at Versailles the year before (fig.44).[10] While the gown was made in Germany, the design and the fabric were French – the bride's parents ordered the silver brocaded silk

from Paris at enormous expense.[11] The distinctive design of the silk – a scalloped lace pattern punctuated by large flowers, is strikingly similar to that shown worn by Marie Antoinette in a print depicting the wedding that is known to have been a faithful representation (fig.45).[12]

The *grand habit* or *robe de cour*, the official court dress, was an article of the utmost luxury, spectacle and expense, and could only be worn by the women of the royal family and members of the court who had been presented to the king and queen.[13] The gown was composed of a stiffened bodice (*grand corps*), skirt and a detachable train which could be gathered decorously in the middle or tied to one side. Critical to the impressive girth of the gown was the under-structure, a panier (or pannier) composed of three to four hoops encased in canvas or silk. The gown and bodice were of the costliest silks which were elaborately brocaded or embroidered and trimmed, all with silver and/or gold thread. An exquisite and rare pale pink satin *grand corps* bodice in the V&A is embellished with rows of scalloped silver lace that descend into a point to further exaggerate the narrowness of the wearer's cinched waist (fig.46).[14]

The spectacular effect of the formal court gown was completed by sleeves of frothy tiered lace and a profusion of trimmings: real or silk flowers, gold and silver lace, ribbons, bows, fur, strings of pearls and jewels that could be pinned to the bodice and the skirt. In her first official full-length portrait as queen and aged nineteen when it was painted and displayed in the Hall of Mirrors, Marie Antoinette's bodice is adorned with diamond solitaires, clusters and a large diamond bow, while silk lilies symbolizing France decorate the gold-shot silk gauze swags that span the skirt (fig.48). In a later monumental portrait that her mother adored, the 22-year-old wears a white silk taffeta court gown that demonstrates the move away from more elaborately patterned silks to plain silks and solid colours, the opulence lent instead by elaborate swags, bows, gold fringe trimming and heavy gold tassels (fig.49). For important ceremonies, Marie Antoinette also added the royal mantle of ermine-lined velvet embroidered with *fleurs-de-lis*, visible in both these portraits.[15] The distinctive bodice and lace sleeves of the *grand habit* can also be seen in many of the young queen's smaller portraits and were considered a key element of official representations of the queen (see fig.39).

Due to the exceptionally high content of metal from the silver and gold brocaded silks and metal lace trimmings, and the long train that attached to the waist with metal hooks, the weight of these formal gowns could be unbearable. The aforementioned wedding gown of Princess Hedvig, which is similar to that worn by Marie Antoinette, was reported by a senior courtier as 'magnificent' but 'terribly

47. JEUNE DAME DE QUALITÉ EN GRANDE ROBE
COËFFÉE AVEC UN BONNET OU POUF ÉLÉGANT
DIT LA VICTOIRE, c.1778
(YOUNG WOMAN OF QUALITY IN COURT
DRESS WITH A BONNET OR ELEGANT POUF
HAIRSTYLE CALLED LA VICTOIRE), FASHION
PLATE FROM THE GALLERIE DES MODES
(8ÈME CAHIER), ÉTIENNE CLAUDE VOYSARD
(1746–1807) AFTER CLAUDE-LOUIS DESRAIS
(1746–1816), PARIS, HAND-COLOURED ETCHING,
23.8 × 16.5 CM. V&A: E.21584–1957

48. *MARIE ANTOINETTE IN COURT DRESS* (AGED 19), 1775
JEAN-BAPTISTE ANDRÉ GAUTIER-DAGOTY (1740–1786), OIL ON CANVAS, 160 × 128 CM. MUSÉE NATIONAL DES CHÂTEAUX DE VERSAILLES ET DE TRIANON: INV. MV 8061

49. *MARIE ANTOINETTE IN COURT DRESS* (AGED 22 OR 23), 1778–9
ÉLISABETH VIGÉE LE BRUN (1755–1842), OIL ON CANVAS, 223 × 158 CM. MUSÉE NATIONAL DES CHÂTEAUX DE VERSAILLES ET DE TRIANON: INV. MV 3892

**50. FRAGMENT FROM A *ROBE DE COUR* OR
ROBE PARÉE, PROBABLY BELONGING TO
MARIE ANTOINETTE, c.1780–91**
FRANCE, IVORY SILK SATIN WITH APPLIED
GREEN VELVET, GOLD THREAD AND SILVER
FOIL-BACKED PASTE GEMS AND SOLID SILVER-
GILT SPANGLES. LONDON MUSEUM: 2014.34/2

heavy, which makes me believe that the princess will redraw with relief on her wedding day'.[16] This was also the case with the gown worn by Marie Antoinette to Louis XVI's coronation at Reims Cathedral on 11 June 1775.[17] This was a spectacular *grand habit* arranged by Rose Bertin that was so rich in metal thread that its weight caused some difficulties in terms of packing and transporting it to Reims.[18] The queen can be glimpsed wearing this gown in a drawing made from life and the corresponding print published later.[19] From her elevated position in the gallery above the altar, the wide paniers, bodice and lace sleeves of Marie Antoinette's formal court dress are visible, the queen further adorned with jewels, a feathered coiffure and an open fan.

In addition to its weight, the French bodice that made up part of the *grand habit*, the stiff-boned *corps*, was rigid and known to be worn exceptionally tightly laced. Marie Antoinette's mother, Maria Theresa, offered to send her some from Vienna instead as, 'They say that those from Paris are too strong'.[20] Marie Antoinette's paniers were made by a seamstress at Versailles and her *grand corps* were made by the Paris tailor, Sigly, who supplied the royal family.[21] A silk bodice believed to have belonged to Marie Antoinette, which was found pressed between the pages of the account book of one of her *marchandes de modes*, Madame Éloffe, is in the style of a *corps* but has removable boning. It was probably designed to be worn during pregnancy or periods of ill-health, or possibly, given the constellation of pin holes, to trial ornaments and trimmings (fig.51). It is not surprising that Marie Antoinette famously came to despise the *grand habit* and Madame Campan recalled that as soon as she reached her private apartments she would remove her train and paniers. Once she became queen, Marie Antoinette asked Louis XVI to retire it, whereupon formal court dress was gradually replaced by other more fashionable styles.[22]

A petticoat fragment, probably from one of Marie Antoinette's *robes de cour* or *robes parés* dating from this later period, shows the breathtaking refinement and luxury of these gowns (fig.50). The length of ivory silk satin is richly embellished with solid silver-gilt spangles (sequins), coloured paste gems, appliquéd velvet and metal-thread embroidery giving a wonderful *trompe-l'œil* effect of trailing stems of pink and white roses and blue cornflowers, tied with bows and tassels simulating the swags of silk, gold fringe and other three-dimensional trimmings conventionally used on *grands habits*.[23] This was part of the period's taste for visual trickery which can be seen in wallpapers, marquetry and even porcelain imitating textile effects (see fig.24).

Other common types of court dress included the *habit de bal*, the ball dress, which was bell-shaped – shorter and narrower than other dresses thereby facilitating dancing. The queen was known to be a skilled dancer and the English writer and

52. A DOMINO FOR A MAN OR WOMAN, 1765–70
ENGLAND, PINK SILK LUSTRING WITH CAPE
AND HOOD. V&A: T.195–1968

**53. *L'ENTRÉE DU TAPIS VERT À VERSAILLES*
(SHOWING MARIE ANTOINETTE AGED 20), 1775**
HUBERT ROBERT (1733–1808), OIL ON CANVAS,
124 × 191 CM. MUSÉE NATIONAL DES CHÂTEAUX
DE VERSAILLES ET DE TRIANON: INV. MV 774

politician, Horace Walpole, was witness to the sensation Marie Antoinette made at a Versailles *bal paré* in 1775, exclaiming, 'it was impossible to see anything but the Queen! Hebes, and Floras, and Helens and Graces, are streetwalkers to her.' Walpole went on to describe her exact attire, 'She was dressed in silver scattered over with laurierroses [oleanders]; few diamonds, and feathers…'.[24]

The queen's ball costumes and those of her ladies-in-waiting, often commissioned from Rose Bertin and featuring costly gold and silver thread accessories, came out of the entertainment budget of the *Menus-Plaisirs*, the department in charge of court ceremonies and festivities.[25] When the King of Sweden, Gustav III, visited Versailles in June 1784, Madame Bertin dressed all the ladies of the court for a masked ball held in his honour, which Marie Antoinette's lady-in-waiting, the princesse de Lamballe reported, created a 'beautiful spectacle', exclaiming that Bertin 'surpassed herself in grace and magnificence on this day, thus, you can imagine, what a wonderful thing!'[26] These were not always a success however, the superintendent of the *Menus-Plaisirs*, Denis-Pierre-Jean Papillon de La Ferté, complained of shoddy work in some of Bertin's completed costumes but mindful of the futility of questioning one so powerful said that he would pay her bills 'nonetheless'.[27]

For public balls and masquerades, where, as one fashion journal put it, 'one goes not to dance, but to enjoy the spectacle without being recognized',[28] men and women would cover their ensembles with a domino, an elegant and voluminous hooded silk cape that fastened in the front with bows and was worn with a black velvet mask (fig.52). Marie Antoinette and Louis XVI can be seen wearing dominos in 1782 while attending a masked ball in Paris held to celebrate the birth of their son, the dauphin.[29]

'All wished instantly to have the same dress as the Queen'
Madame Campan, *Memoirs*, 1823[30]

In addition to court (ceremonial and formal) dress, Marie Antoinette adopted and drove trends in a market for fashionable dress that, with its acceleration in pace, emerging fashion press, and the powerful influence of a select number from the trade, foreshadowed the fashion industry we know today. One early example of the queen wearing fashionable dress comes from a painting commissioned by Louis XVI in 1775 of the royal family in the gardens of Versailles. In a small yet charming detail, Marie Antoinette can be glimpsed playing with the daughters of her ladies-in-waiting and wearing an ivory *robe à la polonaise* with pleated trimming, pink bows, a knotted fichu and a dainty *bergère* hat (fig.53). The little

girls in their dresses also worn *retroussée* (drawn up) are like miniature versions of the queen who was not, in fact, so very much older than them. The painting was executed at the height of the fashion for the *robe à la polonaise* during the 1770s and Marie Antoinette can also be seen wearing this style in her portrait by Élisabeth Vigée Le Brun (fig.55). Although it took many forms it was essentially an open gown that was not fitted to the waist, the skirts of which were drawn up and fastened with ribbons or cords to create the enchanting effect of airy puffs of silk.[31] The loose waist and open front revealed the fitted bodice and petticoat worn underneath. Other styles of gowns could also be worn *retroussée* to give a similar effect, an exquisite surviving example is a pink, white and green, floral and striped *robe à la française* with a beautifully embellished stomacher that is confection-like in its prettiness (fig.54).

One of the most notorious episodes in the queen's reign was triggered by her fashion forwardness: the *chemise* dress scandal of 1783 (see Banić and Harpley in this volume, p.113).[32] The gown (and portrait) that replaced it, while more appropriate, were no less fashionable. In this now iconic depiction, the most famous of all portraits of the queen, Marie Antoinette wears a steel-blue silk satin gown, the inverted 'V' shape of the front of the gown and the visible triangle of silk behind her back indicating it is most likely a 'polonaise longue' – a *robe à la polonaise* worn unbustled or long (fig.55).[33] The very fine blonde (silk) lace trimmings, and the collar were much in vogue but it is the satin in particular that was undergoing a period of intense popularity and is thought to demonstrate the queen's support of the silk-weaving industry.

Another silk satin gown and likely survival from Marie Antoinette's wardrobe are the fragments of a beautiful *robe à l'anglaise* of a salmon-pink silk satin decorated with spangles and embroidered ermine tails (fig.56). Both are traditionally associated with royalty but also testify to the 1780s craze for animal print of every description, from leopard to zebra – the queen has some examples in her wardrobe book of 1782.[34] The luxurious quality and likely royal provenance are reinforced by the fact that the spangles are made of pure silver.[35]

Much, if not all, of the dress and accessories worn in Marie Antoinette's portraits were based on her real wardrobe. Trimmings and accessories were lent to artists so that they could capture the detail after the sittings had finished. This was the case for the miniaturist François Dumont who had been lent a small black *collerette* and a coral necklace for his portraits of the queen which his descendants still had in their possession in the 1930s.[36] This is surely the same *collerette* seen in his miniature of the queen which was subsequently set into an earlier snuff box

55. *MARIE ANTOINETTE À LA ROSE* (AGED 27), 1783
ÉLISABETH VIGÉE LE BRUN (1755–1842), OIL ON CANVAS, 116 × 88 CM. MUSÉE NATIONAL DES CHÂTEAUX DE VERSAILLES ET DE TRIANON: INV. MV 3893

56. FRAGMENT OF PETTICOAT FROM AN OPEN CLOSE-BODIED COURT GOWN, PROBABLY BELONGING TO MARIE ANTOINETTE, c.1780–91
FRANCE, SALMON-PINK SILK SATIN WITH SOLID SILVER SPANGLES AND EMBROIDERED EMBELLISHMENTS TO RESEMBLE ERMINE. LONDON MUSEUM: G.32.149;149A;149B;149C; 149D;149E

57. SNUFFBOX WITH PORTRAIT OF MARIE ANTOINETTE, c.1780 (MINIATURE), 1768 (BOX)
PORTRAIT: FRANÇOIS DUMONT (1751–1831);
BOX: PIERRE-FRANÇOIS-MATHIS DE BEAULIEU (1750–1819), WATERCOLOUR ON IVORY IN A GOLD AND ENAMEL BOX. THE CLEVELAND MUSEUM OF ART: 1957.408. GIFT OF MRS. EDWARD B. GREENE

58. MARIE ANTOINETTE'S COLLERETTE (DECORATIVE LACE COLLAR), LATE 18TH CENTURY
BLACK COTTON LACE AND BLACK RIBBON. MUSÉE CARNAVALET, PARIS: INV. OM 272

59. MARIE ANTOINETTE WITH HER TWO CHILDREN WALKING IN THE PARK OF THE TRIANON (SHOWING MARIE ANTOINETTE AGED 30), 1785
ADOLF-ULRIK WERTMÜLLER (1751–1811), OIL ON CANVAS, 276 × 194 CM. NATIONALMUSEUM SWEDEN: NM 1032

(fig.57). A black lace *collerette* belonging to Marie Antoinette, once believed to be a mourning headband, could well be the original accessory (fig.58). A woman was employed within Marie Antoinette's garderobe just to make her collerettes.[37]

A fine example of fashionable dress worn by the queen is that of the shot-silk taffeta *robe à la turque* seen in her portrait with her children (fig.59). This was based on a real gown, commissioned specially for the portrait, the silk chosen not just as a highly fashionable fabric but for the beautiful effects it would create in paint.[38] Madame Campan, who organized the details, reminded the artist that everything had to be perfect as, 'this enterprise will draw the eyes and the criticism of all of Paris'.[39] A deep purple shot with orange, the shoes are matched in the same silk, and the harmonious effect is continued by the purple ribbon in the queen's coiffure.

A.Wertmüller. Svedois
à Paris 1785.

In fashionable dress Marie Antoinette embraced and modelled the latest silhouettes and trends, such as Anglomania, and was pivotal in advancing the new informality in dress. Fashions were extremely personal to the queen and her accounts make frequent mention of gowns hand-selected by her, such as a dress of Toile de Jouy she wore in the spring/autumn of 1779. Even the colours she chose had personal significance: Marie Antoinette wore one satin *grand habit* in a shade of blue replicating the colour of Louis XVI's eyes, known as 'king's eye', and had another *grand habit* embroidered with flowers from the Petit Trianon. Her favourite Trianon flower, the cornflower, appears as a frequent motif on a number of gowns. Similarly, in 1781, the same year her 'pearls and cornflowers' service with its fashionable ground colour of 'merde d'oie', or goose dung (i.e. a muted green), was delivered, she wore several informal gowns in a matching shade.[40] During the hostile Tuileries years of 1789–92, when the royal family was under virtual house arrest, part of Marie Antoinette's wardrobe was retrieved from Versailles but new purchases also had to be made, many of which can be found in the journal of her *marchande de modes*, Madame Éloffe, which covers the period 1787–93. Following the Revolution in 1789, for example, she purchased large quantities of 'national ribbon', in pink, white and blue satin, for the trimming of gowns and hats in an appropriately patriotic display as well as numerous cockades (cockades worn at court were pink, white and blue, other cockades were the more conventional poppy-red, white and blue; fig.60).[41]

The baron du Frénilly later recalled that all fashionable women of this time wore 'flat shoes, fitted/narrow skirts and the Pierrot'.[42] In 1781 the queen had 11 different pierrots in a variety of fabrics in her spring wardrobe.[43] Marie Antoinette can be seen wearing a striped silk pierrot or redingote in a portrait from 1788, which can be compared to a strikingly similar extant example of blue silk taffeta with thin yellow, red, green and black satin stripes and fringed braid (figs 61 and 62). The 1792 wardrobe book of Marie Antoinette's sister-in-law, Madame Élisabeth, is an invaluable window onto the later gowns and fabrics the queen was wearing. It shows samples for *grands habits* in striped and chiné silks of a bruised palette of purple, chestnut and black, an increasingly sombre palette for unsettled times.[44]

In eighteenth-century France, the term 'garde-robe', or wardrobe, referred both to the physical space in which garments were stored, the modern-day equivalent of which would be a dressing room, with the furniture required of such a space, and to the contents of the wardrobe itself – all the garments, accessories, undergarments and linen. Marie Antoinette's *garde-robe* at Versailles was composed of three large rooms bordered with *armoires* (wardrobes) providing both shelves and hanging space, and large tables in the centre of the room on which to lay out, alter and mend garments.[45] Her wardrobe

Overleaf left
61. *MARIE ANTOINETTE* (AGED 33), 1788
ADOLF-ULRIK WERTMÜLLER (1751–1811), OIL ON
CANVAS, 65.5 × 54.4 CM. MUSÉE NATIONAL
DES CHÂTEAUX DE VERSAILLES ET DE TRIANON:
INV. MV 8211

Overleaf right
**62. STRIPED SILK CARACO (PIERROT) JACKET
AND EMBROIDERED PETTICOAT, c.1790**
FRANCE, BLUE SILK WITH FINE YELLOW AND
BLACK STRIPES, EDGED WITH PINK, YELLOW
AND GREEN FRINGED SILK BRAID; MUSLIN
PETTICOAT EMBROIDERED WITH COLOURED
SILKS. V&A: T.1, 2, 3–2023

was a royal chattel and could even be viewed by the public. A young Englishwoman, Anna Cradock, came to Versailles to see it in July 1784 and marvelled at the spectacle:

> [We came to] see part of the Queen's wardrobe. The great gowns are, all at once, of an inconceivable richness and elegance. Most of them in pink, blue, or other coloured satin, are finely embroidered with pearls and trimmed either with magnificent lace, or with pleated ribbons, or with gold or silver braids.[46]

The queen's wardrobe was composed of 105–8 gowns for the year, of which 90 per cent were new orders. There were 36 for each of the three seasons: winter; summer; spring/autumn. These were categorized by degree of formality: 12 *grands habits* (formal court gowns); 12 'rich' gowns (gowns made of costly textiles or embellished) on paniers; and 12 more informal gowns.[47] Purchases were made seasonally and with specific events, settings and etiquette in mind, but gowns were frequently retained and worn again. In the winter of 1779, for example, two new *grands habits* were ordered for All Saints' Day and New Year, two of the most important feast days in the calendar, and the queen re-wore two of the previous year's formal gowns for Christmas and Candlemas.[48] Everyday gowns, those of a simpler design and made from less expensive fabrics such as cotton and muslin, were not included in this overall figure and were kept and worn for several years. While there is therefore no substance to the myth that Marie Antoinette never wore a gown more than once, the number of new gowns ordered every year was still an extravagance only possible for the royal family. For her courtiers, *grands habits* were so costly that it was preferable to repair, replace or update them rather than order an entirely new ensemble.

The queen's wardrobe expenditure is also complex. When Marie Antoinette became queen in 1774, she was given a set wardrobe budget of 120,000 *livres* (£775,000 in today's money). However, this budget had not been increased in almost 50 years, since it was first set in 1725, when Marie Leszczyńska became queen. It was inevitable then, that Marie Antoinette would exceed it to some degree. Nonetheless, Marie Antoinette's spending on her wardrobe increased steadily and then rose dramatically under the influence of the *marchande de modes*, Rose Bertin, who charged a staggering amount for her services and wares. In 1782, for example, almost half of the queen's annual wardrobe expenditure of 186,057 *livres* went directly on bills to Bertin.[49] Throughout the 1780s, the rise in the use of accessories and trimmings meant that these now accounted for well over half of the total bill – the amount spent on the actual silks and other textiles from which the gowns were made was markedly less. Madame Campan felt strongly that it was Bertin's arrival

on the scene that set Marie Antoinette's downfall in motion. To compound matters,
as early as 1772 the Austrian ambassador, the comte de Mercy-Argenteau, attributed
the overspending to mismanagement of the wardrobe by the queen's *dame d'atours*,
whose responsibility it was to place orders and maintain the accounts and in whose
interest it was to spend lavishly as she stood to benefit from the items that would be
passed on to her to be resold at the end of the year.[50] He noted the absurd amounts
and quantity of some articles that, unbeknown to the queen, were being ordered
and which would never be used. This was a contributing factor, as were the inflated
commissions charged by the *marchandes de modes*, yet still the queen did not take
an active role in bringing the budget under control. The maximum amount Marie
Antoinette spent in one year on her wardrobe was 258,002 *livres* in 1785 (£1.6 million
in today's money) although this was exceptional.[51] But herein lay the central paradox,
for while the queen's role as consort required her to support and promote native
luxury trades – the silk-weaving industry for example – and, as Madame Campan
pointed out, her subjects expected a regal and brilliant display from their sovereigns,
she was continuously pilloried for her spending and her interest in fashion.[52]

Marie Antoinette's wardrobe was regularly pruned and divested of its contents,
which were distributed to her *dame d'atours* for whom the re-use or sale of such items
were considered a privilege of her office and part of her remuneration. Thus the
wardrobe, as it existed in 1789 when the Revolution erupted, did not comprise every
single garment that she had ever worn since her arrival in France in 1770. Nevertheless,
it was a significant asset, its contents highly valuable and also symbolic. During the
attack on the Tuileries palace of 10 August 1792, when the royal family escaped with
their lives but 700 of their guards, courtiers and servants were killed,[53] mayhem ensued
and Marie Antoinette's wardrobe was looted and dispersed. What few articles remained
were sold off with the palace contents the following year.[54]

In the Temple prison, the queen was accorded a modest allowance for her wardrobe,
and stylish to the very end, some of the final articles of dress she ordered were a
redingote and 'pierrots of percale [cotton], pink and white, blue and white: a pierrot
of toile de Jouy'.[55] However, by the time she reached the Conciergerie, at which point
the monarchy had lost all its authority and aura of inviolability, her belongings had
dwindled to a mere handful of items, including her fine chemise, which survives to
this day and has assumed a relic-like reverence (fig.63). On the day of her execution,
the queen put aside the black mourning she had worn continuously since Louis XVI's
death earlier that year and donned the final article of clothing she would ever wear, a
plain white chemise dress (*déshabillé*) of cotton piqué, a knotted white muslin fichu and
a white cap over her hair, newly shorn for the guillotine blade.

28

32

33

34

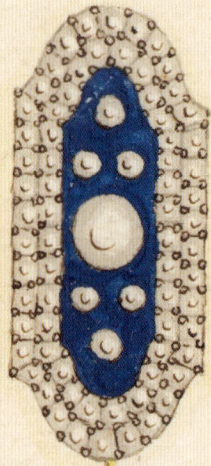

QUEEN OF SPARKLE: DIAMONDS, FASHION AND POLITICS

Vincent Meylan

The letter is dated February 1776. It is kept in the Archives nationales in Paris, in the dossier of Ange-Joseph Aubert (1736–1785) jeweller to the French Crown, and is addressed to Monsieur de Malesherbes, Minister of the Maison du Roi (the King's Household) of King Louis XVI:

> I just received an order from the Queen (Marie Antoinette) via a letter from sieur Bazin, manservant to the King, to deliver to Mademoiselle Bertin, *marchande de modes* [fashion merchant/milliner], all the Crown diamonds she might need to embellish the outfit that the Queen has ordered from her … I was at Madame Bertin's [*sic*], and gave her 814 chatons (cushion-cut diamonds) and rose-cut diamonds belonging to the Crown and had them itemized.[1]

Ange-Joseph Aubert maintained, modified, restored or created jewellery *parures* (sets) made with the precious stones belonging to the state. A large part of this treasure, notably the king's regalia and the queen's parures, were kept at Versailles, but the unused stones – numbering in the hundreds – were deposited at his atelier in the Tuileries. The request of Mademoiselle Bertin, fashion merchant to the queen, was very unusual, but illustrates the new way the young Queen Marie Antoinette intended to use the Crown diamonds. All previous sovereigns had worn them as symbols of pomp and power, at times even with tedium, whereas she simply associated them with fashion.

Less than two years previously, Louis XVI had ascended the throne of France. The excitement of those first months now in the past, the young 20-year-old queen found herself isolated in her sumptuous apartments at the palace of Versailles. The long days dragged for Marie Antoinette, who was no intellectual, and who was neglected by her husband. Her passions were gambling, music, dance, theatre and fashion. Rose Bertin, who she had recently discovered, was the fashionable stylist – to use a contemporary term – of the mid-1770s. She was not a dressmaker, but was known as a *marchande de modes* or fashion merchant.[2] Her job was to embellish the queen's dresses. Her Majesty chose the fabrics, the seamstresses did the sewing and Mademoiselle Bertin decorated the finished gown with garlands of fabric flowers, with gold, silver or silk lace, and with embroidery. Precious jewels were one of the tools of her trade. In the eighteenth century, they were often sewn onto fabric to create sumptuous embroidery, particularly on the bodice of a dress. We will probably never know what the famous 'outfit' was, ordered specially by the Queen of France from Mademoiselle Bertin, but it was certainly lavish enough to have several hundreds of Crown diamonds sewn onto it.

64. DESIGNS FOR BLUE ENAMEL AND DIAMOND BEZEL-SET GOLD RINGS AND OTHER JEWELS (DETAIL OF FIG.76)

65. GOLD RING WITH RUBY AND DIAMOND DOUBLE HEART BEZEL, c.1780
WESTERN EUROPE. SIMILAR DIAMOND AND RUBY HEART RINGS ARE DESCRIBED IN A REVOLUTIONARY INVENTORY OF MARIE ANTOINETTE'S JEWELS. V&A: M.171–2007

66. DESIGNS FOR BLUE ENAMEL AND DIAMOND BEZEL-SET GOLD RINGS AND OTHER JEWELS, 1780s
EUROPE, INK AND COLOURED GOUACHE ON PAPER. A SIMILAR RING WAS WORN BY MARIE ANTOINETTE IN HER 1785 PORTRAIT (FIG.59). V&A: D.320–1899

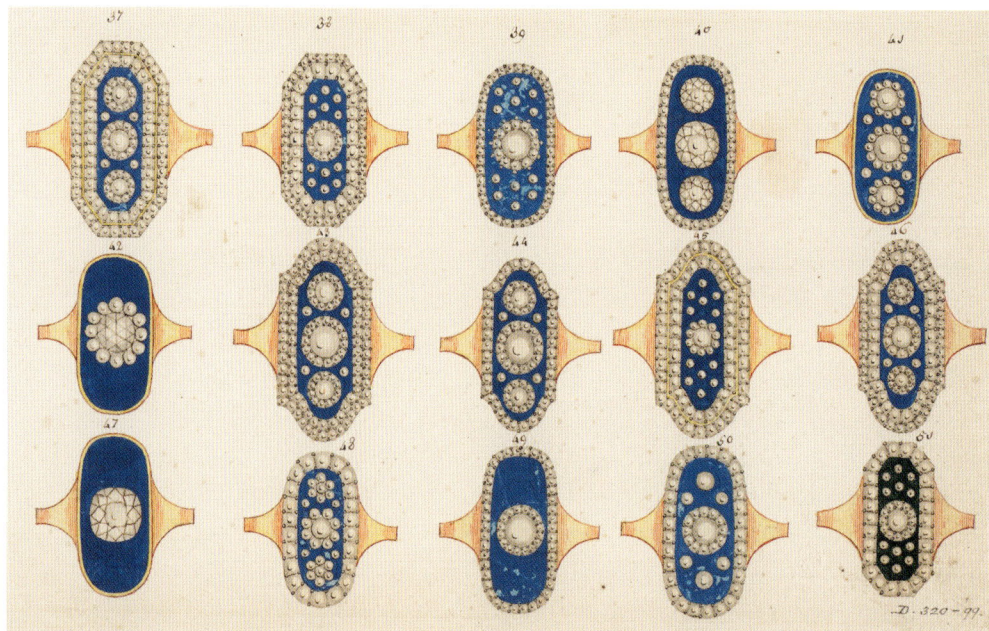

At this time, Marie Antoinette possessed an extraordinary number of diamonds, which were divided into two distinct collections: those belonging to the Crown and her personal jewels (fig.67). The most significant diamonds from the Crown collection – the 140-carat Regent diamond, the 55-carat Sancy diamond (both now in the Louvre), Louis XIV's great 69-carat French Blue diamond and the 30-carat 'Mirror of Portugal' diamond – were set in the king's regalia, but the queen sometimes wore them as a pendant or pinned into her hair. She also had at her disposal a ruby and diamond parure, a string of very large pearls and several hundred unmounted stones. She could use these sets as she wished, but they did not belong to her. However, her personal collection was her private property, and was very significant. Its first mention can be found in the Austrian State Archives in Vienna. The comte de Mercy-Argenteau, Austrian ambassador to Versailles, oversaw all the preparations for the union of the archduchess Marie Antoinette and the future Louis XVI. This marriage, which took place in 1770, was above all a political one. A year before the ceremony, Mercy-Argenteau warned Empress Maria Theresa of Austria, mother of Marie Antoinette, of the special role that the diamonds – at the time the term referred to all precious stones – would play in the marriage of the future queens of France:

67. MARIE ANTOINETTE'S JEWELLERY BOX, 1770–5
MARTIN CARLIN (1730–1785), OAK AND ROSEWOOD WITH SÈVRES PORCELAIN PLAQUES, 95 × 55.5 × 37.5 CM. MUSÉE NATIONAL DES CHÂTEAUX DE VERSAILLES ET DE TRIANON: INV. V 5807

… diamonds, as well as gold jewellery, being the only effects that are not vulnerable to the plunder of court offices, and thus becoming the only asset that the archduchess could keep, he advised, for the benefit of the princess, that it pleased Her Majesty to give her as little as possible in clothing and to convert into jewellery and gemstones the rest of the sum allocated for the provision of her royal highness.[3]

The young archduchess was delivered to the French court, not entirely naked as is often erroneously claimed, but without any clothing of foreign origin. The ceremony unfolded on an island on the Rhine near Strasbourg. The archduchess changed her dress in a *cabinet de toilette* under the watch of her Austrian lady-in-waiting, the princesse de Paar, her French lady-in-waiting, the comtesse de Noailles, and her *dame d'atours*, the duchesse de Villars, who had chosen her new trousseau.[4] Only then did she appear in the state drawing room, before emerging on the French side with her new court. The empress had followed her ambassador's advice. In terms of clothing, her daughter had received only a travel outfit and a few gowns. The entirety of the 400,000 French *livres* allocated by the empress for her daughter's trousseau was used to buy jewels. This list is also preserved in the Austrian State Archives. The first piece is a necklace 'complete with bow and pendant, *esclavage* and pendant'.[5] The piece is actually a double necklace. The single necklace is in effect a choker, decorated at the centre with a bow and pendant (fig.68). The *esclavage* or 'slave' necklace is a wider piece which skims the neckline, and also features a pendant. The two pieces can be worn together. The next piece is an aigrette in two parts. Aigrettes were the perfect ornament for the still somewhat flat hairstyles of the 1770s (see fig.48). Next were two diamond girandole earrings, four pairs of diamond shoe buckles, two clips, two rings, thirteen jewelled buttons, twenty-nine diamond-headed pins – pins were indispensable because some elements of a woman's attire, such as lace or cuffs, were removable – a diamond bow from which to hang Austria's diamond Order of the Cross, several miniatures surrounded by diamonds, and a 'ribbon' (i.e. a flexible necklace) with eight diamond motifs. The only pieces that were not exclusively decorated with diamonds were two bracelets made of several strands of pearls fastened with diamond clasps (fig.69).[6]

Upon her arrival at the court of Versailles, Marie Antoinette received another set of precious stones. King Louis XV had purchased all the jewels from the estate of his daughter-in-law, the dauphine Maria Josepha of Saxony, who died in 1767. The ensemble was estimated at two million *livres*, that is to say, five times the value of the jewels given by Empress Maria Theresa to her daughter. The most significant of these

was a 'stomacher' or bodice ornament made of several thousand diamonds. It had been created around 1745 by Jean-Baptiste Leblanc, Jeweller to the French Crown at the time. The stomacher was the quintessential court jewel, and Marie Antoinette's was lavish. It was part of the *grand habit de cour*, the required formal dress for ladies at the French court. The diamond stomacher created by Leblanc is in the form of three bows of decreasing size, embellished with pendants, scrolls and ribbons, set with large and small diamonds, and was sewn onto the main body of the dress. The accompanying epaulettes were attached to the top of the bodice sleeves, the lace ruffles descending from these fastened to the shoulders with diamond-headed pins. The four *tailles* (waist clasps), two for the front and two for the back, concealed the hooks that fasten together the petticoat and bodice. The *trousse-côtés*, two strands of large diamonds with hooks at each end, 'trussed' or raised the train left and right. The *trousse-queue* served the same purpose at the back. Next were pairs of diamond *boutons de compère* or bodice studs, attached to areas of the dress the woman wanted to highlight. The hair was set with more studs, an aigrette and possibly strands of pearls. In addition to the stomacher, the four *tailles*, the *trousse-côtés*, the *trousse-queue* and the studs, the parure Marie Antoinette received included a necklace and two pairs of earrings, one in the form of simple pendants and the other girandoles. This personal collection was completed by a set of pearls, comprising two necklaces (one with six strands) and a pair of bracelets, as well as two parures of coloured stones, one of rubies and the other of emeralds. These last two comprised brooches, pendant earrings and aigrettes.[7] Thus when Marie Antoinette became queen of France in May 1774, she had her own private collection of diamonds and precious stones worth around two and a half million French *livres*. For the time, and even among European queens, few could rival this.

Once queen, she continued to add to her collection. As a New Year's gift at the beginning of 1775, King Louis XVI gave her an aigrette and a watch, both entirely set with diamonds. These two pieces of jewellery, purchased from Aubert, were invoiced at 25,440 and 11,000 *livres* respectively.[8] In January 1776, the queen bought from Charles-Auguste Boehmer, a young jeweller of German origin, a pair of pendant earrings for 348,000 *livres*. The original price was 480,000 *livres*, but in offering to replace the two round diamonds that attached the pendants to the ear with two round diamonds of her own, the queen obtained a discount of 132,000 *livres*. She paid 48,000 *livres* in cash and planned on settling the balance – 300,000 *livres* – in two or three years by making savings from the annual allowance paid to her by the Treasury for her personal expenses. Six months later, during the summer of 1776, she acquired, again from Boehmer, a pair of diamond bracelets for 250,000 *livres* (fig.72). Each was made of three strands of 17 diamonds, with a clasp of large diamonds. Her debt to the jeweller was now 550,000 *livres* – two and a half times her annual allowance. Her purse now depleted, she paid a deposit in kind for the bracelets, offering Boehmer to choose from the older jewellery she no longer wanted. The jeweller accepted a diamond jewellery set that he estimated at 80,000 *livres*, but the queen still owed him 470,000 *livres*.

In November, with gambling debts adding to those linked to the diamond purchases, Marie Antoinette was forced to admit her personal bankruptcy to Louis, who assumed the debt. He negotiated its repayment in 34 instalments. His personal account book, kept at the Bibliothèque nationale in Paris, records these payments, including interest, up to December 1782.[9]

At the beginning of 1780, in keeping with the times, the queen's collection underwent a fairly radical change in style. With the rise of neoclassicism dress became much simpler. Hairstyles, too, evolved. The structured, powdered chignons on which elegant women heaped aigrettes, strands of pearls and feathers were replaced by styles that were fuller and looser, but equally sophisticated. It was for one of these new styles that the queen ordered from Aubert, in July 1782, a series of 12 diamond ears of wheat, for which she provided the stones. The cost of making them was 2,400 *livres*.[10] A year later, in June 1783, she ordered from Aubert a lavish

70. *TRAITÉ DES PIERRES PRÉCIEUSES ET DE LA MANIÈRE DE LES EMPLOYER EN PARURE* (TREATISE ON PRECIOUS STONES AND THE ART OF USING THEM IN ADORNMENT), 1762
JEAN HENRI PROSPER POUGET (D. 1769), DESIGNS FOR DIAMOND BOW NECKLACE AND BODICE ORNAMENTS AND HEART PENDANTS, POUGET FILS, PARIS. V&A, NAL: 38041800751745

71. BOW ORNAMENTS, *c.*1760
EUROPE, BRILLIANT-CUT DIAMONDS SET IN SILVER. V&A: M.93, 94&A–1951

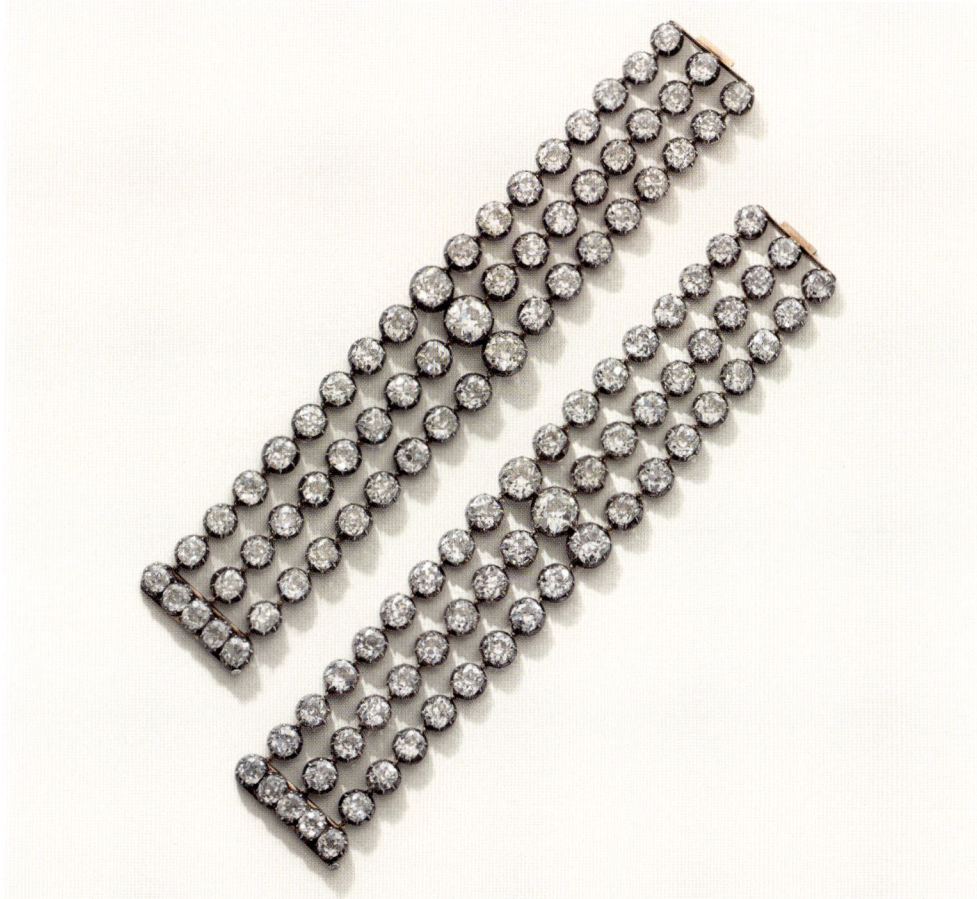

belt buckle. It was made of 18 diamonds, which must have been quite large, as it cost 52,260 *livres*.[11] But the most significant order dates from 30 July 1783. The queen asked Aubert to completely reset the *pièce de corps* or jewelled stomacher that she had inherited from Maria Josepha of Saxony. This ensemble, all scrolls, foliage and swirls of diamonds, was the epitome of the rococo style – and the absolute antithesis of the new fashions. The new, more restrained *pièce de corps*, is the one found in the inventory of queen's jewellery drawn up on 10 February 1794 in Brussels.

Article 1
A *pièce de corps* made of seven buttons, one of which is pear shaped, six strands of chatons [cushion-cut diamonds] made of 136 chatons and tassels, all in diamonds.[12]

The manufacture of this new *pièce de corps* was invoiced at 5,000 *livres* and its case at 84 *livres*.[13] During this same month of July 1783 the queen sold Aubert all the gems which had been set in the rococo-style *pièce de corps* that she had inherited from her mother-in-law, that is to say, 9,207 gems weighing 694 carats for a total of 58,809 *livres*.[14] In August 1784 a second set of gems was delivered to Aubert for a total amount of 23,574 *livres*.[15] In November, as compensation for these losses, Louis XVI gave his wife all the jewels belonging to his deceased aunt, Princess Maria Christina of Saxony. As the princess had been heavily in debt, the king purchased her jewels from the estate for a sum of 158,000 *livres*.[16] The last significant addition to the queen's collection took place on 13 March 1785. Since her marriage she had made use of a number of jewels belonging to the French Crown, notably a diamond and ruby parure estimated at 145,000 *livres*. She often wore this set, which she mixed with stones given to her by Louis at the time of their marriage. She also added some other pieces purchased from Aubert, meaning it was impossible to distinguish which jewels belonged to the Crown, and which were from the queen's personal collection. The king therefore signed a special decree, removing the jewels from the Crown treasury, in order to give them to the queen as her own property.[17] The gift of the ruby parure from the Crown was the last act recorded by Aubert before offering his resignation a few weeks later. In his letter, he cited reasons of health and suggested the jeweller Boehmer, as his replacement. Boehmer was no stranger, having previously sold diamonds to the queen, but he was to become extremely well known a few months later, during the infamous 'Affair of the Diamond Necklace'.

The scandal erupted on 15 August 1785. The entire court was assembled in the Hall of Mirrors to watch the procession for the feast of Assumption, one of the most important dates in the religious calendar. In front of everyone, the cardinal de Rohan, Grand Almoner of France, in full regalia of red robe and lace surplice, was arrested by order of the king and sent to the Bastille. The comtesse de la Motte, a descendant of the kings of France, now fallen into penury, soon joined him. As did the comte de Cagliostro, a Sicilian adventurer (real name: Joseph Balsamo); a young woman of easy virtue, Nicole Le Guay d'Oliva, and a forger, chevalier de Rétaux de Villette. All were implicated in the theft of a magnificent diamond necklace created by the jewellers Boehmer and Bassenge. The jewel was made of 674 diamonds, totalling 2,842 carats (fig. 74). The central part contained 17 diamonds ranging from five to eight carats, supporting swags from which hung six enormous pear-shaped diamonds. The central necklace was framed by triple-stranded bands of large diamonds, terminating in diamond tassels. The jewellers had created it for Madame du Barry, favourite of Louis XV, but alas the king had died before the necklace was finished. They therefore offered it to Louis XVI for Marie Antoinette, for the colossal price of 1,600,000 *livres*.

74. REPLICA OF THE BOEHMER AND BASSENGE DIAMOND NECKLACE, FROM THE AFFAIR OF THE DIAMOND NECKLACE OF 1784–5, COMMISSIONED BY KING LOUIS XV FOR MADAME DU BARRY IN 1772
WHITE SAPPHIRES, PEARLS, SILVER AND SILK, 1960–3. MUSÉE NATIONAL DES CHÂTEAUX DE VERSAILLES ET DE TRIANON: INV. V 3925

75. NECKLACE CONTAINING THE SUTHERLAND DIAMONDS, 18TH CENTURY (SOME STONES 17TH CENTURY)
TWENTY LARGE OLD BRILLIANT-CUT DIAMONDS IN SILVER-TOPPED GOLD COLLETS. V&A: M.10:1 TO 3–2022. ACCEPTED IN LIEU OF INHERITANCE TAX BY HM GOVERNMENT AND ALLOCATED TO THE V&A, 2022

The king agreed to the cost, but the queen, who was already very unpopular and owned so many diamonds, felt it prudent to refuse the gift.

It was this official refusal that Madame de la Motte, her husband, and her lover, Rétaux de Villette, would use to set up their scam. They convinced the jewellers that the queen had not dared to accept the necklace publicly, but that she dreamed of owning it. To lend credibility to their scheme, they decided to entrust the negotiation to the cardinal de Rohan. During his embassy to Vienna, the cardinal had greatly irritated the queen's mother, and he was ready to do anything to gain Marie Antoinette's favour. Madame de la Motte gave him a letter forged by Villette, purportedly from the queen. A fake meeting was organized, to take place at night in the park of Versailles, with Mademoiselle d'Oliva, a Parisian prostitute who resembled the queen. Wearing a veil and standing several metres away from the cardinal, she was convincing. Rohan took

charge of contacting the jewellers on the queen's behalf, paying for the small deposit himself. The necklace was entrusted to him, and he passed it on to Rétaux de Villette, who was posing as one of the queen's valets. The comte de la Motte had the diamonds removed and sent to London, where they were discreetly sold.

A few months after the theft, the jewellers became worried that they had not seen the queen wearing the necklace. Most concerning of all, the instalments they had agreed to pay for the necklace had not been honoured. Boehmer, Crown Jeweller, demanded an audience with the queen. She, of course, knew nothing of the situation and informed the king. Rather than settle the whole business discreetly, the queen called for a public trial. The investigation would last a year. The questioning that took place in London in December 1785, by representatives of the French judicial system with the cooperation of the British government, gave precise details of the fate of the necklace.[18] Two British jewellers, William Gray (son of Robert Gray) of New Bond Street and Nathanial Jefferys of Piccadilly, acknowledged having met the comte de la Motte in April 1785, when he offered them a very large quantity of diamonds. Nathanial Jefferys's offer was rejected by La Motte as too little, but William Gray bought several hundred diamonds for more than 10,000 pounds sterling. For each group of diamonds, Gray specified which part of the necklace they had come from. However, he gave few details about the jewellery he had made with the diamonds, with the exception of a necklace made of 41 large diamonds and a pair of ear studs made from a single diamond each.

After a year of proceedings, the cardinal de Rohan was exonerated, although he agreed to pay the jewellers for the necklace. Madame de la Motte was sentenced to be marked with a branding iron and life imprisonment, from which she escaped. But no matter who was guilty or innocent, for a large number of French people the real culprit was their queen. The perception of Marie Antoinette pillaging the coffers of France to finance her entertainment and amass diamonds and jewels was lent support by the whole affair. Diamonds would become one of the political symbols of the Revolution. For many historians, the 'Affair of the Diamond Necklace' was the prelude to it.

The rest is well known. The Fall of the Bastille in July 1789. The March on Versailles at the beginning of October 1789, to bring the royal family back to Paris. The virtual house arrest of King Louis XVI, Queen Marie Antoinette and their family at the Tuileries palace. Their attempted escape and subsequent arrest at Varennes in June 1791. The Storming of the Tuileries on 10 August, the trials of the king and queen and their respective executions on 21 January 1793 and 16 October 1793. The execution of the king's sister, Madame Élisabeth, on 10 May 1794. The sovereigns' son, the young Louis XVII, dying practically alone in the Temple prison at the age of 10, after months of appalling detention.

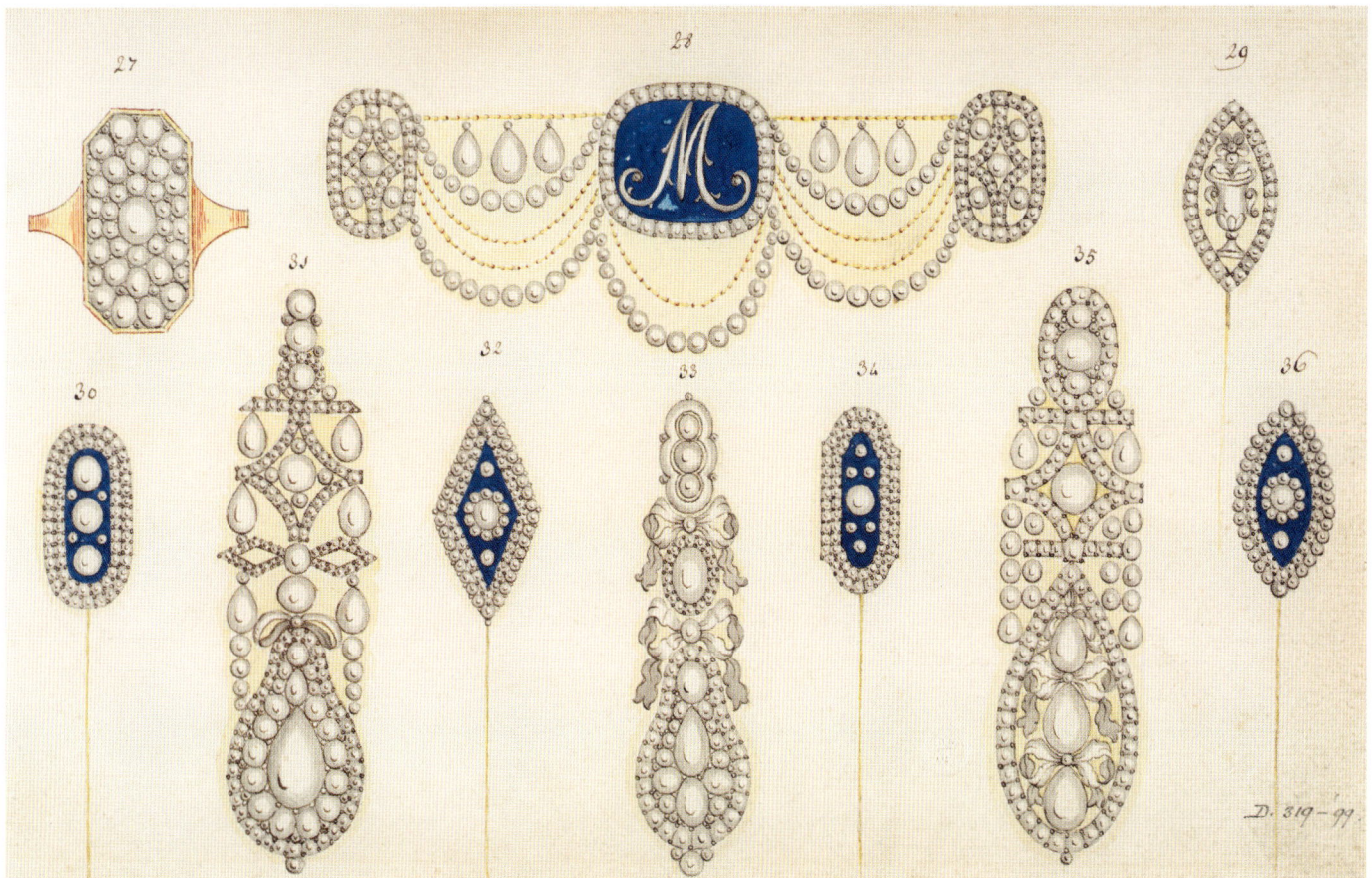

The only survivor was the sovereigns' daughter, Marie Thérèse, known as Madame Royale. She was released from prison the day of her seventeenth birthday, 19 December 1795, and went into exile in Austria, then Latvia, where she married her cousin the duc d'Angoulême on 9 June 1799. She returned to France in 1814 with her uncle, King Louis XVIII, before going into exile once more in 1830. She died in Austria in 1851. Madame Royale is not very well known to the wider public, but she should be to fans of jewellery, because it was thanks to her that Marie Antoinette's jewels survived the Revolution. On 4 March 1791, a small chest was smuggled out of the Tuileries palace. A special courier had been tasked with bringing it to Brussels, to the comte de Mercy-Argenteau. From there, it was taken to Vienna, where it was given to Madame Royale. The inventory of these jewels, preserved in the Austrian State Archives in Vienna, lists three parures of diamonds, emeralds and rubies, and a set of unmounted pearls which had belonged to Marie Antoinette, the most notorious queen in the history of France.[19] The famous ruby parure was sold by Madame Royale to her cousin the Emperor of Austria. It would be worn by subsequent Austrian sovereigns, notably Empress Sisi, and would disappear in the revolutionary upheavals following the end of the First World War and the long years of exile of the Habsburg dynasty after the loss of their throne in 1918. Certain pieces, set with diamonds and pearls, remained with the descendants of the nephews of Madame Royale for more than 150 years. They were sold in 2018 and 2021 at auction in Geneva by Sotheby's and Christie's respectively (figs 77 and 78).

79. *SALON DE VÉNUS* **BRACELET FROM THE**
***DIOR À VERSAILLES* COLLECTION, 2016**
VICTOIRE DE CASTELLANE FOR DIOR, WHITE
GOLD, BLACKENED SILVER, DIAMONDS AND
PINK SAPPHIRE

80. FILM STILL OF *MARIE ANTOINETTE,*
DIRECTED BY SOFIA COPPOLA, 2006
KIRSTEN DUNST AS MARIE ANTOINETTE

One last detail from this inventory of Marie Antoinette's personal jewellery, dated 10 February 1794 and preserved in the Austrian State Archives, is worth mentioning. It gives an idea of the elegance of the Queen of France. This inventory describes the different pieces in the two parures of coloured stones. In each of the two descriptions, the last line reads, '44 small motifs in rubies and diamonds and 44 small motifs in emeralds and diamonds'.[20] They were to be embroidered by the chambermaid onto the heels of the queen's slippers.

TOILES DE JOUY: MARIE ANTOINETTE AND COTTAGECORE

Silvija Banić & Jessica Harpley

In 1783, Marie Antoinette commissioned a new portrait of herself that caused such a furore it was promptly removed from display and repainted. The controversy? Her choice of attire. Depicted wearing a semi-transparent chemise dress and straw hat, the queen's appearance in the portrait *Marie Antoinette en chemise* was the epitome of *déshabillé* (or 'undress'), the most informal mode of dress that a lady would wear only in her private chambers, far from prying eyes (fig.81). The exact origins of what would become known as the *chemise à la reine* style are still debated by scholars – it may have been inspired by the prevailing fashion for *déshabillé*; by the light dresses worn by the French elite and local inhabitants in the heat of the colonial French West Indies; or even by children's dress.[1] Although deemed inappropriate for a royal portrait, it was nonetheless a faithful representation of the queen, who had spent years fleeing to the Petit Trianon, her rural abode, where she could escape the rigid formality of court life and fashion at Versailles. Among thatch-roofed cottages and a functioning farm, Marie Antoinette enjoyed a simpler, pastoral lifestyle – one that required a wardrobe to match. Eschewing ostentatious fashions for more practical, muted attire, the queen adopted a style that harmonized with her surroundings. Garments were loosely cut with paniers removed and floor-sweeping skirts raised. Silks in saturated colours were swapped for airy muslin or linen in pale tones. Elaborate headdresses and heavily powdered *toilettes* were toned down with straw hats, lace bonnets and naturally flushed cheeks. And excessive embellishments and jewels were discarded for modest garnishes of ribbons and wildflowers.

Over two centuries later, the rustic style of dress worn by Marie Antoinette would again find favour with a generation seeking escapism through fashion. Fatigued by the prevailing extremes of artificial cyber-aesthetics and plain 'normcore' fashion, a new trend emerged on the cusp of the 2020s that offered something different. 'Cottagecore' was the antidote, presenting a more authentic, romantic mode of dressing inspired by country living in a bygone age. Taking its cue from the humble undergarments and informal wear of times past, cottagecore is characterized by prim and pragmatic garments feminized with genteel, home-spun accents: shirring and smocking, bows and frills, crochet and lace, all rendered in natural materials. By the early 2020s, cottagecore was catapulted into the mainstream as the global COVID-19 pandemic brought modern life to a halt. Amid a wave of nostalgia for simpler, slower living, cottagecore came to the fore – offering not only a new wardrobe, but crucially a new, back-to-basics way of life. Many rediscovered an appreciation of nature, turning to the great outdoors as a space of solace and nurturing home-grown produce.

p. 112

**81. *MARIE ANTOINETTE IN A MUSLIN DRESS*
(AGED 27), AFTER 1783**
AFTER ÉLISABETH VIGÉE LE BRUN (1755–1842),
OIL ON CANVAS, 92.7 × 73.1 CM. NATIONAL
GALLERY OF ART, WASHINGTON. TIMKEN
COLLECTION: 1960.6.41

**82. *ROBE EN CHEMISE* ONCE BELONGING TO
MADAME OBERKAMPF, LATE 18TH CENTURY**
EMBROIDERED COTTON AND MUSLIN. MUSÉE
DE LA TOILE DE JOUY: 000.4.10_MTJ

83. *MARIE CLAIRE AUSTRALIA*, FEBRUARY 2021
JONATHAN ANDERSON FOR LOEWE
READY-TO-WEAR SPRING/SUMMER 2021.
PHOTOGRAPH BY DARREN MCDONALD

Just as Marie Antoinette fled to her peaceful retreat at the Petit Trianon, playing the part of a shepherdess on stage in her theatre, the fantasy of cottagecore provided relief from stifling periods of enforced confinement and uncertainty. Perhaps the original pioneer of cottagecore, Marie Antoinette and her style have become touchstones of the trend, frequently referencing her love of printed cotton. The queen surrounded herself with what is commonly known today as toile de Jouy – often shortened to simply 'toile' – using the printed cotton to add a decorative touch to her outfits and her private chambers. In the centuries following her death, toile de Jouy has become a familiar design to many. Eternally linked to the queen, it conjures thoughts of quaint country homes and delicate eighteenth-century aesthetics. Today, though, the term largely refers to one quintessential category: monochromatic arrangements of figures set in scenic vignettes on a white background. Unlike today, this eye-catching version of toile was originally intended for curtains, wall coverings and bed hangings, not garments. But in its steady evolution from interior design classic to contemporary fashion favourite, toile has charmed successive generations, drawn by its unique ability to be both classic and yet open to endless reinterpretations.

Of all the textile industries in eighteenth-century France, cotton was the most dynamic. But to unravel the story of the art of printed cotton or *toile imprimée*, one needs to take a step further back in time, for this revolution in textile production had started in the early seventeenth century with the importation of printed and painted cottons from Asia. With the establishment of the French East India Company in 1664, increasing quantities of these fabrics were imported directly into France. They were known as *toiles peintes*, *chites*, *perses*, *suratas* or *patnas*, but the name most commonly given to them by French merchants was simply *indiennes*. Produced and imported for the upper-class luxury market, they had a more subtle texture due to the fine quality of the threads and the higher thread count and were far superior to the block-printed linens printed in Europe. Their attraction lay in the precision of their design and in their bright, multicoloured and colour-fast patterns. Blues were achieved using indigo, which was 10 times more concentrated than its European equivalent, woad, which is highly light sensitive and fugitive (fig.85).

The more expensive *indiennes* had a glazed finish that mimicked the light-reflective properties of silks and was sometimes further enhanced by gilding and silvering. So high was the demand for clothes and furnishings made from the *indiennes* that they started to be copied in the workshops across the country, alarming the silk and wool manufacturers who persuaded the government to outlaw both the import of the printed cottons and native copies.

When the ban was lifted in 1759, it was an able and creative German who became the most famous manufacturer of the printed fabrics in France and one favoured by the court. Christophe-Philippe Oberkampf (1738–1815), arguably one of the most innovative entrepreneurs of his time, came from a family of Protestant dyers in Württemberg. Although he allegedly did not speak a word of French, Oberkampf immigrated to Paris in 1758 where a Swiss, called Tavanne, soon noticed his talents and took him on as an associate. The result was the establishment of a small factory in Jouy-en-Josas, on the route between Versailles and Paris. The choice of location was a critical one, being close to the major centres of consumption and to the banks of the river Bièvre, famous for the purity of its water: a prerequisite for obtaining high-quality dyes.

During the first decade, all of Oberkampf's fabrics were printed solely using woodblocks. The technique limited the dimensions of the pattern to the size of the block, normally no bigger than could be held comfortably in the hand. The more colours used, the longer the work took, and the more expensive the final product. The cotton of an exquisite example of a *robe à l'anglaise* (fig.86) is woodblock-printed in seven colours. The Jouy firm made a fortune on such fabrics, called *perses*, where the colours, shapes and the arrangements of the Persian-style blossoming branches and sprigs recall the appearance of *indienne* prints; the queen used these to spectacular effect in her interiors in the main Palace of Versailles and in the Petit Trianon (see Delalex in this volume). Dresses made from glazed *perses*, which were highly sought after during the last third of the eighteenth century, made their way into the wardrobe of the queen herself. While she was still dauphine, Marie Antoinette visited the Jouy manufactory together with the children of Louis XV and enjoyed walking in the gardens where she could hear Oberkampf and his companions speaking German.[2]

The era of unparalleled prosperity began in 1770, the year when Oberkampf introduced copperplate printing. This technique, perfected in Ireland about two decades earlier, allowed the pattern with a repeat of about a metre high to be printed in one movement. Motifs were no longer small and monotonously repeated. Moreover, the engraved metal plates permitted figurative subjects to be treated with

a greater degree of detail and a delicacy of execution than could be achieved by block printing. On the other hand, only one colour was possible, though this could range from light to dark according to the thickness of the lines. The preferred colours were normally red, blue, purple or sepia. Although monochrome, these *meubles à personnages* quickly became popular for bed hangings and upholstery.

The first design for a copperplate-printed textile that Jean-Baptiste Huet (1745–1811) drew for Oberkampf is also probably their most important collaboration: *Les travaux de la manufacture* from 1783 shows a series of vignettes from the firm, including the press for copperplate printing. The toile was commissioned to commemorate the definitive event in the manufactory's history to that point: the visit of Louis XVI and Marie Antoinette that year. The king subsequently granted Oberkampf the privilege and patent protection of distinguishing his products with the stamp 'Manufacture Royale', which bestowed the highest approval in the realm.

Thanks to their pictorial possibilities, copperplate-printed cottons were frequently used to depict or reflect on contemporary events. *La Fête de la Fédération* was designed by Huet to commemorate the Revolution's first anniversary and the new constitutional monarchy. The composition is more symbolic than realistic (fig.89). On the left of an altar in the antique style is an allegorical figure of Liberty, brandishing a Phrygian cap at the end of a pike. On the right, the king takes the oath to the new nation. Depicted at the foot of the podium are Marie Antoinette with the dauphin on the left, while her daughter, Madame Royale, and sister-in-law, Madame Élisabeth, are on the right, all with their right arms outstretched, repeating the same oath. Around the central motif, smaller scenes recall the enthusiasm of the event. On a tree is the sign 'Ici … on danse' (here we dance) and in the vicinity, young women and soldiers dance on the ruins of the Bastille. Despite the evolution of events, the last pieces of this design were still being sold in 1795.

The final technological invention introduced to Jouy was roller printing, an innovation that changed the industry not only technically and economically, but also in terms of design. Regardless of the printing technique employed, figurative toiles remained perennial favourites within interior design but the crossover from their use for dressing spaces to dressing bodies was gradual.

Throughout the nineteenth century, womenswear typically featured small-scale roller-printed textiles, and it would have been unusual for figurative toiles, originally made as furnishing fabrics, to be used for clothing.[3] By the early twentieth century, however, fashionable new uses for these textiles began to be experimented with. After decades of heavy, ornate womenswear, fashion exhibited a softer and more natural feel, with toile adding a complementary touch to the latest modes. While modern imitation toiles were in production, original eighteenth-century examples were favoured for their superior quality, genuine rococo designs and gently faded colours.[4] Reconfigured for the new century, the by-now antique furnishing fabric was used to line garments or accent cuffs and collars. Indeed, despite being described by *Vogue* as the 'craze of the summer' in 1907, toile was used with restraint, being 'so decorative and of such a rich intricate design, that a narrow strip … is most effective'.[5] Another approach involved cutting out individual toile motifs and appliquéing them onto garments and accessories, before outlining them with embroidery or beading.[6] In these early decades of the century, toile was a popular pattern for childrenswear and women's gardening and beach clothes, bestowing the textile with a cheerful, outdoorsy spirit. And while the range of toiles being welcomed into wardrobes

88. *THE DRINKING TROUGH* **(DETAIL), c.1792**
FRANCE, DESIGNED BY JEAN-BAPTISTE
HUET (1745–1811) FOR THE MANUFACTURE
OBERKAMPF, JOUY-EN-JOSAS. V&A: T.1–1961

89. VALANCE DEPICTING *LA FÊTE DE LA
FÉDÉRATION* **(DETAIL), c.1790**
FRANCE, DESIGNED BY JEAN-BAPTISTE
HUET (1745–1811) FOR THE MANUFACTURE
OBERKAMPF, JOUY-EN-JOSAS, 84 × 192 CM.
V&A: 1682–1899

ICI. ON
DANSE

was expanding beyond florals – now incorporating neoclassical and what were considered 'exotic' designs – it would be several years yet before the figurative toiles we associate with the textile today would fully envelop garments.

In 1947, Christian Dior opened his first boutique, *Colifichets*, on the ground floor of his Parisian couture salon. Under the direction of artist Christian Bérard, the boutique was covered in toile – from the walls and drapery to the furniture – fulfilling Dior's wish to emulate 'eighteenth-century shops which sold luxurious trifles'.[7] Successive Dior designers John Galliano, Maria Grazia Chiuri and Kim Jones, would later return to the print in their designs for the fashion house, most notably in the Dior Homme Spring/Summer 2019 collection for which Jones reprised the original neoclassical toile used by Dior in 1947. It was in the post-war climate that entire garments constructed from toile had begun to appear, fashioned from material printed specifically for clothing. Advances in screen-printing meant increasingly complex, large-scale designs could be more affordably produced, bypassing toile's original copper-plate printing process. Coinciding with an appetite for novelty prints, which brought levity into fashion again after the sombre war years, toile emerged as fresh option for womenswear – particularly apt for summer – with its light cottons and soft colourways.[8] Moreover, toile's depiction of carefree, outdoor living provided an appropriate, aspirational even, pattern for the warmer weather, creating light-hearted fashions tinged with wistful nostalgia.[9] Such nostalgia was carried into the 1960s and 1970s with brands such as Gunne Sax and Laura Ashley, whose proto-cottagecore style revived antiquated modes of rustic dress, often rendered in toile, known in Britain as chintz. Establishing a lifestyle brand of fashion and interiors that swept the British high street, Laura Ashley reinforced toile's sentimental, old-world associations, using it to infuse homes and wardrobes with an approachable country charm that signalled refinement without resorting to grandeur.[10] Laura Ashley's polite treatment of toile was shaken up towards the end of the century, when fashion renegades John Galliano, Jean Paul Gaultier, Christian Lacroix and Vivienne Westwood used the textile to more rebellious effect. Incorporated into sumptuous, deconstructed designs that reference hyper-feminine silhouettes of the past, toile was a poetic choice for such *déshabillé* looks, which recalled the alfresco romps so often depicted within (fig.90).

Fashion's love affair with toile continued into the twenty-first century. By now familiar but also transportive, it is used by a diverse roster of designers catering to a spectrum of sartorial tastes.[11] Whether evoking demure summertime femininity, eighteenth-century rococo excess or something altogether more punkish, toile is re-cut and reconfigured with each passing season. And with the expediency of

91. ANIME TOILE DE JOUY PANIER DRESS,
MOSCHINO, AUTUMN/WINTER 2020
DESIGNED BY JEREMY SCOTT

92. *LA DANSE DES NOIRS* (THE DANCE OF THE
BLACK MEN), c.1784
FRANCE, BLOCK-PRINTED COTTON IN SEVEN
COLOURS, MANUFACTURE OBERKAMPF,
JOUY-EN-JOSAS. V&A: T.440–1919

computer-aided design and digital printing, the ease with which a brand can create a bespoke toile aligning with its aesthetic has propelled its use within fashion. For its Autumn/Winter 2019 collection, Chloé developed a *Highlands* toile, featuring a couple dressed in modern streetwear walking in a Scottish landscape. In the same year, Staud included a toile as part of its Resort collection, playfully incorporating 'office dogs' belonging to company staff into the design. And for the Marie Antoinette-inspired Moschino Autumn/Winter 2020–2021 collection, garments were cut from a toile that could at first glance pass for an eighteenth-century original, were it not for its vivid blue colouring. A closer look, however, reveals a collision of worlds, as the figures frolicking outside in fashionable eighteenth-century French dress are in fact Japanese anime characters.

Classic from a distance, but with the potential to counter expectations, toile is a textile ripe for visual storytelling and sociopolitical commentary. Myriad artists have populated toile's vignettes with subversive imagery, replacing rose-tinted depictions of rural enjoyment with something more realistic.[12] Scottish design duo Timorous Beasties exposed the seedy side of urban life in their *Glasgow* (2004) and *London* (2009) toiles, a similar approach taken by fashion brand Sibling, whose 2012 toile documents the violence of London's 2011 riots.[13] In 1992, American artist Renée Green designed a toile illustrating the horrors of the slave trade and the Haitian Revolution, taking a quintessentially French medium to present an unfiltered view

93. *HARLEM TOILE* BY SHEILA BRIDGES, 2006
HAND SCREEN-PRINTED WALLPAPER, BLACK
AND WHITE VIGNETTES ON A YELLOW
GROUND, PATTERN REPEAT, 68 × 76.2 CM.
V&A: E.539–2024

Overleaf

94. VICTOR GLEMAUD WITH HIS DESIGN
TOUSSAINT TOILE FOR SCHUMACHER LTD., 2022
PRINTED WALLPAPER AND TEXTILE.
V&A: E.234–2024. PHOTOGRAPH BY
JASON THOMAS GEERING

95. *MISS CELIE* DRESS CONSTRUCTED FROM
ZULU PRINCESS TOILE BY SINDISO KHUMALO,
SPRING/SUMMER 2020 COLLECTION
CAPE TOWN, SOUTH AFRICA, PRINTED
COTTON. V&A: T.2437:1,2–2021

of France's colonial past.[14] It recalls the racialized imagery seen in eighteenth-century sources, such as the toile produced by Oberkampf commemorating France's role in securing American independence depicting a ring of Black men dancing around a palm tree, surmounted by a Phrygian cap – the cap of Liberty – and the first French and American flags (fig.92).

American artist Sheila Bridges would later use the conventions of toiles to satirize 'some of the stereotypes deeply woven into the African American experience'.[15] Incorporating basketball and boomboxes into her *Harlem Toile*, Bridges places African American culture at the centre of her practice and humanizes her subjects, seeking to counter racist historical depictions of Black peoples (fig.93). In 2022, American fashion designer Victor Glemaud designed the *Toussaint Toile* in collaboration with interior firm Schumacher, which has manufactured toiles since the late nineteenth century. Based on the life of Haitian revolutionary Toussaint Louverture, Glemaud recounts a story of Black liberation, usurping the place of French colonizers who historically populated toile's designs (fig.94). In a similarly celebratory approach, South African fashion designer Sindiso Khumalo makes frequent use of toile within her cottagecore designs. In her specially commissioned *Zulu Princess* toile, French landscapes are replaced with South African vistas, and Khumalo's mother is affectionately represented wearing an *inkehli*, a traditional Zulu headdress (fig.95). Khumalo's design is not based on an imagined Utopia; it is an uplifting and personal expression of cultural heritage, inserting African perspectives into the European histories that so frequently excluded them.

Figurative toiles from the second half of the eighteenth century survive today in greater quantities than woodblock-printed dress fabrics, and have therefore come to be associated with the term toiles de Jouy. The enduring charm and exceptional quality of these lively textiles ensured they were appreciated and carefully looked after over generations. Evidently, the visual appeal of these textiles that so enchanted Marie Antoinette still stands today.

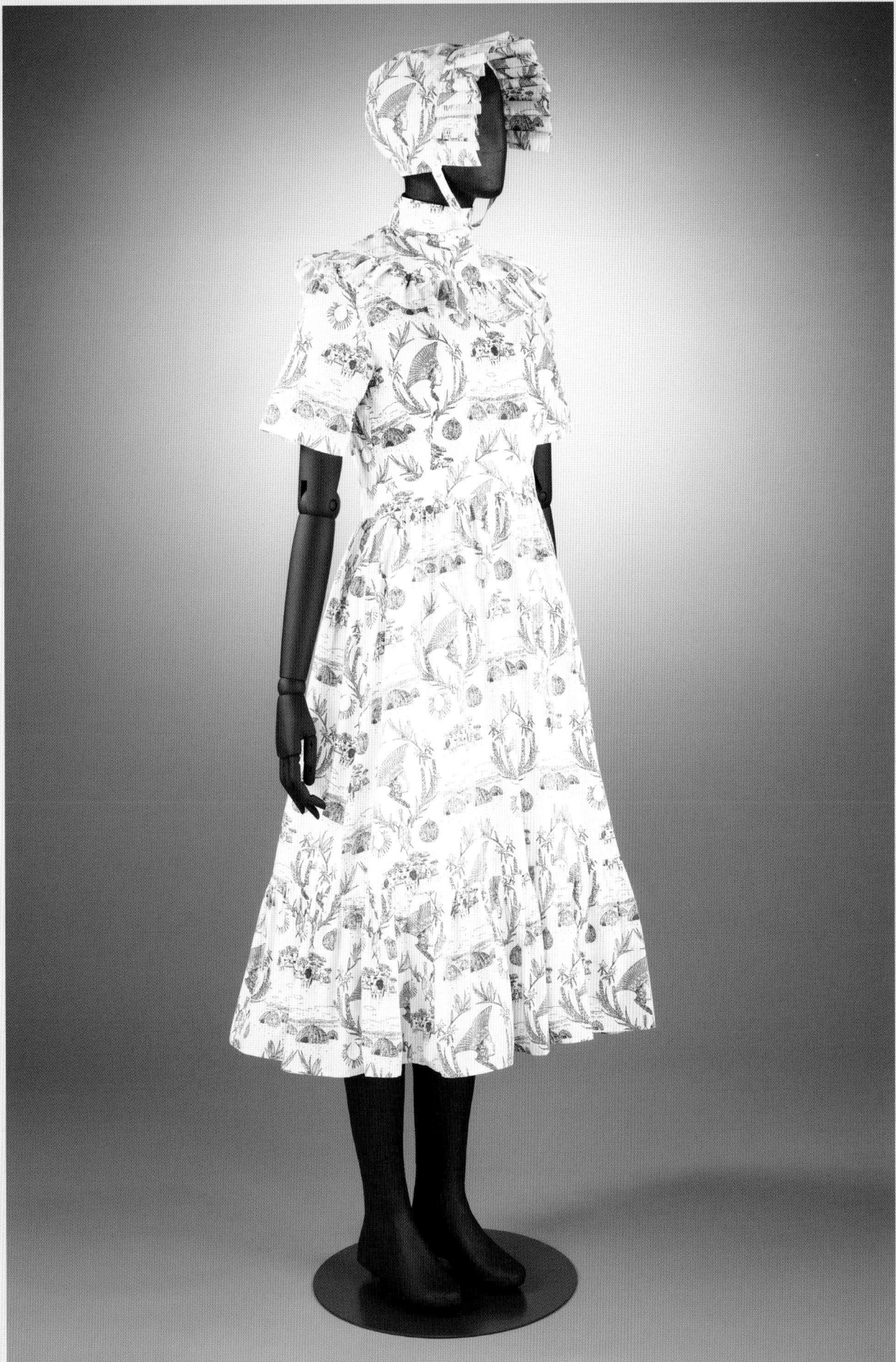

THE PERFUMED PALACE: MARIE ANTOINETTE AND SCENT

Sarah Grant

Heralding Marie Antoinette's arrival in France, as an innocent young bride full of promise, one gazette reported that she 'smelled of springtime'.[1] Once installed at Versailles, the dauphine and later, queen, embraced and inhabited a highly fragrant world. During her reign, men and women liberally perfumed themselves, their fashion accessories and their interiors. In her palaces Marie Antoinette was surrounded by visual representations of scent – bouquets of flowers spilled out across the silk cladding, marquetry furniture, porcelain services and painted mouldings of her apartments; in her portraits she clutched aromatic posies of lily-of-the-valley and narcissus. Her gardens at the Petit Trianon exhaled the sweet scent of thousands of hyacinths, violets, roses, jasmine, orange blossom and 'copses of fragrant lilac, populated with nightingales', the baronne d'Oberkirch recalling, 'the air was full of balmy fragrance' (fig.96).[2]

Of course there were malodours too. At Versailles, Marie Antoinette shared her palace with over 1,000 courtiers and servants residing across 226 apartments, with many thousands more in the adjoining court buildings and still more bodies passing through daily to work in or visit the court.[3] An overcrowded château naturally created some problems; when he visited in 1767 the diplomat and founding father of the USA, Benjamin Franklin, was astonished by the combination of both great splendour and squalid neglect.[4] Kitchen hands threw waste directly out of the windows, creating, according to one courtier's report, 'an indecent stench'.[5] The courtyards were constantly befouled by the sheer numbers of carriage horses coming and going, the waste channels did not drain correctly and this together with stagnant water created in 1774, the year Marie Antoinette became queen, an 'unbearable smell' one courtier complained.[6] Add to this the haze of soot leeching from chimneys, lanterns and candles, the emptying of latrines and the odours escaping from the château's 29 cesspits, and it is not surprising that scent was a subject that preoccupied everyone from the servants to the king and queen themselves.[7]

Scent at Marie-Antoinette's court therefore played a vital role, not just to mask odours, nor just for its perceived medicinal and purifying properties, but for the sensory and therapeutic pleasures it generated, which were widely recognized, and its undeniable ability to convey an individual's power, status and allure.

The court was supplied by a handful of the over 250 perfumers operating in Paris, the best of whom were based on the rue Saint-Honoré, still a luxury shopping address in Paris today.[8] Clients could arrange to have products delivered to the French provinces and even abroad; glass and porcelain bottles and pots were sealed with the merchant's seal to ward off counterfeits.[9] Jean-Louis Fargeon (1748–1806) has long been assumed the queen's official perfumer following a claim he advanced in a

p.132

96. THE FRENCH GARDEN AT THE PETIT TRIANON, VERSAILLES
MUSÉE NATIONAL DES CHÂTEAUX DE VERSAILLES ET DE TRIANON

97. MARIE ANTOINETTE'S POMADE POT WITH HER MONOGRAM, ONE OF A PAIR FROM HER *NÉCESSAIRE DE VOYAGE* (TRAVEL TOILETTE CASE), c.1775
PROBABLY THE DUC D'ORLÉANS'S PORCELAIN MANUFACTORY, PAINTED AND GILDED PORCELAIN. MUSÉE DU LOUVRE: OA 9594 26 A

treatise published after her death.[10] While Fargeon's bills show he did indeed supply the court, he was not the exclusive perfumer to the queen.[11] In 1781 the main Paris perfumer supplying Marie Antoinette was Claude-François Prévost on the rue de l'Arbre-Sec, the queen spending 6,289 *livres* per year on perfume. She obtained her orange blossom pomade from Beauclin and her rouge from Dubuisson, both in Paris. A local supplier in Versailles, Tissot, also furnished her with cleansing pastes.[12]

Perfumers boasted of 'exotic' scents and ingredients, such as incense, myrrh and sandalwood, sourced from the Middle East and India, but in reality the majority of their production was based on European-derived ingredients and scents found locally. 'Essences of rose, lavender, jasmine, citrus, carnation, lilac', together with

98. MARIE ANTOINETTE'S POWDER POT WITH HER MONOGRAM FROM HER *NÉCESSAIRE DE VOYAGE* (TRAVEL TOILETTE CASE), c.1787–8
JEAN-PIERRE CHARPENAT, SILVER WITH LEATHER LINING, ENGRAVED WITH 'MA' IN CENTRE AND ON COVER. MUSÉE DU LOUVRE: OA 9594 21

orange blossom, rose, tuberose and acacia, with flowers, botanicals and citrus fruits, formed the basis for most of the production, particularly for scented waters which were the cornerstone of the toilette.[13]

Thus Marie Antoinette used the lavender water made by the nuns of the Paris convent, La Madeleine de Traisnel,[14] and turned to orange-flower water as a calming scent.[15] She also favoured the rose-water based 'Eau de Bouquet' scent and rose-scented pomade from the perfumer Jean-François Houbigant (1752–1807).[16] A pair of the queen's porcelain pomade pots from her travel toilette case bear a painted pattern of garlands of pink roses and a gilded plum finial, an indication of the contents within (fig.97). Like most of the articles in the queen's toilette case they bear

99. MARIE ANTOINETTE'S EAU DE COLOGNE
BOTTLE, FROM *HER NÉCESSAIRE DE VOYAGE*
(TRAVEL TOILETTE KIT), 1788
CRYSTAL. MUSÉE DU LOUVRE: OA 959412J

100. *PORTRAIT OF MARIE ANTOINETTE IN*
COURT DRESS (DETAIL OF FIG.68)

her prominent and distinctive gilded monogram, 'MA'. This pomade was used to set and scent her coiffure. These and other cosmetics were highly fragranced: 'In the last century', recalled Madame de Genlis in 1818, 'women were much more perfumed than today, because pomade and powder were excessively [perfumed]. For the same reason, men were as well'.[17] At the height of Anglomania, the queen ordered, by post, 'the most beautiful pomades from England', her courtier reported.[18]

Also in the queen's travel toilette case was a silver powder pot lined with leather (fig.98). Dulac, a glove and perfumer maker on the rue Saint-Honoré, sold coloured and scented powders of every description, in a dizzying range of scents: violet; tuberose; jasmine; carnation; chypre; bergamot; narcissus; and amber along with accompanying swansdown powder puffs.[19] In a striking illustration of the connection between scent and other luxury goods, Dulac also sold jewels, advertising diamond earrings and bracelets alongside gold boxes in which to house rouge and other cosmetics.

Another pot in the queen's case may have been for rouge. François-Hubert Drouais's portrait shows the young dauphine highly powdered and rouged, as was then the fashion and for which she was mercilessly teased by her brother Joseph II when he visited Versailles (fig.100). In 1783 Marie Antoinette used and gave her royal endorsement to the rouge made by the enterprising valet of one of her friends, the princesse de Lamballe. The recipe contained French safflower, which yielded shades of cherry-red and pink.[20]

The queen's scent bottle from her 1788 toilette case is a simple yet elegant faceted crystal Eau de Cologne bottle, with a handwritten label (fig.99). This was designed for travel and a silver funnel was included in the case to replenish the contents. Fragile bottles such as these were kept in carefully lined and cushioned toilette cases or individually enclosed in a leather or shagreen case to protect them from breakage. It was understood that scent was individual to the person: when Marie Antoinette arranged to send her old toilette case to her elder sister, archduchess Christina, she instructed that the perfume bottles be emptied as she knew Christina would want to fill them with her own scents.[21]

Armed with bottles of scent, cosmetics and an array of perfumed accessories including gloves, fans, silk flowers and fur muffs, Marie Antoinette was scented from the tip of her coiffure to the toe of her slipper, a process that began in the bathroom and culminated in her public *toilette*. The queen's pastel-blue bathroom at Versailles, although she did not live to use it, was fit for a water nymph, with its decorative mouldings of swans, dolphins, reeds, branches of coral, shells, pearls and arabesques (fig.101). Her preferred bathing ritual was to sit with a cup of chocolate

or coffee in hand, immersed in waters scented with various concoctions to treat the skin, accompanied by scented soaps. In 1777, the general recommendation was that a bath be taken every 8 to 10 days, both for cleanliness and as a health treatment.[22] Madame Campan recalled that on the days the queen did not bathe a *femme de chambre* would wash her legs.

The final touch in the creation of an atmosphere fit for a queen, was the scenting of her interiors. This could be done in all manner of ways, from perfumes disseminated in a pot-pourri (a vase or vessel filled with aromatics), scented sachets, essences diffused in a *bain-marie* or scented lozenges burnt in a *cassolette* (perfume burner).[23] The *cassolette* was derived from ancient Greek and Roman ornamental tripod vases and urns, used to light interiors and burn perfumes, which became fashionable in the eighteenth century at the height of the taste for the Antique. In Marie Antoinette's allegorical portrait as a vestal, a priestess of ancient Rome associated with the domestic realm who is often depicted burning incense, she is pictured with both a flaming altar and a *cassolette*, and they can also be spied in the portraits of a number of other royal sitters (fig.102).[24]

One such scent burner belonging to the queen and decorated with neoclassical symbols was displayed by her on the chimneypiece of the *Cabinet de la Méridienne* in her private apartments at Versailles (fig.103). Pastilles, lozenges or incense would have been burnt within, with a metal liner fitted to protect the precious stone. An indication of how instrumental and ubiquitous these scent burners became is conveyed by their incorporation into the decoration of the queen's interiors. For example, a *cassolette* can be found in the Etruscan gilded mouldings of Marie Antoinette's interior apartments at Versailles (1783), and in *trompe-l'oeil* form in the exquisite painted decoration of her *boudoir turc* at Fontainebleau where, in an extraordinary conceit, the miniature three-dimensional *cassolettes* were capable of releasing real scent through the use of lozenges or pot-pourri.[25] Similarly, in the Belvedere pavilion of the Petit Trianon, where the queen staged musical concerts and entertainments, the painted arabesques feature smoking perfume burners and baskets of flowers evoking both manufactured and natural scents, a sight enhanced by views onto the verdant beauty of the gardens beyond (fig.104).

Marie Antoinette left a trail of scent in her wake all the way to the scaffold. During her residence at the Temple prison from August 1792 to August 1793 she was granted an allowance for perfumes and toiletries and among the modest array of plain glass bottles and a porcelain powder pot is a little scent bottle with a gilded glass stopper, which still contains the residue of one of her perfumes (fig.105). Its decoration is typical of scent bottles of the time, on which gilded friezes reference gardens,

102. *PORTRAIT OF MARIE ANTOINETTE AS A VESTAL*, 1776–8
CHARLES LECLERCQ (1753–1821) OIL ON CANVAS, 41 × 33 CM. MUSÉE NATIONAL DES CHÂTEAUX DE VERSAILLES ET DE TRIANON: INV. V.2018.26

103. MARIE ANTOINETTE'S PERFUME BURNER FROM THE *CABINET DE LA MÉRIDIENNE* (MIDDAY ROOM) IN HER PRIVATE APARTMENTS AT VERSAILLES, 1773–5
PIERRE GOUTHIÈRE AND FRANÇOIS-JOSEPH BELANGER, JASPER AND GILT BRONZE DECORATED WITH A SERPENT, RAMS' HOOVES, SATYRS' HEADS AND GRAPES, 48.3 × BOWL D. 21.7 CM (PURCHASED IN 1782 FROM THE SALE OF THE DUC D'AUMONT'S COLLECTION). WALLACE COLLECTION, LONDON: F292

104. PAINTED INTERIOR OF THE BELVEDERE PAVILION, PETIT TRIANON, VERSAILLES, 1781
ARCHITECT: RICHARD MIQUE; PAINTER: SÉBASTIEN FRANÇOIS LERICHE. MUSÉE NATIONAL DES CHÂTEAUX DE VERSAILLES ET DE TRIANON

105. MARIE ANTOINETTE'S SCENT BOTTLE FROM THE TEMPLE PRISON, c.1792
GILDED GLASS. MUSÉE CARNAVALET, PARIS: OM2103

courtship and floral ornament. In her confinement, scent had become one of the queen's sole remaining pleasures, a form of escapism. Her attendant at the Temple recalled the queen sprinkling scented powder in her hair and 'rubbing her hands with scent and waving them near my face so that I might smell the scent, which was very sweet'.[26] From time to time a small bouquet of flowers was smuggled in to introduce a vernal note to the oppressive space and to recall to Marie Antoinette, stranded Rapunzel-like, high in her medieval prison tower, the flower gardens she had once wandered daily.[27]

THE UNIVERSE AT HER FEET: MARIE ANTOINETTE'S SHOES

Helena Cox

'Monsieur de Bièvre bowed, and seeing the queen was wearing green slippers exclaimed, "her majesty's desires are orders, the universe is at her feet".'[1]

In certain portraits of Marie Antoinette,[2] the tip of her shoe is glimpsed – often pointed, no doubt heeled – leaving to the imagination what lies beneath. Her shoe size was a 36.5, most likely corresponding to a height of around 1.65 metres.[3] For the aristocracy, long before the outbreak of revolution,[4] shoes told a tale of status, privilege and glittering prestige. In the eighteenth century, Paris was the epicentre for stylish shoemaking, and consumerism thrived; 'the first thing to be done, in Paris, is always to send for a Taylor, a Peruke maker and a shoemaker', claimed one American visitor.[5] The extravagantly eccentric Prince Potemkin once despatched an express messenger from Russia to Paris to bring back ball slippers for his mistress, Princess Dolgoruki.[6] Marie Antoinette received four new pairs of shoes a week[7] – undoubtedly bespoke – and though excess has become a byword for the French queen, it is worth noting that in 1777 her brother-in-law, Artois, ordered 365 shoes so that he could have a new pair for each day of the year.[8] In 1781 the queen's official shoemaker was Monsier Gilles, rue Saint Martin, and that year she spent 2,590 *livres* on shoes.[9]

For Marie Antoinette and her circle, the rising hems of popular dress styles were '*retroussée*'[10] (pulled up) revealing both ankles and shoes (fig.107), which were now much lower-heeled than was fashionable in the previous Louis-XV period. Luxurious materials such as leather, silk, damask and brocade were accessorized with buckles, jewels and trimmings. Carriage rides, the dwindling use of sedan chairs and an adorned, pampered existence lessened wear and tear, although inclement weather and venturing outdoors necessitated more practical footwear.[11] Then, as now, there was always the unexpected. In 1770, when Marie Antoinette accompanied the 'Mesdames Tantes' (the so-called daughters of Louis XV) on the royal hunt, their carriage got stuck in the marshland. The unfazed dauphine got out, eager to continue, losing one of her shoes in the mud.[12]

Undoubtedly enhanced by her dancing master Noverre's instruction, moving with elegance came naturally to Marie Antoinette. Horace Walpole claimed that 'When she moves she is Grace incarnate.'[13] Arriving at the French court, she mastered the so-called 'Versailles glide', where ladies moved effortlessly, their feet seemingly not touching the ground beneath them.[14] She adored dancing and from December 1770 organized little dances in her apartments, attended by the dauphin and intimates.[15] The most formal court dress – the *grand habit* – was accompanied by high-heeled mules, exemplified by the queen's sumptuous silk pair (fig.108). Featuring a high, curved heel and pointed toe, they are intricately embroidered

Le Clerc del.   Jaminet direx. Woeiriot Sculp.

Robe à l'Anglaise retrouſſée pour donner de l'aiſance à danſer.

à Paris chez Esnauts et Rapilly, rue St Jacques à la Ville de Coutances· A.P.D.R.

p.144

106. 18TH CENTURY SHOES, FROM THE COLLECTION OF LILIAN WILLIAMS
PHOTOGRAPH BY DEIDI VON SCHAEWEN

107. 'ROBE À L'ANGLAISE RETROUSSÉE POUR DONNER DE L'AISANCE À DANSER' (*ROBE À L'ANGLAISE* **PULLED UP TO ALLOW EASE OF DANCING), 1782 (1912 RESTRIKE)**
FASHION PLATE FROM *GALLERIE DES MODES ET COSTUMES FRANÇAIS*, J.P. VOSSINIK (FL. 1755–65), AFTER JEAN-FRANÇOIS JANINET (1752–1814) AND PIERRE THOMAS LE CLERC (1739–1791). RIJKSMUSEUM, AMSTERDAM: RP-P-2009-1195

108. MARIE ANTOINETTE'S BEADED COURT MULES, c.1770–80
PINK SILK AND GLASS BEADS. MUSÉE CARNAVALET, PARIS: OM3435

with white and black beads along the vamp and edges. Heeled mules contributed to a tottering, slow, almost hypnotic gait; however, effortless gliding down the parquet floors of Versailles was not without tribulation, as recalled by the marquise de La Tour du Pin, for whom attending balls 'transformed dancing into a kind of torture. Narrow heels three inches high, which put the foot in the position where it is when one raises on tiptoe to reach a book on the highest shelf of a library', making it 'impossible to dance with pleasure'.[16] The comte de Vaublanc was less sympathetic, comparing women wearing heels to rough-legged pigeons.[17]

The eighteenth-century shoe[18] was laden with sensual allure, becoming a totem of desire, femininity and seduction – a sartorial endnote to the femininely performative ritual of dressing. Shoe obsession and foot fetishism disclosed hidden desires. In England, Lady Coventry's dainty feet became such a topic of gossip and intrigue that a Worcester shoemaker received two and a half guineas from exhibiting her shoes.[19] French writers revelled in the fictive propensity for erotic and sensual tales, from Choderlos De Laclos's swooning ingenue Cécile de Volanges in *Dangerous Liaisons* (fig.109),[20] who mistakes a visiting shoemaker for a potential suitor as he kneels and asks for her foot, to Restif de la Bretonne's heroine in *Le pied de fanchette*, whose pretty little foot and magnificently embroidered mules bewitch men, inviting trouble. A shoe style called 'Venez-y-voir' (come and take a peek) played upon secret coquetry, with diamond or gem-encrusted shoes glimpsed under a dress. There was even a shoe using silk of a colour named after Marie Antoinette's hair – 'cheveux de la reine' – and in a particular example embroidered with diamonds 'en coups perfides' (devious strokes) that the celebrated courtesan Rosalie Duthé wore to the Paris Opera in 1788.[21]

Marie Antoinette's surviving shoes are freighted with reliquary status, evoking both absence and presence.[22] Her remaining shoe collection reveals that she had a favourite classic style – pointed, low heeled (often the so-called 'Saint Huberty,' measuring the height of two thumbs and named after the singer who launched the style),[23] made of silk, elegantly embellished with a concoction of feminine bows, fringing and frou-frous, decorative ruching and embroidery. The Metropolitan Museum of Art's gold, pointed, low-curved heels (fig.110) are indicative of the characteristic exquisite workmanship and *passementerie* of the queen's shoes, the patterned silk fabric decorated with fringed trim along the edges. Auction sales over the past 15 years have witnessed skyrocketing results.[24] Drouot's sold pair of pointed green and pink silk slippers are a delightful beribboned confection (fig.111); in remarkable condition, they are an eye-catching statement most likely designed to match a dress. It was customary for articles of clothing to be passed down to servants. This pair was gifted by the queen to Alexandre-Bernard Ju-Des-Retz, a gentleman in her service, in 1775 and it is evident that instead of being enjoyed as regal cast-offs by his female intimates (if the slippers had fit!), they were conserved and passed down the family. Revelatory of the dispersal and scattering of the queen's wardrobe, an Osenat sale[25] of a single, ecru-coloured pointed shoe with delicate pleated ribbons and a 4.7 cm heel perfectly matches the Ashmolean Museum's silk and kidskin leather shoe (fig.112).

As the authority of the *ancien régime* crumbled, the queen's style and her love of fashion was turned against her. The title of an anti-Marie-Antoinette pamphlet,

110. MARIE ANTOINETTE'S SILK SLIPPER,
c.1770–85
BROOKLYN MUSEUM COSTUME COLLECTION
AT THE METROPOLITAN MUSEUM OF ART,
NEW YORK: 2009.300.4128A, B. GIFT OF MRS.
CLARENCE R. HYDE, 1928

MARIE ANTOINETTE *Style*

Portefeuille d'un talon rouge (1783), uses the Sun King's red heels from the previous century as its political leitmotif, libelling the queen's lust for power and the corrupt court. With the outbreak of revolution, sumptuous style statements and luxury became seen as the enemy of republicanism. Patriotic devotion gave rise to an outbreak of silver buckle removals, and to be caught with any on shoes was akin to self-incrimination.[26] Instead, symbolic buckles became the order of the day: 'à la bastille', 'au Tiers-Etat' and 'à la nation'.[27] Allegiance to the Revolution found stylistic expression in patriotic shoes embellished with revolutionary cockades, a trend adopted by Marie Antoinette, and she reputedly wore her pair of tricoloured silk-ribboned mules to the Fête de la Fédération, celebrating the anniversary of the Fall of the Bastille in 1790. The shoes tell a tale of the queen's political self-fashioning via her wardrobe – a sartorial display of solidarity to the revolutionary cause.

Marie Antoinette spent her final years imprisoned. When the Tuileries was stormed by a revolutionary mob in August 1792, the royal family were forced to flee. Marie Antoinette lost a beige silk faille and leather shoe (fig.113), with its distinctive brown rosette bow and criss-crossed ribbon trimming, which was subsequently snatched from the hands of the invading revolutionaries by Monsieur d'Ennecey de Champuis as he defended the palace.

Arriving at the Temple prison, the queen was wearing a shoe so worn and damaged that her foot was sticking out,[28] wryly remarking: 'you would not believe that the Queen of France was in need of shoes.'[29] From this period, fashion merchant Madame Éloffe's account book is strewn with entries of repaired and re-trimmed shoes for the queen, myriad descriptions revealing the salvaged luxury of her diminished shoe collection: 'canary yellow with violet undertones' – 'blue on white' – 'bold green taffeta'– 'violet taffeta'– 'blue satin'– 'pink satin'– 'grey galou' – 'puce' (a brownish purple, translating to flea in French), 'bright coral nacarat' – 'comet-streaked puce' – 'grey comet'.[30] Designs were often named after contemporary events, such as the aforementioned 'comète' style, relating to a fashion trend sparked by a 1743 comet apparition,[31] which incorporated a comet trail ribbon in shoe designs. Such shoes were advertised in fashion journals (fig.114), where the pictured silk shoes feature *comète*-ribboned trimmings and rosettes. Yet despite the repair of old shoes during Marie Antoinette's imprisonment, new shoes were still ordered, quickly fuelling further accusations that she was conspiring and corresponding with the outside world. In April 1793, in one noted occurrence, the Commune commenced an investigation, after citizen Wolff, a shoemaker, had presented himself with six pairs of shoes for the royal prisoners – suspicions being raised, the shoes were subsequently checked by the guards for smuggled messages.[32] Revolutionary Hébert was also deeply suspicious about

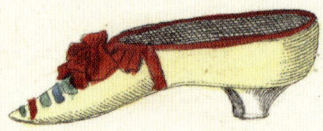

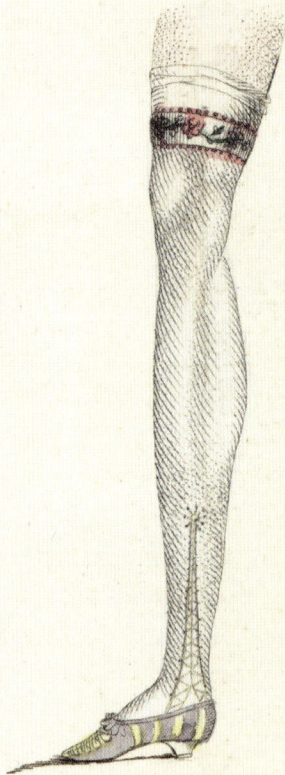
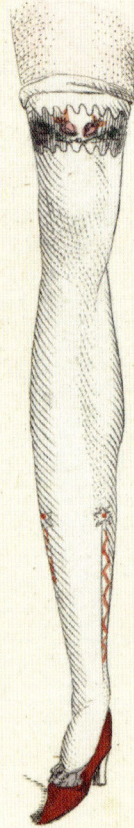

114. FASHION PLATE OF SHOE STYLES, 'SOULIER MASQUÉ', 'SOULIER JAUNE', 'SOU-LIER À LA CAVALIÈRE', 'SOULIERS D'ÉTOFFE DE SOIE' (MASKED SHOE, YELLOW SHOE, CAVALIER SHOE, SILK FABRIC SHOES)
CABINET DES MODES, 13ÈME CAHIER, 25 JUNE 1790

115. MARIE ANTOINETTE'S SILK SLIPPERS, WORN AT THE TEMPLE PRISON, c.1792
PRIVATE COLLECTION

potential message-shoe conspiracies, noting that the supply of shoes was considerable, amounting to 14 to 15 pairs a month.[33] A pair of *eau-de-nil* flat-soled silk slippers[34] with exaggerated points and decorative ruching survives from the Temple (fig.115), which tallies with recorded requests for shoes in either blue or grey from this time.[35]

When Marie Antoinette was imprisoned in the Conciergerie, a servant girl called Rosalie Lamorlière looked after her; she later recalled that when the queen got up, she put on little slippers, and every two days, Rosalie would brush her 'souliers noirs de prunelle' with their Saint-Huberty heel.[36] In one unforgettable incidence, the queen's shoes became so filthy that a sympathetic guard, taking pity, scraped the damp rust from the bricks off her soles with the point of his sword.[37]

On the day of her execution, Marie Antoinette was denied the right to wear black mourning, so she stepped out in white. The shoes she wore remain an unresolved enigma, seemingly escaping notice from eyewitnesses that day, except for Rosalie who maintained that she wore 'souliers de prunelle'.[38] 'Prunelle' denoted not a plum colour but a type of fabric, corresponding with a bill for two pairs of shoes in 'raz de Saint-Cyr noir' (an equivalent to 'prunelle' material that would explain Rosalie's description), suggesting that this element of her ensemble went unnoticed and that the queen in fact wore a small token of mourning – her shoes.[39] Taking Rosalie as a reliable witness with intimate access, augmented by the gravity of the queen's final moments before she left the Conciergerie, her record certainly seems imbued with truth. However, to complicate matters, a fawn leather shoe[40] (fig.116) is upheld as the assumed execution shoe that Marie Antoinette lost as she ascended the steps to the guillotine like a doomed Cinderella.[41] While the 'Caen' shoe does not match Rosalie's description, it is undeniably in keeping with the queen's shoe styles, with its green braid, beige silk ruffling and Saint-Huberty heel.

Marie Antoinette's final steps were supposedly 'firm and dignified',[42] while other accounts noted her swiftness and 'légèreté'[43] (lightness or frivolity), a word that has become synonymous with Marie Antoinette. Reputedly, when Marie Antoinette encountered her executioner, she stepped on his foot, uttering her final words: 'Pardonnez-moi, Monsieur. Je ne l'ai pas fait exprès' (Excuse me, sir, I did not do it on purpose).[44] There are even contemporary engravings bringing to life this very incident and quoting these final words.[45]

Following Marie Antoinette's death, the *savoir-faire* of luxury shoemaking in France declined with the democratization of fashion. Marat forewarned in the *Ami du Peuple*: 'I would not be surprised if in twenty years, not a single worker in Paris will know how to make a hat or a pair of shoes.'[46] As the century drew to a close, the new Republic revelled in a spirit of antique revival as neoclassical styles took over, women sensually draped akin to statues, accessorized with flat-soled pumps (often ribboned complementing the *à-la-victim* styles alluding to the reign of terror), or Greek sandals *cothurnes*. The eighteenth-century shoe that danced the minuet, stepped into carriages and glided down the parquet floors of the Hall of Mirrors was a shadow of the past.

After the Bourbon Restoration in 1815, when the bodies of Marie Antoinette and Louis XIV were exhumed in the old Madeleine cemetery, notably, no shoes were found in the debris.[47] Yet many of her shoes have survived – over 230 years since her death – symbols of a rarified world of privilege, intimate relics of a tragic end; potent reminders that there was once a time when the queen had the universe at her feet.

NEVER WITHOUT A FAN

Helena Cox

Fans were an enduring style staple in Marie Antoinette's *garde-robe*, intricately woven into her story. Unfurling examples from the queen's time holds a mirror up to her life and to France's path towards revolution. Both majestic status symbol and omnipresent trapping of court fashion, the eighteenth century was the ultimate golden age.

Fans evoke a bygone age. As with handbags today, they were an essential accessory, a ubiquitous sight.[1] Yet their primary function – to provide a cooling breeze in the heat – was eclipsed as fans became veritable works of art, style statements and conveyors of expression. They never left the hand and were carried even in winter, according to Diderot's *Encyclopédie*, to 'enhance a look'.[2] Originating in China and Japan, the folding fan arrived in Europe via Portugal and Spain in the sixteenth century, becoming a vital accoutrement of female dress. Catherine de' Medici is credited with its introduction to the French court in 1549, and her son, Henry III, became such a fanatic that he was mocked. The flourishing of the market was matched by the extraordinary creativity of the makers who approached the leaf as a folding canvas.

Fans were available across a spectrum of prices for women of every class – from the inexpensive and utilitarian to the extravagantly custom-made and bejewelled. They became ambassadorial items of French elegance. In 1770 there were 150 fan workshops in Paris, employing around 6,000 workers.[3] The fabrication process was collaborative, with 15 to 20 workers handling each piece, from gilding, gluing the leaf, setting the rivet and painting.[4] The synergy with porcelain painting was such that when the Sèvres porcelain factory experienced a scarcity of painters, fan painters were brought in.[5]

Etiquette books provided women with a guide for using their fans and satirical repartee was rampant with descriptions of women 'armed with fans as men with swords'.[6] No accessory could be more of a paradox – decorous yet flirtatious. There were fans with puzzles, lotteries of love, and fortune-telling for playful diversion. The 1790s *Ladies Conversation Fan* or *Fanology*, designed by Charles Francis Badini, even had a rubric for communicating in code, with letters of the alphabet grouped to convey different hand positions and fan-lady pictograms of signals to spell out words.[7] Despite much debate, the myth of fan language predominately stems from the nineteenth century as a savvy marketing tool by Parisian fan maker Duvelleroy, who cemented the game of coquetry and intrigue. According to Duvelleroy, twirling the fan in the left hand meant 'we are watched'; carrying it in the right hand before the face: 'follow me'; carrying it in left hand, open: 'come and talk to me'; and placing it on the left ear: 'I wish to get rid of you'.

For Marie Antoinette and her circle, fans completed an outfit and were both communicative accessories and conversation starters. In 1771, when Marie Antoinette wilfully snubbed Louis XV's mistress Madame du Barry by refusing to speak to her,

the Austrian ambassador, the comte de Mercy-Argenteau, wrote to the dauphine's mother, Empress Maria Theresa, about her daughter's obligation to acknowledge and address the king's favourite, advising that she could comment on her fan.[8] Fans could be exhibitionist statements and self-referential; a leaf inscribed with lines from the *Marriage of Figaro* (1778) conveyed that its owner had seen Beaumarchais's provocative new play and was glad to flaunt it. Current affairs sparked *à la mode* trends in fan design, enabling women to showcase they were well-informed with the news (following the Montgolfier balloon ascent in 1783, balloon mania was myriad). Fans commemorated important events and acted as tokens and souvenirs, such as (fig.118), celebrating Marie Antoinette's marriage to the future Louis XVI in 1770, with public festivities and fireworks celebrating the couple.

In her portrait at Innsbruck Palace, Marie Antoinette is dressed in a *robe de cour*, delicately holding a closed fan between her hands (fig.119). Such a pose is prevalent in court portraiture, where the fan is akin to a feminine sceptre,[9] bestowing queenly status and majesty. When Marie Antoinette arrived in France in 1770, Louis XV gifted her with a dazzling fan encrusted with diamonds.[10] Notably, her custom-made bridal fan, attributed to Jean-Honoré Fragonard, came up for auction in 1882.[11] It depicts the dauphine seated on a billowing cloud, surrounded by putti – one preparing to crown her with laurel, the other holding aloft the marriage contract she prepares to sign, overseen by the god of marriage (fig.120). At the court of Versailles, these accessories were bound by etiquette. The royal fan (and gloves) were carried within a basket covered with yards of green taffeta, which was replaced daily.[12] Baronne d'Oberkirch recounted in her court memoirs that it was forbidden to open a fan in the presence of the queen.[13] The only exception was if someone had something to present, whereby the item would be balanced on an open fan leaf – a gesture which once resulted in the baronne's mortification when she dropped a bracelet and broke her fan.[14] Despite ceremonial protocol, fans persisted as accessories of coquetry and dissimulation. During the period of mourning for Louis XV, the marquise de Clermont-Tonnerre, bored by the long ceremony, started sly mischief-making to divert the court ladies around her, which soon caught Marie Antoinette's eye as she tried to hide her amusement, shielding her face with her fan.[15] Madame Campan, the queen's *femme de chambre*,

ANTONIA.
ERZHERZOGIN V OESTER-
REICH. GEMAHLIN DES
DAVPHIN

recounted that this did not go unnoticed by the severe older court ladies, who declared the queen's levity derided those there to pay her respect, and consequently, Marie Antoinette was branded a 'moqueuse' (mocker).[16] The following day a satirical song circulated with a foreboding prophesy: 'Little Queen, you must not be so saucy, with your twenty years; your ill-used courtiers soon will see you pass.'[17]

Motherhood marked a turning point in Marie Antoinette's life as she invested herself in the care and education of her children. Élisabeth Vigée Le Brun's expressive chalk study (fig.122) depicts her outside, dressed in a *robe à la polonaise*, armed with her fan. Marie Antoinette's *marchande de modes*, Rose Bertin, recounted in her memoirs an anecdote revelatory of the queen's style of parenting. When Marie Antoinette's young daughter, Marie-Thérèse, dropped her fan, she commanded her nursemaid to pick it up – which she did. The queen promptly took the fan and threw it back to the ground, ordering her daughter to pick it up herself.[18]

Marie Antoinette frequently gave her own fans as gifts. When the future Tsar and Empress of Russia visited Versailles in 1782, while they were watching a play

Plate 21.

Marie Antoinette's Marriage Fan. French.
380.

from the royal box, Marie Antoinette gave Maria Feodorovna a fan adorned with diamonds containing a lorgnette in the rivet, remarking as she did that she too was shortsighted.[19] So-called lorgnette 'peeping fans' were popular at the theatre and opera for enhanced surveillance, and Marie Antoinette was observed making use of hers at the Royal Chapel in 1787.[20] While little remains, Marie Antoinette undoubtedly had a formidable fan collection.[21] After all, her expenditure on accessories in 1776 was 100,000 *livres*.[22] Her fan seller is recorded as 'la dame Berthelot'.[23] In 1770, when Marie Antoinette made her carriage journey from Vienna to Versailles, crowds celebrated her arrival in Strasbourg, Alsatian girls greeting her with bouquets, which prompted the dauphine to reciprocate, giving her fan with a rococo-esque music scene to one of the girls (fig.123).

Images of Marie Antoinette also graced fan leaves of her time, as both muse and fashionable contemporary subject. A comparison of two works reflecting current affairs reveals the juxtaposed fortunes of the queen and a tale of two reputations: one fan cultivates her image, while the other deconstructs it. The example from about 1773 (fig.124), depicts the dauphine's commended act of compassion, which was reported in newspapers and widely disseminated on engravings and fans.[24] On the fan leaf, having

leapt from her nearby carriage, the dauphine comforts a peasant woman whose husband was injured by a stag during the royal hunt at Fontainbleau. The comte de Mercy-Argenteau recorded that the scene moved bystanders,[25] and such accessories undoubtedly transmitted favourable publicity of the compassionate future queen. Some 12 years later, the decline in Marie Antoinette's reputation is splashed across a fan acting as a piece of contemporary journalism unfolding the infamous 'Affair of the Diamond Necklace', which implicated the queen in scandal in 1784–5 (fig.125). Strands of diamonds are held aloft by putti with ribbons and *fleurs-de-lis*, accompanied by medallions of the principal plot schemer, Jeanne de la Motte with the Comte de Cagliostro. The existence of other similarly themed fans in collections[26] reveals not only that these were the latest trend, but also how fan-owners were complicit in a sartorial promulgation of the queen's tarnished reputation. The mystery remains whether possessing such fans signified anti-monarchical sentiment or whether they were simply style statements – perhaps both.

On the brink of revolution in May 1789, following the meeting of the Estates-General, Marie Antoinette watched her husband address the deputies at Versailles. Her anxious awareness of the spiralling political situation was palpable, according to the nearby Madame de La Tour du Pin, who noted how she fanned herself in an 'almost compulsive way' with her large fan.[27] A month later the queen lost her son; all periods of mourning calling for black fans.[28] After the Fall of the Bastille in July, fans made from papers emblazoned with the fortress became both souvenirs and political statements parading patriotic allegiance.[29] While fan usage never waned, the luxury market was at an end. Fashion journals now portrayed women patriots to emulate. One fashion plate (fig.126) dating from October 1791, shows a 'Palais Royal' woman proudly brandishing an 'éventail à la Mirabeau' (the Mirabeau medallion, a homage to the death of the comte de Mirabeau in what was to be a fleeting status as a national hero of the Revolution). In another fashion plate (fig.127), a cockaded patriot toys with her yo-yo, armed with a fan; while the imagery is indiscernible, the accompanying caption cites it as an 'éventail à la Montmédy'. Montmédy, associated with royalist support, was the royal family's intended destination in their 1791 escape from France, which unravelled

Comte de Cagliostro

Comtesse de la...

T 24.

1791.

T 30.

1791.

as an aborted plan in their 'Flight to Varennes' where they were discovered, arrested and escorted back to Paris. Within this political context of thwarted royalist escape a Montmédy fan can therefore be viewed as an anti-monarchic jeer.

Nevertheless, in their powerful capacity to both signal and express, fans could function as facades, and flaunting revolutionary fans did not necessarily reflect genuine allegiance (after all, once the cockade became mandatory in 1792, the royal family – no doubt propelled by self-preservation – adopted tricolour accessories to show national support for *La Partie*). In contrast to the conspicuous nature of pro-revolutionary fans, counter-revolutionary accessories were codified with secret royalist imagery (supporting and later commemorating the deposed Bourbon monarchy). Fan painters artfully planted seditious royalist motifs that would escape casual observation: the guillotined queen appearing on a fan leaf when it was held up to the light;[30] transparent profiles projected by magic lanterns;[31] anthropomorphic royal faces concealed in the contours of a funeral urn and the trunks of a weeping willow;[32] and innocuous sequined floral imagery transforming into a defiant 'Vive le Roi' and *fleurs-de-lis* when the fan leaves were partially closed.[33] To possess such a royalist fan (albeit with concealed imagery) in a climate of suspicion, revolutionary accusation and violence was to risk potential discovery and accusations of treason against the Republic. In 1796, the *Journal de la justice civile* reported a Frenchwoman accused of conspiring against the Republic; one of the incriminating pieces of evidence found against her was a fan found in her home printed with an effigy of the 'famille Capet' with the words 'domine salvum fac regem' (Lord, save the King).[34] The accused defended her royalist fan ownership, claiming that it had been a present given to her before the fall of the Bastille.[35]

In the years after Marie Antoinette's death, as the century culminated, Mercier noted in *Le Nouveau Paris* (1798) that fans with the royal *fleur-de-lis* were no longer used.[36] At the *bals des victimes* commemorating the Reign of Terror, attended by the hedonistic *Incroyables* and *Merveilleuses*, the women 'stick their fan in their belt',[37] suggestive perhaps of a stylistic invigoration – a pointed contrast to the former courtly portraiture where the fan acted as a regal sceptre denoting majesty. After the Revolution, in the new Republic, the memory of the old regime was cast off as the fan was now treated like a scabbard, charged with vigour and vigilance.

Yet, nostalgia for the time of Marie Antoinette – the queen who was never without a fan – was to be revived in the early nineteenth century, following the Bourbon Restoration (1814). Fancy-dress balls became both an escape and a return to the past. At the duchesse de Berry's ball in 1829, guests participated in a treasure hunt for old court fans supplied by Vanier, which they used as props as with a mood of reverie and wistfulness for what once was, the vanished decadence of Marie Antoinette's court re-emerged with the flash of a fan.

IN HER OWN WORDS: MARIE ANTOINETTE'S LETTERS

Catriona Seth

In 1816, papers confiscated during the Revolution were seized on behalf of the recently enthroned Louis XVIII. Among them was an unsigned letter written in a small precise hand over a little more than two sides of paper. It was said to have been previously found hidden under Robespierre's bed. Composed before dawn on 16 October 1793, at the Conciergerie, it was addressed by Marie Antoinette to her sister-in-law, who never received it. The late queen's last missive (whose authenticity has sometimes been contested) asked her children to forsake ideas of revenge. Striving to assert his legitimacy and appease partisan tensions, the new King of France had it published and circulated it widely to complement other moves designed to commemorate his unfortunate predecessors, like the reburying of their remains.[1] This constituted an important stage in the rehabilitation of the much-maligned Marie Antoinette but also contributed to the development of a market in royal souvenirs.

It is paradoxical that correspondence played such a part in shaping public appreciation of a controversial historical figure. For much of her life, Marie Antoinette was reluctant to take up her pen. As a child, like her siblings, she sent occasional notes (in French) to family members and court officials. She followed tradition during her last weeks in Vienna: before departing to marry foreign princes, archduchesses wrote personal messages on the back of holy images distributed to their entourage. Valued by their recipients, several such mementoes survive (fig.129).[2] On one, a devotional watercolour representing St Helena, 'Antoine', as the future dauphine was known before her marriage, addressed a few lines of gratitude and hope to the empress:[3] her mother's advice, she affirmed, would be the greatest help and her only solace when she was far away.

This brief note inaugurates an essential correspondence. From her marriage in 1770 to Maria Theresa's death 10 years later, Marie Antoinette regularly exchanged news with her mother. Sent to Versailles at 14 with no proper instructions or support, the dauphine strove to please. The empress always remained in command. She condemned her daughter's frivolity. She deplored a youthful love of elaborate hairstyles – often far more overblown than the one depicted on Drouais's portrait (fig.128)[4] – and fine jewellery. More seriously still, she bullied the hapless adolescent about her childless marriage, repeating that all she wanted was a grandson to inherit the French throne. There was little Marie Antoinette, whose union was not consummated for seven years, could do. Her answers are often heartbreakingly naïve. 'It is distressing for me that my dear mother believed often erroneous and almost always exaggerated reports to my discredit', she affirms in June 1776.[5] And her letters always contain deep-felt expressions of love for the distant parent who usually treated her, even when Queen of France, as an immature child.

128. *MARIE ANTOINETTE*, c.1778–81
FRENCH SCHOOL, (ATTRIBUTED TO
FRANÇOIS-HUBERT DROUAIS), OIL ON
CANVAS, 120 × 100 CM. HÔTEL LE
BRISTOL, PARIS, OETKER COLLECTION

**129. AUTOGRAPH PIECE ADDRESSED BY THE
YOUNG ARCHDUCHESS MARIE ANTOINETTE TO
HER LADY-IN-WAITING, TWO DAYS BEFORE HER
DEPARTURE FOR FRANCE, 1770**
SOLD BY CHRISTIE'S PARIS, 3 NOVEMBER 2015

In October 1777, Marie Antoinette writes characteristically, hoping the length of her missive would not constitute an abuse of her correspondent's kindness: 'May I end by embracing her tenderly and assuring her that nobody in the world is more tenderly and more respectfully devoted to her or desires to continue to deserve her benevolence more than me?'[6]

While strain is often evident in her letters to her mother, Marie Antoinette was freer with other correspondents. Early in their marriage, the dauphin and his wife seemed polar opposites: she loved partying, he only wanted to hunt. He rose early, she went to bed late. Writing to Count Rosenberg, the young queen alluded to the king's interest in the locksmith's art (fig.130).[7] She quipped that she could not play the role of Vulcan and that he would be taken aback if she took on that of Venus. Maria Theresa was scandalized when her attention was drawn to one of her daughter's missives to Rosenberg: it was not the tone she expected from an archduchess.

Letters like those to Rosenberg illustrate the importance for Marie Antoinette of her closest circles. A true champion of people whose company she appreciated, she often wrote to reassure friends or to meet their requests in times of need. She was generous with her actions and her expressions, lending support when she could. Cynical acquaintances sometimes abused her kindness and many people put pressure on her to serve particular interests, none more so than the comte de Mercy-Argenteau, the empress's representative in Paris. Marie Antoinette considered him to be an ally and never suspected him of betraying her trust, though he spied on her on her mother's behalf. He put pressure on her to lobby for the Empire, even against her own good, and rarely shone a positive light on the woman he felt was too little invested in Austria's interests. Though determined to remain loyal to France, something he failed to understand, she bent over backwards to meet his requests as her frequent notes to him show. While some of these were sealed with wax bearing her coat of arms or her cypher (fig.131),[8] like most of her personal letters, they were generally unsigned.

In 1784, the cardinal de Rohan, a high-ranking priest and courtier, disliked by Maria Theresa but who hoped to ingratiate himself with her daughter, received a missive signed 'Marie Antoinette de France'. The cardinal should have realized that 'de France' never figured in royal signatures and that this was a fake but he fell into the trap of confidence tricksters who used him to get their hands on precious jewellery which they claimed the queen coveted. Though she was innocent of any involvement in the so-called 'Affair of the Diamond Necklace', Marie Antoinette suffered a loss of reputation: many wrongly thought there was no smoke without fire.

When the Revolution came, those close to the queen, like the devoted princesse de Lamballe and the ambitious duchesse de Polignac – one of the members of her

Auspice Deo

Soyez persuadée chere Durieu
que je penserai toujours
a vous et que je n'oublirai
jamais les peines que vous
avez eu avec moi c'est
dont vous assure

ce 19 Avrie   Votre tres fidelle
    1770   Antoine Archiduc.

S: IOANN: BAPTISTA:

regret par sa niece, on ne parle plus du
tout de cette tracasserie.
notre vie actuel ne ressemble en rien a
celle du carnaval, admiré mon malheur
les devotions de la semaine sainte mont
beaucoup plus enrhume que tout les bals
vous trouvez surement que cela est bien
fait pour cela, j'ai etabli chez moi un
concert tout les lundi qui est charmant
toute etiquette en est ôté, j'y chante avec
une societé de dames choisie, qui y chante aussi
il y a, quelques hommes aimables mais
qui ne sont pas de la jeunesse, il y a
Mr de Durcos, le Duc de Noailles, le baron de
besenwalde, d'Esterhazy, Mr de polignac
de Guemene, et deux ou trois autres
cela dure depuis six heures jusqu'à neuf est
ne paroit long a personne.
je suis bien fachée que vous ayez de si
bonne raison de ne pas continuer les voyages
c'est un grand malheur pour mon frere,
j'espere que vous l'aurai bien preché avant
son depart vous savez qu'il faut stile un peu
vif, pour l'animer, dieu veuille, que vous en
soyez venu a bout. je ne vous pardonne pas
vos excuses sur la longueur de votre lettre, il faut
droit que vous me crussiez bien injuste pour douter
de mes sentiments pour vous et du plaisir que
j'aurai a recevoir de vos lettres, j'y compte
ce 17 avril   antoinette

**130. LETTER FROM MARIE ANTOINETTE TO
COUNT ROSENBERG, 1775**
STEFAN ZWEIG COLLECTION, VOL.CLXXI,
BRITISH LIBRARY, LONDON: ZWEIG MS 171

**131. DETAIL OF A LETTER SEAL FROM MARIE
ANTOINETTE'S LETTER TO COUNT ROSENBERG**
BRITISH LIBRARY, LONDON: ZWEIG MS 171

circle who sometimes abused Marie Antoinette's kind-heartedness – were singled out as enemies of the people. After the storming of the Bastille, fearful of popular reprisals, Madame de Polignac left Versailles. A poignant note betrays the queen's concerns: 'Farewell, the most tender of friends. It's an awful word, but needs must. Here is the order for the horses; I only have enough strength to embrace you.'[9] While such hasty messages were characteristic of court life – delivered by hand by a footman or a lady-in-waiting – long letters sent overseas became a means for Marie Antoinette to seek agency once the royal family had been led to Paris in October 1789. Spending considerable time on her correspondence as the king sank into depression and inertia, the queen was no longer a carefree adolescent or the wealthy mistress of Trianon, whose refuge from court obligations had remained characteristically luxurious as her splendid fall-front desk shows (fig.132). She had, however, not renounced her appreciation of the finer things in life: her travel case contains everything from a porcelain teapot to a silver warming-pan and writing implements (fig.133). Marie Antoinette wanted it with her in exile when the royal family escaped from Paris only to be apprehended in Varennes.

Under virtual house arrest in the Tuileries, Marie Antoinette wrote to Mercy regularly and contacted her brothers and other European sovereigns such as the King of Sweden and Empress of Russia, sending clandestine messages via a network of allies and loyal messengers to contradict overt ones, which appeared to pander to the revolutionaries' desires. Sometimes she used secret codes that changed for every letter. Both correspondents had a copy of the same book from which the keyword would be plucked. On other occasions, passages were drafted in invisible ink and there are records of correspondents not being able to decipher what was written.

Great pains were taken for the missives to reach their destinations: they were hidden in false-bottomed boxes or presented as recycled rough paper. Carriers were often unaware of their contents. At different stages during the Revolution, the royal family had papers destroyed, fearing they might compromise their allies. Other documents were entrusted for safe-keeping to faithful members of their entourage, which means surprising bundles have survived such as the letters Marie Antoinette exchanged with Antoine Barnave, one of the revolutionary representatives who escorted the king and queen back to Paris after their arrest at Varennes. She had won him over to her cause and was trying to make use of every scrap of information, particularly when corresponding with anyone likely to be able to influence foreign heads of state.

Marie Antoinette displayed considerable political acumen, encouraging her correspondents to take sides and intervene to restore the monarchy to its former

132. MARIE ANTOINETTE'S *SECRÉTAIRE* FROM HER BOUDOIR AT THE PETIT TRIANON, 1783
JEAN-HENRI RIESENER (1734–1806), OAK, PURPLEWOOD, SATINÉ, TULIPWOOD, STAINED WOODS, BURR WOOD, EBONY OR EBONIZED WOOD, BOX, GILT BRONZE AND CARRARA MARBLE. WALLACE COLLECTION, LONDON: F302

133. SILVER AND EBONY SEAL WITH MARIE ANTOINETTE'S CYPHER, FROM THE QUEEN'S *NÉCESSAIRE DE TOILETTE* (TRAVELLING TOILETTE CASE), 1787–8
MUSÉE DU LOUVRE: OA 9594 11

glory, planning a congress, seeking funds and envisaging where troops should be stationed. At times she despaired: 'We are told, and the King's brothers constantly assure us [from exile] that we should refuse everything, and that we will be supported. By whom? It seems to me that the foreign powers are not making great efforts to assist us',[10] she complained in August 1791. Detained under increasingly draconian conditions, Marie Antoinette hoped Mercy would push Austria to wage war on France: 'I like to think that I share in the sentiment which bound you to my mother. Now is the time to give me great proof of this by saving us, me and my family, me, if there is still time'[11] are the sentences which end her final letter to him in July 1792. He advised successive emperors to play the waiting game. As a result, the deposed queen was abandoned by her birth family to her grisly fate.

Possibly the most intriguing of Marie Antoinette's letters are those addressed to Axel von Fersen. The Swede sought to alleviate the royal family's conditions and was one of the organizers of the ill-fated escape attempt, which ended at Varennes. The missives she wrote him were smuggled out, often with unidentifiable seals, and frequently written in code or in invisible ink. Those that survived, in Fersen's family archives, include redacted passages. Many readers presumed these hid details of an affair between the nobleman and the queen. Spectroscopic analysis of the inks shows that while suppressed lines often concern sensitive diplomatic information, some contain terms of endearment like 'beloved' or 'tender friend', which hint at the bonds between the correspondents (fig.134).[12] Emotional intensity was characteristic of Marie Antoinette's revolutionary exchanges as a July 1792 letter to her childhood friend the Landgravine of Hesse-Darmstadt shows: 'Farewell, my princess. They have taken everything from me save my heart which will always remain to love you, never doubt this; that is the only misfortune I could not bear'.[13]

Marie Antoinette's execution on 16 October 1793 was seen by many as gratuitously cruel. Under French *ancien régime* law, a queen was nothing more than the king's wife and had no official power. In royalist eyes, her death turned her into a martyr. Added to her reputation for elegance and style, even during her own lifetime as so many portraits and texts confirm, her tragic end made her into an iconic figure. Collecting relics, from shoes to jewels or signatures was all the rage. This led in turn to counterfeiting by – often talented – mavericks such as Feuillet de Conches.[14] The fashion for autographs fuelled the market and spurious publications complicate even serious historians' jobs to this day.

In the second half of the nineteenth century, Alfred von Arneth carried out extraordinary editorial work. He published letters from the imperial archives in Vienna, particularly those exchanged by Maria Theresa and her daughter.[15] Along with reading Freud, this correspondence proved invaluable to Stefan Zweig when he wrote his biographical essay on Marie Antoinette, attempting to uncover the individual behind the public figure with neither hagiographical nor denunciatory zeal.[16] Zweig, tellingly enough, acquired one of Marie Antoinette's missives to Rosenberg for his collection.

There are museums and libraries whose prized letters 'by Marie Antoinette' are fakes.[17] Respectable auction houses sometimes offer dubious missives purportedly by her for sale. Fortunately, though, there are still authentic documents to be discovered in public and private archives and a project is underway to locate and publish them all.[18] They tell the story of a complex woman sent as a teenager to France, far from her family and friends, ill-equipped to live in a foreign court, who doubtless used partying as a means of escape from her adolescent solitude, and who discovered fulfilment in motherhood. She was someone who had been taught to believe that God had ordained her elevated station in life but who was highly sensitive to the suffering of others. Beyond the rumours, the adulatory comments and scurrilous gossip, it is only in her correspondence that we can discover Marie Antoinette in her own words.

le porteur de tous ces papiers ne sait pas, par qui ils me sont venu, et il ne faut pas lui en parler. le memoire est bien mal faite et on voit que les gens on pense mais pour notre sureté personnelle il faut encore les menager; et surtout leurs inspirer confiance par notre conduite icy. on vous expliquera tout cela, ainsi que les raisons pourquoi souvent je ne peu pas vous avertire d'avance de ce qu'on va faire. mon homme n'est pas encore revenu je voudrois pourtant bien avoir des nouvelles d'ou vous etez, ~~que~~ que veut dire cette declaration subite de l'emp: pourquoi ce

silence profond de vienne, et menee de brux: envers moi, je m'y perd, mais ce que je sais bien c'est que si c'est prudence ou politique qui fait qu'on ne me dit rien on a bien tort, et ont m'ex pose beaucoup puisque personne ne croira, que je sois dans cette ignorance, et il seroit pourtant necessaire que je puisse regler mes propos et ma conduite d'apres ce qui se passe, c'est ce que je charge la personne de dire a mr. de mercy je vais finir [redacted passage]

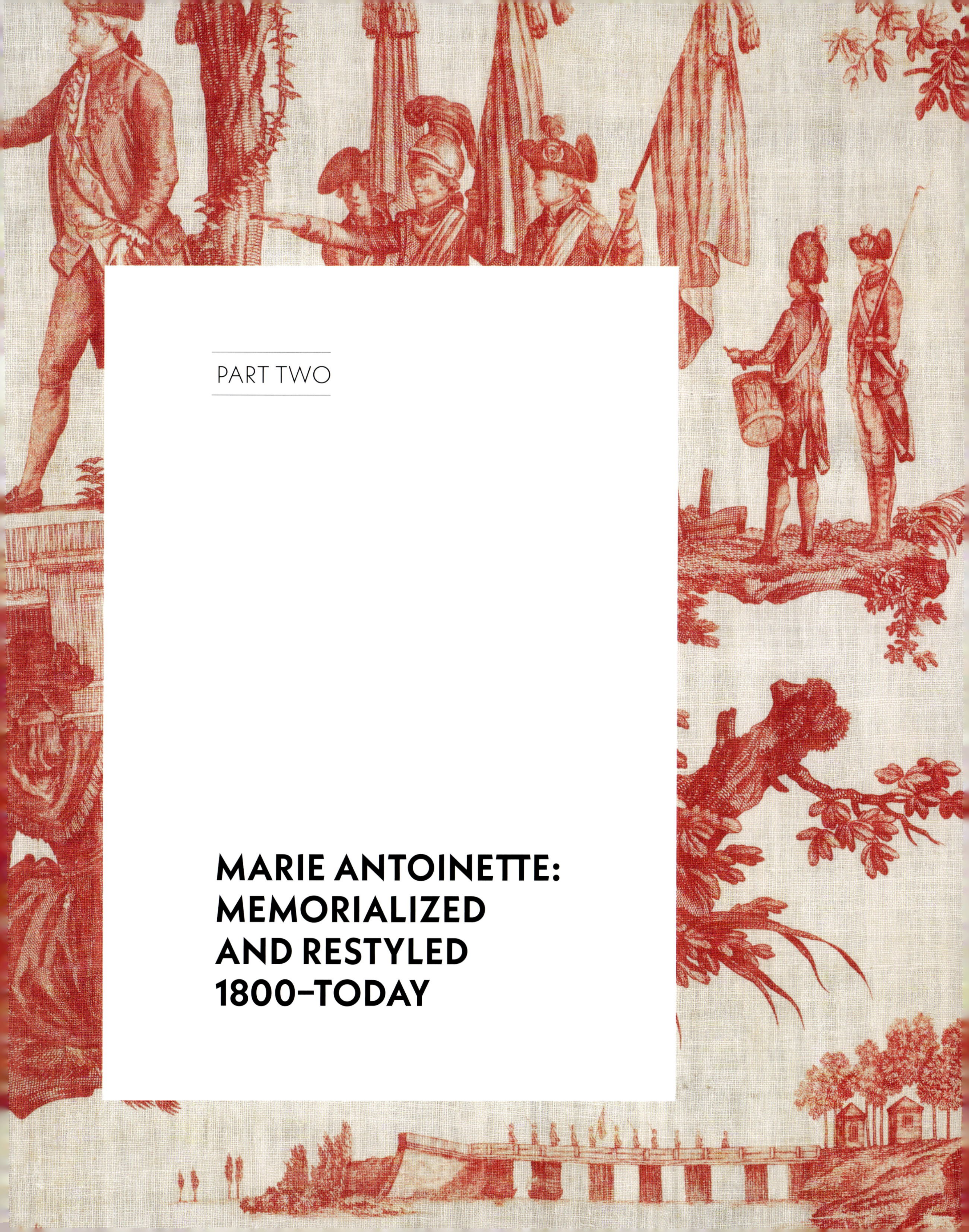

PART TWO

MARIE ANTOINETTE: MEMORIALIZED AND RESTYLED 1800–TODAY

INSPIRATIONS:
CAPTURING MARIE ANTOINETTE

Antonia Fraser

'That will be quite a journey', said my husband Harold, when I broke it to him that I intended to try and write a biography of the French queen, Marie Antoinette. At the time what I said was: 'we shall journey together'. But in my secret heart I felt both fearfully nervous and deeply excited. This was something I had always wanted to do ever since I wrote *Mary Queen of Scots*, 25 years earlier.

'I expect I shall have to research a lot of formalities', I said, 'in the footsteps of Marie Antoinette. From imperial Austria to royal France and then ….'

'I on the contrary expect to be dancing in the footsteps of a giddy girl', said Harold cheerfully.

What neither of us expected was that six months later, I should be facing two men armed with guns: and it was all part of my research. What was more, I myself was wearing elegant white gloves and that, too, was part of the routine.

It will be obvious that the adventures I had in pursuit of Marie Antoinette were extremely exciting, and it was for that reason I called the book, *Marie Antoinette: The Journey*, leaving the reader to imagine I was referring to the queen's thrilling if ultimately tragic life, rather than the fascinating not-at-all tragic journey of the writer (and her husband).

To begin at the beginning, with Marie Antoinette's own belongings, the explanation for the guns was simple but surprising. It turned out that one of the queen's wardrobe books had survived the Revolution. These were enormously heavy volumes, which would be presented to Her Majesty in the morning by a courtier on their knees. The queen then carefully chose swatches of material for the various dresses she would adopt throughout the day and evening, pricking the book with a pin at the relevant place. We were fascinated to discover that some of the original pins, made of iron, had survived.

So why the guns at the ready? The answer was that this book was a National Treasure, being held appropriately in the national archives. Harold and I might, just might, have attempted to get away with the book: hence the guard. As for the gloves, which looked very pretty and greatly adorned my drab researcher's outfit, that was for reasons of hygiene to protect the eighteenth-century iron pin from a twentieth-century predator.

Compared to this, our experience visiting the Habsburg tomb in Vienna was quite conventional. Except that the imperial crypt contained 143 Habsburgs and one governess – that of Marie Antoinette's mother the Empress Maria Theresa – who died in 1750. The flowers on every tomb were extremely impressive, including that of the governess, where I decided to say a special prayer for all those born into the world who were not Habsburgs. It was also noticeable how the atmosphere in the Habsburg crypt, including visitors, contrasted with the vault of the Bourbons in the Basilica Cathedral of Saint-Denis in Paris. Although I visited the latter three times in my five years of research, I was always quite alone in the French gloom, as opposed to the Austrian good cheer.

135. ROYAL ALBERT HALL NEW YEAR'S BALL PROGRAMME, 31 DECEMBER 1925
DEPICTING 'CARNIVAL' BY FELIX DE GRAY (1889–1925), REPRODUCED IN *THE SKETCH*.
ROYAL ALBERT HALL ARCHIVE, LONDON

Flowers and guns; and then there were the comments of our fellow visitors to the exhibitions, the palaces and the exhibitions in the palaces. These varied from tears at the thought of the tragic queen's story (including mine) to denunciations. 'La reine méchante', were words I heard once or twice, said in explanation by a teacher or guide-like figure pointing to the pictures on the wall. The second time, I stepped forward indignantly to complain: 'She wasn't the evil queen. It was the other lot who were evil'. Only to be restrained by Harold, not normally the calmer partner in our marriage.

'Darling', he said gently, 'do nothing. Write your book.'

And so I did.

INSPIRATIONS: MARIE ANTOINETTE ON SCREEN

Sofia Coppola

When I consider why Marie Antoinette endures as such a fascinating figure for us, I think about what she represents: glamour, decadence, beauty, obliviousness and being a bad girl. She seemed to lick whipped cream off her finger while people in need suffered. She was blamed for the troubles of her times, as other women in history seemed to be. The more I learned about her, the more she seemed to have been in an impossible position, with a big heart but no power to do much outside of her life, a life that she made her creative outlet, drowning herself in beauty and indulgences. I don't know about you, but I think as girls we were all told to be good, to be polite, not to make people uncomfortable and not to be selfish, so maybe there's a side of ourselves that wants to throw our head back and say 'Let them eat cake' – which Marie Antoinette never said, and we wouldn't either. I'm lifting a glass to the misunderstood bad girls of history, the queen of all queens, and to the importance of surrounding yourself with what you find beautiful.

136. *MARIE ANTOINETTE*, DIRECTED BY
SOFIA COPPOLA, 2006
KIRSTEN DUNST ON SET. PHOTOGRAPH
BY SOFIA COPPOLA

EMPRESS EUGÉNIE'S FASCINATION WITH QUEEN MARIE ANTOINETTE

Alison McQueen

In February 1853, less than two weeks after the Spanish-born Eugenia, Countess of Teba (1826–1920), married Emperor Louis-Napoléon Bonaparte (Napoléon III), the new Empress Eugénie, as she was known in France, had an experience with a profound impact. The couple were on a tour of the newly installed *musée des Souverains* (Museum of Sovereigns), in a wing of the Louvre. Among the displays of objects connected with previous French rulers was the final letter of Marie Antoinette, addressed to her sister-in-law within hours of her death. Eugénie asked if the curator could read the letter aloud and he recorded how she 'listened in silence and with tears in her eyes, the final words of a queen ready to mount the guillotine, of a mother who, in this terrible moment, cannot even embrace the children she leaves in the hands of her executioners'.[1] It is the earliest document to describe Eugénie's interest in Marie Antoinette and provides an evocative testament of the empress's feelings about the queen's lived experiences. Throughout the nearly two decades of their reign, Eugénie remained concerned her family would meet with an equally terrible fate. She was also passionate about eighteenth-century design, especially from Marie Antoinette's era. Those parallel experiences combined into a complicated fascination with a historical figure that merged admiration of fortitude and resilience with appreciation of taste and style.[2]

Eugénie declared her affiliation with Marie Antoinette publicly for the first time at the Salon of 1857, with the display of her portrait with her newborn son (fig.137). Eugénie commissioned the painting from the prominent European court portraitist Franz Xaver Winterhalter and presented herself in a luxurious garnet red velvet dress trimmed with sable fur. The gesture of her right hand and outward glance suggests she offers the Prince Imperial to the viewer, meaning for the country. He is dressed in the symbolic red, white and blue of the *tricolor* flag of revolutionaries from 1789. Curiously, mid-nineteenth-century viewers seemed not to register, or at least did not comment on, the contrast between the Prince Imperial's outfit as a sign of France's republican past, while Eugénie's clothing made direct reference to the *ancien régime* political structure of absolutist rule that was dismantled by the Revolution. One wonders whether few people besides Eugénie and the artist realized that her dress was inspired by Marie Antoinette's outfit in the group portrait of the queen with her children by acclaimed painter Élisabeth Vigée Le Brun. Eugénie admired the work and felt a connection with this representation of the queen as a maternal figure. Soon after she gave birth Eugénie arranged for a large tapestry of the painting (fig.138) to be hung at the château de Saint-Cloud, outside Paris, where the imperial family spent a large portion of their time.[3] The portrait of *Empress Eugénie with the Prince Imperial Seated on her Lap* was displayed in a prominent position at the Salon, surrounded by portraits of military and political figures.[4] The display reveals

MARIE ANTOINETTE *Style*

p. 186

137. *EMPRESS EUGÉNIE WITH THE PRINCE IMPERIAL SEATED ON HER LAP*, 1857
FRANZ XAVER WINTERHALTER (1805–1873), OIL ON CANVAS, 243 × 158 CM. PRIVATE COLLECTION

138. *MARIE ANTOINETTE SURROUNDED BY HER CHILDREN*, AFTER ÉLISABETH VIGÉE LE BRUN'S PAINTING COMPLETED IN 1787
GOBELINS MANUFACTORY, TAPESTRY PRODUCED 1818–22 IN THE STUDIO OF LAFOREST, 212 × 282 CM. MOBILIER NATIONAL

139. *EMPRESS EUGÉNIE*, 1854
FRANZ XAVER WINTERHALTER (1805–1873), OIL ON CANVAS, 92.7 × 73.7 CM. METROPOLITAN MUSEUM OF ART, NEW YORK: 1978.403. PURCHASE, MR. AND MRS. CLAUS VON BÜLOW GIFT, 1978

how Eugénie felt comfortable making a statement about her admiration of Marie Antoinette as a consort, mother and important public figure in French history.

Within the semi-public sphere of the court, Eugénie began to express her interest in the late queen's fashions even before she became a mother. Fancy-dress balls were a significant part of court social practices during the Second Empire and offered Eugénie opportunities to appear in the guise of a mythological or historical French figure. She enjoyed costumes styled after *ancien-régime* elite and royal society, and in 1854 commissioned Winterhalter to paint her portrait in eighteenth-century dress (fig.139). Most likely working from a photograph, he captured her heavily embellished two-tiered silk dress, festooned with bows, strands of pearls and *passementerie*, as the fringe and applied designs were known. This fantasy-like

140. 'LES TRAVESTIS DE S.M. L'IMPERATRICE EUGÉNIE', *FÉMINA*, 15 FEBRUARY 1911, ISSUE 242
ARTICLE FROM FRENCH SOCIETY MAGAZINE ILLUSTRATED WITH PRIVATE PHOTOGRAPHS OF EUGÉNIE IN FANCY DRESS

141. EVENING BODICE FROM EMPRESS EUGÉNIE'S WARDROBE
CHINÉ SILK TRIMMED WITH BLONDE LACE (c.1855), ACCOMPANIED BY A REPLICA SKIRT BY LUCA COSTAGLIOLO, PRINT DESIGN BY LEON MAURICE (2017). BOWES MUSEUM, BARNARD CASTLE: CST.91/1059.47

portrait, set in a lush, imaginary landscape, was not a large painting but it was a significant work for Eugénie. She never loaned it to an exhibition and chose instead to display it at the château de Saint-Cloud, in the *salon des dames* of her private quarters, where she and her guests could enjoy it.[5] Photographs taken over a period of years reinforce how clothing from the era of Marie Antoinette continued to be Eugénie's favourite historical costume (fig.140).[6]

Surviving pieces of Eugénie's wardrobe from the 1850s reveal how she valued chiné silk and blonde lace trim, which Marie Antoinette had also cherished (fig.141). For much of the time Eugénie was empress, the skirt portion of a dress was circular, shaped initially by layers of fabric and then a metal cage-crinoline. However, in the later 1860s, the skirt front flattened and became less pronounced, with underpadding used to increase the volume at the back, creating a bustle. A photograph of Eugénie

142. PORTRAIT PHOTOGRAPH OF EUGÉNIE DE MONTIJO, 19TH CENTURY
W. & D. DOWNEY, WILLIAM DOWNEY
(1829–1915) AND DANIEL DOWNEY (1831–1881).
MUSÉE CARNAVALET, PARIS: PH50193

143. STRIPED GREEN SILK DAY DRESS WITH BUSTLE IN THE *ROBE À LA POLONAISE* STYLE, 1868
BRITAIN, SILK TRIMMED WITH BRAID, SATIN, LINEN, CRYSTAL BEADS, BRASS, BOBBIN LACE AND SILK FRINGE, LINED WITH COTTON AND BONED. V&A: T.37 TO C–1984

144. WRITING TABLE WITH LECTERN, 1784
FRANÇOIS RÉMOND (c.1747–1812) AND ADAM
WEISWEILER (c.1750–1810), OAK, SYCAMORE,
EBONY, JAPANESE LACQUER, STEEL, BRONZE
AND GILDING, 73.7 × 81.2 × 45.2 CM. MUSÉE DU
LOUVRE: OA 5509

shows how ornamentation and the cut of a dress bodice could accentuate the new style (fig.142). An overlayer was equally effective at adding to the form, as is evident from the back of a dress created in Britain around 1868 (fig.143). The portrait of Empress Eugénie in eighteenth-century dress suggests the *ancien-régime* origins of the style, with raised sections of the overskirt creating a dramatic profile (fig.139).

In addition to sartorial connections, Eugénie expressed her interest in eighteenth-century interior design at imperial residences, including her renovated quarters in the Tuileries wing of the Louvre. Her audience room, the *salon bleu*, was one of three semi-public spaces ornamented with what a contemporary described as 'gracious arabesques, svelte volutes, delicate garlands, and refined carvings',[7] characteristic of the Second Empire's fusion of eighteenth-century revival styles, later named *style Louis XVI-Impératrice* (Louis XVI-Empress style).[8] In 1865 Eugénie acquired a writing desk that was once in Marie Antoinette's cabinet at Saint-Cloud (fig.144). Eugénie secured it at auction with her privy purse and communicated reverence for the queen and her taste by placing it in her audience room.[9] In an earlier commission of overdoor paintings for the *salon bleu*, Eugénie had six contemporary women metaphorically presented as her companions, while she conducted meetings and

received diplomats. In adding the desk, Eugénie strengthened the symbolic system that surrounded her as she undertook the challenging work of a French consort. For her private office, Eugénie drew on the collection of the *Mobilier national* (National Furniture Collection) and incorporated a roll-top desk and large clock that were in Marie Antoinette's apartment at the Tuileries, as well as an *encoignure* (corner piece) emblazoned with the queen's initials.[10] She also had original objects recreated and commissioned a silk company in Lyon to produce embroidered wall hangings, refashioning elements of the queen's interior cabinet at Versailles.[11] In the empress's two principal living quarters, furnishings and décor created sites of memory, commemorating Marie Antoinette's life and memorializing her taste.

Eugénie declared her admiration to national and international visitors during the Exposition Universelle of 1867, when she spearheaded an exhibition in the queen's honour. The show was mounted in Marie Antoinette's cherished Petit Trianon on the grounds of Versailles and included nearly 150 objects from private collections (fig.145). A photograph dated around 1867 shows how Marie Antoinette's bedroom was recreated with a replica Louis XVI bed next to an original chair carved with the queen's initials, that was part of a set of four by Jean-Baptiste Bernard Demay (fig.146). Those objects had furnished different rooms and were loaned from the *Garde meuble* (state furniture holdings).[12] From her apartments at Saint-Cloud, Eugénie lent a *guéridon*, a round-topped table, that had also belonged to the queen and carried her initials.[13] Eugénie further contributed 11 objects that evoked the daily life of the royal couple, including a portrait medallion of the king, a small marble bust of the queen, Marie Antoinette's fruit knife and religious books, an ivory-handled cane that was with Louis XVI in prison, and the ring he gave his confessor shortly before his execution.[14]

Eugénie's efforts to promote Marie Antoinette as a significant figure in French history, one who made valuable social and cultural contributions including through style and décor, were then turned against her. Eugénie was regent in Paris during the Franco-Prussian war in 1870 when her husband capitulated and was imprisoned. While Marie Antoinette and her family were unsuccessful when they attempted to flee in 1791, Eugénie and a female companion escaped to England with the help of her American dentist. When press restrictions were lifted for a period during the tumultuous early months of the Third Republic, and Commune of 1871, caricatures of political figures proliferated. Eugénie was lambasted as *l'espagnole* (the Spaniard) just as Marie Antoinette had been labelled *l'autrichienne* (the Austrian). A caricature representing them as Empire and Monarchy, prancing off while the Republic cleans their dirty laundry, reminds us just how often and inappropriately they are

Page 94.

PETIT TRIANON

Page 99.

LA BERGERIE

146. CHAIR FROM A SET OF FOUR, WITH THE 'MA' MONOGRAM, AFTER 1784
JEAN-BAPTISTE BERNARD DEMAY (1758–1848), CARVED AND PAINTED WOOD, COTTON AND SILK. MUSÉE NATIONAL DES CHÂTEAUX DE VERSAILLES ET DE TRIANON

147. LARGE DIAMOND BODICE BOW BELONGING TO EMPRESS EUGÉNIE, 1855
FRANÇOIS KRAMER, CONTAINING 2,438 DIAMOND BRILLIANTS AND 196 ROSE-CUT DIAMONDS. MUSÉE DU LOUVRE: OA 12238

blamed for their husbands' political agendas. The crown atop Marie Antoinette's head represented the royal and imperial luxury abhorred by the Third Republic government and it organized an auction of the Crown jewels. Some pieces were bought and disassembled by jewellers while others were acquired by private collectors who treasured their original form. Among the pieces that remain intact is the large bow belonging to Empress Eugénie (fig.147), which she wore as a brooch connected by rows of gemstones to create a necklace styled in the manner of the Louis XVI era.[15] It is through the remarkable survival of objects like the brooch and letter with which we began, that we can best approach historical figures like Marie Antoinette and Eugénie, whose fortitude and style we continue to admire today.

MARIE ANTOINETTE AND THE *BAL POUDRÉ* IN VICTORIAN FANCY DRESS

Susan North

Marie Antoinette and her sartorial style exerted considerable influence on Victorian Britain, through two versions of fancy-dress costume and contemporary fashion. The first of these three phenomena is the focus of this chapter. Marie Antoinette's court dress and the ensembles depicted in portraits by Élisabeth Vigée Le Brun inspired many Marie Antoinette fancy-dress costumes from the 1840s until the First World War, particularly for the *bal poudré* (eighteenth-century themed parties). Surviving costumes, designs, prints and photographs illustrate these ensembles; newspaper articles and advertisements describe many more.

Dressing up in costumes representing historical figures, 'exotically' dressed foreigners, romantic peasants, literary characters and allegorical figures has a long history in Britain. The eighteenth-century masquerade mixed costumed strangers of various classes and backgrounds, wearing disguises, in public places that people paid to attend. By the early nineteenth century, the social subversion this engendered was increasingly censured.[1] However, Queen Victoria loved dressing up and she set a new trend for fancy-dress events that endured well beyond her reign.[2] Fancy-dress balls became annual private parties, often held over Christmas and New Year, while public and paid versions were organized to support a variety of worthy causes – connecting frivolity with charity aligned with Victorian moral virtue.[3]

Queen Victoria's second fancy-dress ball, held in 1845, was a *bal poudré*, so-called because participants wore powdered hair or wigs. It revived the court dress of the 1740s and 1750s, for which the queen wore appropriate costume (fig.148). Eighteenth-century French court dress had, in fact, appeared at Queen Victoria's first costume ball, the Plantagenet ball in 1842. Although themed on the reign of King Edward III and Queen Philippa in the fourteenth century, there were a few outliers. The Viscountess Drumlanrig had appeared in the 'costume of the time of Marie Antoinette' wearing a 'robe of rich crimson velvet, elegantly decorated with point lace, opened in front, over a rich white satin; the body and sleeves of velvet, richly ornamented with lace and diamonds; coiffure, powdered hair and diamonds'.[4] Queen Victoria's *bal poudré* initiated the fancy-dress theme of French court dress broadly covering the reigns of Louis XV and Louis XVI, at which Marie Antoinette proved a popular figure to impersonate. She also appeared at many fancy-dress events without a theme, as many newspaper reports illustrate, for example, 'The Grand Ball at Eastwood Park ... Lady Georgina Codrington, Marie Antoinette...'.[5] In 1873, three ladies attended an Easter fancy-dress ball in Bath as Marie Antoinette, 'all more or less carrying out the same idea; hair drawn high off the forehead, poudré and wreathed with pearls and feathers, rich brocades looped up over bright satin jupes, long pointed bodices richly jewelled'.[6]

148. *QUEEN VICTORIA IN COSTUME FOR THE 1745 FANCY BALL*, 6 JUNE 1845
LOUIS HAGHE (1806–1885), WATERCOLOUR AND BODYCOLOUR OVER PENCIL, 27.6 × 19.8 CM. ROYAL COLLECTIONS TRUST / HM KING CHARLES III: RCIN 913347

149. DAISY GREVILLE, COUNTESS OF WARWICK (1861–1938), AS MARIE ANTOINETTE, 1897
LAFAYETTE STUDIO. V&A LAFAYETTE NEGATIVE ARCHIVE: 1178955

Victorians loved fancy dress because it allowed them to escape the strict etiquette of everyday and fashionable dress by wearing clothing that might otherwise be regarded as risqué.[7] The courts of the *ancien régime* were considered gaudy and frivolous, qualities which eighteenth-century fancy dress with its powder, feathers, lace and braid tacitly represented. For men and women, the *bal poudré* also allowed the blatant wearing of make-up – completely forbidden for the former and severely criticized for the latter in any other context.[8] Powdered hair made one's face look sallow and the caricature of the eighteenth-century French courtier included patches and rouge; 'even plain faces look well with the necessary and judiciously applied rouge, and a coquettish patch or two here and there'.[9] Advertisements for fancy-dress accoutrements included wigs, facial hair, rouge, powder, eyebrow pencils and 'every other requisite required for the Fancy Dress Balls'.[10]

Of the many versions of Marie Antoinette reported between 1845 and 1914, Daisy Greville, Countess of Warwick (1851–1938), was the most luxurious at the lavish *bal poudré* she held on 1 February 1895.

> Anyone who was fortunate enough to be present at the Warwick Castle Bal Poudré on the 1st inst. might well be excused if for the moment he (or she) imagined the Wheel of Time to have forgotten itself – and calmly revolved back a hundred years or so – landing us amidst the famous beauties, the gallant courtiers, and all the courtly train that made up the brilliant throng at the Court of the Tuileries.[11]

Daisy's ensemble (fig.149) – possibly inspired by a portrait at Versailles of Marie Antoinette in court dress (see fig.48) – was

> of the palest pinkiest white, clusters of pink flowers and smaller blue ones forming a rich design all over it ... the superb velvet train of an almost sapphire hue fell in folds from the shoulders, and was embroidered with large golden fleurs-de-lis, and caught from shoulder to shoulder with a magnificent rivière of diamonds.[12]

Daisy's *bal* was eclipsed by the ball held on 2 July 1897 by the Duchess of Devonshire (1832–1911), celebrating Queen Victoria's Diamond Jubilee – although perhaps only because the latter was recorded in photographs, whereas grainy newspaper prints illustrated the former. The Devonshire ball had five historical themes, including the courts of Louis XV and Louis XVI. Demonstrating remarkable thrift, Daisy wore her Marie Antoinette costume again, in which she was photographed. Surviving in the Victoria and Albert Museum's collections is the Louis XV-themed riding costume worn by Lady Isobel Stanley (1875–1963;

fig.150). Her future sister-in-law, Lady Alexandra Acheson (1878–1958), wore a very similar ensemble, suggesting a collaboration in costumes (fig.151).[13]

The Queen, The Ladies' Newspaper chronicled the popularity of fancy dress in general and the costume of Marie Antoinette in particular, with information on sources of inspiration, styles and makers. Although these costumes now appear anachronistic –

their adherence to the Victorian female silhouette and contemporary fashion overshadowing any eighteenth-century detail – their wearers fretted about authenticity and sought the correct sources. In 1869 *The Queen* noted in 'Hints on Fancy Costume':

> I now come to the costumes after different ages – a matter in which it is easy to fail, but in which success is charming when achieved. To 'get up' correctly the costume of a past age is a matter of some nicety, and requires careful study of pictures, and history, and of biographies. ... Even the 'powder' costumes of Louis XIV, Louis XV and Louis XVI, are not easy to produce correctly. The size of the hoop varied considerably during its long reign. Ruffles, though worn always with powder, were of different sorts of lace, and the wig changed in form greatly; nor is it easy to learn to what precise period each different 'poudré costume' belonged. Yet there are certain mistakes which are unpardonable, and which are the result of leaving the costume to the milliner. Thus I have seen a moiré train hooped up over blonde for a poudré costume à la Louis XV, a time when both moiré and blonde were non-existent.[14]

Another article narrated at length the choice and acquisition of appropriate fancy-dress costume:

> Our first step was to obtain a collection of drawings of costumes; and ... for practical use Lacy's Dramatic Costumes [Thomas Lacy, *Female costumes, historical, national, and dramatic: in 200 plates*, 1865] were by far the best, always remembering that his ideas of costumes are dramatic, viz, such as are worn on the stage, though by no means always strictly correct.[15]

Portraits of Marie Antoinette, especially those by Vigée Le Brun, were frequently mentioned for *bal poudré* costumes. After the restoration and reopening of Versailles in 1837, the British aristocracy who visited could view portraits of Marie Antoinette there. Requests for illustrations and advice in *The Queen* demonstrated that fancy-dress wearers were concerned about historical accuracy. For example, in 1872, a reader enquired: 'I am anxious to know what is the costume for Marie Antoinette, how the hair should be dressed, and whether it should be powdered'.[16] The reply recommended: '"Modes et Costumes Historique", published by René Pincebourde, 78 Rue Richelieu. I got my copy in London, at Sharp's library, Berkeley Square. There is a portrait in this book of Marie Antoinette, after Mme. Lebrun's picture' (fig.152).[17] The source for this print by Pauquet Frères was Vigée Le Brun's portrait

Marie Antoinette,
Reine de France,
d'après
M.me Vigée Lebrun.
1788.

Pauquet frères, éditeurs.

of Marie Antoinette in blue velvet (fig.153), which had already inspired a fancy-dress costume in 1870: 'Marie Antoinette in blue velvet and point lace, the headdress being that peculiarly becoming high round headdress which so many portraits represent...'[18] Preparations for the Devonshire ball started with picture research.

> Richness of effect and absolute accuracy of detail were the chief things aimed at, and to those ends old family pictures were eagerly scanned, portraits in the National Gallery studied, and the print room at the British Museum invaded, to find suitable models for this historical event.[19]

A painting by Charles-André Van Loo, *Halte de chasse* in the Louvre (fig.154) clearly inspired Isobel's and Alexandra's ensembles.[20]

Labels in surviving garments, newspaper commentary and advertisements document the makers of these sumptuous costumes. The house of Worth, one of the leading couturiers of the 1890s, created several of the Devonshire ball ensembles, including the Duchess of Devonshire's Zenobia costume, and Isobel's and Alexandra's riding outfits.[21] Worth had been making costumes for female performers such as Lillie Langtry and those of the *Comédie-Français,* as well as opera stars Adelina Patti and Nellie Melba, so had long experience creating attractive versions of historical styles.[22] A Worth design for a *bal poudré* ensemble from the 1860s (fig.155) was perhaps inspired by the Vigée Le Brun portrait of Marie Antoinette in blue velvet. Court dressmaker Alice Mason (1823–1901) made Daisy's Marie Antoinette costume in 1895, and 17 other ensembles worn at the Devonshire ball in 1897.[23] Theatrical costumiers also provided appropriate fancy dress, as noted in *The Queen* in 1869:

> When we had decided on our dress, our next step was to pay a visit to the costumiers, Messrs May and Harrison, both in Bow-street, Covent Garden; Nathan in Tichborne street; and Simmons, in Tavistock Street – where we found we could be supplied with any dress we wanted either to buy it or to hire it.[24]

The upmarket department store, Debenham & Freebody, not only sold fancy-dress costumes, but also published a book on the subject in six editions, *Fancy Dresses Described; or, What to Wear at Fancy Balls,* by *The Queen*'s fancy-dress columnist, Ardern Holt.[25]

These expensive, sumptuously decorated ensembles, made expressly for a single event, represent the extravagant extreme of fancy dress. Newspaper articles discussed varying levels of economy for an outfit to be worn once. No doubt many custom-made costumes were passed on to friends, relatives, neighbours and eventually to amateur theatricals and dressing-up boxes. A more economical arrangement – 'we resolved to have ours made at home' – was often selected.[26] Lace accessories, powdered hair and looping a contemporary dress *à la polonaise* over a skirt worn underneath were 'home-made' methods used for amateur theatricals that could also be adapted for fancy dress.[27] Such economies extended to the wardrobes of one's grandmothers. In the pursuit of authenticity, surviving eighteenth-century garments were greatly admired. In 1846, *The Daily Packet* recounted a splendid ball at Clontarf Castle in Dublin and 'Lady Katherine Hely Hutchinson, and Miss Steele, dressed in real court costume of the period of George the Second – the former the richest brocade silk of a dark crimson ground, and bouquets of flowers; the latter, of blue and white brocade'.[28] Daisy's *bal poudré* also featured such originals:

One of the costumes was of old, old, brocade, so fragile with age that the greatest care had to be taken in manipulating it. It dated from the fair owner's great great grandmother's time, when silks and satins 'stood alone', and when gowns did not come into wear for a season only, but were worn and turned and carefully laid away ... One feels a sense of reverence in touching these old relics of bygone days.[29]

Detailed cataloguing of the V&A's collection of eighteenth-century dress has established that rummaging through great-grandmother's trunk for suitable fancy dress was a popular option. More than three-quarters of the museum's 180 gowns/ sacks/mantuas dating from the 1720s to 1790 have been altered for nineteenth-century fancy dress. The Victorian obsession with eighteenth-century fashions did not extend to its silhouette. The surviving garments had to be adapted for different wearers and the underpinnings of the 1860s to the 1890s: various styles of corset, crinolines and bustles – all very different from the eighteenth-century stays and hoops for which these clothes were originally made. Alterations range from slight and invisibly reversible to the irrevocable, such as a once-splendid sack and petticoat of French chiné velvet, that can now only be shown as an example of late Victorian fancy dress (fig.156).

The popularity of the *bal poudré* and Marie Antoinette outlived the reign of Queen Victoria. In 1903 the Lord Lieutenant and Countess of Dudley held one at Dublin Castle. 'Everything had been carefully thought out and arranged so as to ensure the most picturesque effects: quaint and gorgeous dresses of all the powder periods were to be seen'.[30] *The Sketch* noted that there were three 'Marie Antoinettes': Lady Annesley, Lady de Grey and Lady Lurgan; *The Queen* described the first as 'regal in a pale blue brocade sacque over white lace petticoat, trimmed with pink roses, and two large blue feathers arranged on her hair'.[31] Lady Annesley (probably Priscilla Cecilia Armytage Annesley, 1870–1941) appeared as Marie Antoinette again in 1911, in 'the tulle and pearls of Marie Antoinette, a costume which suited her wonderfully' – presumably an entirely new ensemble.[32]

The First World War halted these opulent entertainments. Although fancy-dress parties resumed in the 1920s, newspapers moved on to reporting more noteworthy events and trends in popular fancy dress changed.[33] Dressing up as Marie Antoinette made amateur dress historians of Victorian women, directing them to eighteenth-century portraits, histories of silks and hand-made lace, and family heirlooms, even as the results were interpreted through the lens of late nineteenth-century fashion and aesthetics. While many of their alterations of the latter have destroyed features of their original eighteenth-century styles, without the fancy-dress tradition, these garments might well have vanished entirely, cut up and remade into cushions, curtains and children's clothing.

MARIE ANTOINETTE, ENCHANTMENT AND ILLUSION 1910–40

Sarah Grant

'We have dreamt a pleasant dream, that is all.'
Marie Antoinette, letter to the chevalier de Jarjayes, 1793[1]

Marie Antoinette's words of resignation once she knew her fate was sealed – she refused a final escape attempt from the Temple prison that would have saved her life as she could not contemplate leaving her children behind – could also serve as a poignant reflection on the halcyon days she spent at Versailles. They conjure something of the melancholy tone and dreamlike quality that imbue the Art Deco fascination with Marie Antoinette and makes it such a striking chapter in the many revivals of interest in the queen.

The lure of Marie Antoinette in the 1920s and 1930s, and of the eighteenth century generally, can be attributed to the state of a society emerging, scarred yet resilient, from the death and deprivations of the First World War and the continuing hardships of the Depression. The 'gilded' youth of the 1920s invoked the perceived golden age of the final gasp of the *ancien régime* in all its romanticized reverie, seeing a correlation between the giddy and gay abandon of their own newly reborn generation and the supposed decadence and debauchery of a lost court whose days were passed in a whirl of fashion and romance. The 'Flapper's watchwords' of 'Recklessness, frivolity and self-indulgence' could just as easily have been those of the eighteenth-century forebears they now emulated.[2] During this time a renewed focus was brought to Versailles with the signing of the peace treaty that ended the war in 1919, the château's restoration and recovery of original furniture and furnishings, and the publication of a groundbreaking series of books on Marie Antoinette by its curator, Pierre de Nolhac.[3] The Marie Antoinette style entered a new phase, a form of escapism that suggested, variously: beauty, artifice, sensuality, nostalgia, innocence, intimacy, secrecy, illusion and enchantment.

This coincided with a revolution in fashion, as the industry, stalled by the war, began to find its feet again in a changed world with daring new hemlines, revealing and softening silhouettes and diaphanous modern fabrics of synthetic fibres. 'Glamour is returning', announced Cecil Beaton in 1930. Fashion, he wrote, was becoming 'elaborately graceful' and ladies 'fancifully feminine'.[4] The painted face of the eighteenth century was also revived, as it became acceptable once more, following a hiatus of over 100 years, for women to wear powder and rouge, to which they now added lipstick and nail polish. Echoes of Marie Antoinette's time were everywhere, inflected with a chilly sophistication: diamond brilliants were positioned dewdrop-like in hairstyles, just as they had been at the glittering balls of Versailles.[5]

'This winter will mark the first organized effort at gaiety since the dark night of war', wrote *Harper's Bazaar* in a January 1920 article announcing costume designs for a masked

**157. *CORPS DE NEIGE – CŒUR DE FEU* (BODY OF
SNOW, HEART OF FIRE), COVER DESIGN FOR
HARPER'S BAZAAR, DECEMBER 1917**
ERTÉ (ROMAIN DE TIRTOFF, 1892–1990),
GOUACHE ON PAPER. PRIVATE COLLECTION

**158. DESIGN FOR A COSTUME FROM THE REVUE,
'AU REVEIL DU PASSÉ' (AWAKENING FROM THE
PAST) AT THE ALCAZAR THEATRE IN
MARSEILLE, 1923**
ERTÉ (ROMAIN DE TIRTOFF, 1892–1990),
GOUACHE AND GOLD INK ON PAPER, 37 × 53 CM.
PRIVATE COLLECTION

**159. 'SHE HAS READ ALL THE NEWSPAPERS IN
THE WORLD, AND FORGOTTEN THEM AGAIN,
SO CLEVER IS SHE', 1911**
EDMUND DULAC (1882–1953), ILLUSTRATION
FROM HANS CHRISTIAN ANDERSEN, 'THE SNOW
QUEEN', IN *STORIES FROM HANS ANDERSEN*,
WATERCOLOUR AND BODYCOLOUR, 33 × 25 CM.
PRIVATE COLLECTION

ball in Monte Carlo.[6] The nineteenth-century fancy-dress phenomenon continued into the new century and throughout the 1920s and 1930s, masked balls emboldened a new generation as they had in Marie Antoinette's day, a connection made explicitly at the time.[7]

A particularly elegant iteration of the queen's style can be found in the wave of graphic illustration that emerged, including the work of Erté (Romain de Tirtoff, 1892–1990), who created hundreds of covers for *Harper's Bazaar* between 1915 and 1937 and was himself a collector of the decorative arts of the period. In a snowy Versailles-like garden scene, a caped male snow figure stands at the foot of the stairs, pleading with the imperious Marie-Antoinette-like figure at the top, identifiable from her scattering of beauty spots and high hairstyle of the 1770s (fig.157). His burning ardour is causing him to melt, while she looks on impassively, petting the little dog who rests on her paniers.

Another design by Erté shows a partially clothed Marie Antoinette figure, again signalled by her high powdered coiffure, draped in a garland of pink roses whose petals spell out 'Le Passé' (the past), with an embroidered bodice, enormous panniered court dress and gold tasselled swags (fig.158). The delirious, dreamlike and languid decadence with a dark undercurrent of foreboding witnessed in Erté's work are all characteristics of the Art Deco revival of Marie Antoinette style in which the

queen herself, her physical appearance, also became a feature. Her doll-like figure appears across the graphic arts: hand-printed fashion plates, posters and luminous watercolour illustrations disseminated in high-end publications, in particular, the work of Golden Age illustrators Felix de Gray, George Barbier, Edmund Dulac, Aubrey Beardsley and Kay Nielsen. Marie Antoinette's style took on an association with fantasy, magic and fairy tales, and her image was used to convey a certain antiquity and melancholy beauty. The queen became the paradigm for the stock fairy-tale princess, used, for example, as the model for Aurora in *Sleeping Beauty*, the Fairy Godmother in *Cinderella* and in *The Twelve Dancing Princesses*.[8] In Dulac's illustration for *The Snow Queen*, he imagined Hans Christian Andersen's powerful yet capricious queen as Marie Antoinette-like, seated on her throne and crowned with a diadem of icicles, an aloof and listless figure seeking diversion (fig.159).

Barbier, the most famous illustrator of the Art Deco period, was a key exponent of the late eighteenth-century French revival style.[9] In his illustrations for *Fêtes Galantes*, an anthology of verse with rococo references by the Decadent poet, Paul Verlaine (1844–1896) and in the fashion almanac *Falbalas et Fanfreluches*, Barbier included gardens, statues and other landmarks of the château de Versailles and the Petit Trianon. The queen as mistress of her domain is omnipresent. In one plate, figures play blindman's buff in the pink marble colonnade of the Grand Trianon, while Marie Antoinette's Belvedere is visible in the distance of another (figs 160 and 161).[10] Courting couples play hide and seek beneath the mischievous gaze of a

GEORGE BARBIER 1923

163. 'LETTRE', FROM *FÊTES GALANTES*, BY PAUL
VERLAINE, PIAZZA, PARIS 1928
GEORGE BARBIER (1882–1932), PLATE DATED
1921, HAND-COLOURED POCHOIR PRINT.
V&A, NAL: 95.T.22

164. 'L'ALLÉE' FROM *FÊTES GALANTES*, BY PAUL
VERLAINE, PIAZZA, PARIS 1928
GEORGE BARBIER (1882–1932), HAND-COLOURED
POCHOIR PRINT. THIS COMBINES ELEMENTS
FROM ÉLISABETH VIGÉE LE BRUN'S DRAWING
OF MARIE ANTOINETTE IN A PARK, c.1780–1
(NEW YORK: MET) AND PORTRAITS OF THE
QUEEN BY JEAN-BAPTISTE ANDRÉ GAUTIER-
DAGOTY (1740–1786). V&A, NAL: 95.T.22

Marie Antoinette-style sphinx, a clever nod to the stone sphinxes guarding the
queen's Belvedere and her own interest in Egyptomania. This fashion is marked by
the gilded sphinxes prowling the decorative panelling of Marie Antoinette's *cabinet
doré* at Versailles, and a dazzling pair of gilt-bronze firedogs featuring the mythical
creature which were placed in her formal bedchamber in 1787 (fig.162).[11] In 'Lettre',
a Marie Antoinette-style figure is seated with her little dog on a period-specific
canapé, known as a *veilleuse*, with a lacquer panel inset in the panelling behind
her of the type that she collected (fig.163). Elements were lifted directly from the
modish plates of Moreau le Jeune's *Monument du costume* and the *Galerie des modes
et costumes français* and even from official portraits of Marie Antoinette (fig.164).

Barbier also produced illustrations for a number of new luxury editions of eighteenth-century texts, including an astonishing series for a 1934 edition of Pierre Choderlos de Laclos's (1741–1803) *Les liaisons dangereuses* (Dangerous Liaisons), which manages to evoke both the decadence and glamour of the doomed *ancien régime* and the heady sophistication of his time.

'Dangerous Liaisons', published in 1782, was one of the most successful novels of the eighteenth century, indeed Marie Antoinette herself had a copy in her library at Versailles.[12] An epistolary novel, its premise was that even just one 'dangerous' liaison could bring about complete social ruin, and the plot was probably a veiled, if deliberately titillating, critique of the loose morals and scheming nature of the court to whom the author was closely connected but also, as a member of the rival Orléans household, at odds. The eroticism of Barbier's illustrations reference the imagery seen in the torrent of eighteenth-century pornographic caricatures targeting the queen and in eighteenth-century French erotic novels that circulated on the black market (see Slater in this volume), combined with the aesthetic of Japanese woodcuts from the artist's own collection.[13] The use of pochoir, a hand-stencilling technique incorporating carefully applied washes of translucent gouache, is what gives them their luminous quality, while the designer's attention to period detail, seen in the faithful recreation of interiors, fashions, hairstyles and even textile designs, enriches them further. One striking example is the illustration depicting the downfall of the villain, the marquise de Merteuil (fig.165). Dressed in a black and gold gown, she appears conspicuous amid a sea of pastel, standing isolated at the theatre, shunned by all, as the women whisper behind their fans and the men jeer.

The vignette of a sensual mermaid-Marie Antoinette figure, posing provocatively with her towering hairstyle and jewels, recalls the harpy abominations of the satirical pamphlets that sought to undermine the queen, in which she appeared half-woman half-beast, bare-breasted with a scaled and forked tail (fig.166). Interspersed throughout the two volumes are Barbier's witty illustrated initials, with all the intricacy and humour of an illuminated manuscript: the letter 'M' becomes a kittenish rose-crowned woman putting her finger suggestively to her lips (fig.167).

An eighteenth-century revival was also taking place in the fashions of the time. 'The name of Marie Antoinette is associated with picturesque gowns and amazing head-dresses', announced *Vogue* in 1925.[14] Countless references were made to the queen in the pages of leading magazines throughout the 1920s and 1930s, with features on her fans, gloves, hairstyles, parasols, perfumes, toilette, cabinetmakers, gardens, bedroom, and so on. All the key couturiers sourced inspiration from the queen in their day dresses and evening gowns, giving them a modern twist with the use of the

165. ILLUSTRATION TO LETTER CLXXIII, CHODERLOS DE LACLOS, *LES LIAISONS DANGEREUSES* (PARIS 1934), 2 VOLS
GEORGE BARBIER (1882–1932), HAND-COLOURED POCHOIR PRINTS, 26.6 × 20 CM (SHEET). V&A, NAL: 38041023001803

167. ILLUSTRATED INITIAL 'M' FROM LETTER LXXXVIII, CHODERLOS DE LACLOS, *LES LIAISONS DANGEREUSES* (PARIS 1934), 2 VOLS
GEORGE BARBIER (1882–1932), HAND-COLOURED POCHOIR PRINT, 26.6 × 20 CM (SHEET). V&A, NAL: 38041023001803

166. MERMAID VIGNETTE FROM CHODERLOS DE LACLOS, *LES LIAISONS DANGEREUSES* (PARIS 1934), 2 VOLS
GEORGE BARBIER (1882–1932), HAND-COLOURED POCHOIR PRINT, 26.6 × 20 CM (SHEET). V&A, NAL: 38041023001795

EXEMPLAIRE
N°158

168. *ROBE DE STYLE* DRESS, c.1922–3
JEANNE LANVIN (1867–1946), WHITE SILK
ORGANZA WITH ARTIFICIAL SILK FLOWERS.
V&A: T.54–2013

Overleaf left
169. TEA GOWN, c.1905
CALLOT SOEURS, THE FIRM FOUNDED BY
FOUR SISTERS WHOSE SHOWROOM ON THE
AVENUE MATIGNON WAS FURNISHED WITH
18TH-CENTURY FRENCH FURNITURE. PATTERNED
PINK SILK DAMASK TRIMMED WITH ÉCRU LACE,
LINED WITH PINK SATIN. V&A: T.148–1967

Overleaf right
170. *ROBE DE STYLE* DRESS, c.1922
JEANNE LANVIN (1867–1946), SILK TAFFETA,
METALLIC LACE, SILK GAUZE, WITH GLASS
BEAD AND CRYSTAL EMBROIDERY. LACMA,
LOS ANGELES: CR.83.66-9. GIFT OF
MRS. HOMER BURNABY

diaphanous modern fabrics.[15] In 1921, Paul Poiret designed a 'Marie Antoinette' gown in sheer white organza modelled on the queen's *chemise à la reine*, with the same puffed sleeves and ruffled collar, which he paired with a dark blue transparent voile overdress and sash, the connection with the queen giving it, one fashion magazine observed, 'a little historical cachet that is completely authentic'.[16] Jeanne Lanvin also produced a frothy spin on Marie Antoinette's notorious muslin gown (fig.168). Some references were more oblique: Jeanne Paquin named one of her styles 'Vigée Lebrun[*sic*]', after Marie Antoinette's favourite portrait painter.[17]

A beautiful tea gown by Callot Soeurs draws more directly on the femininity and pastel palette of the queen's wardrobe (fig.169). Made of the palest pink floral damask silk, it features a dramatic sweeping box pleat from the back of the neck and elbow-length sleeves in the style of the *robe à la française* and is trimmed with écru floral-patterned lace in the style of the 'blonde' lace so beloved of Marie Antoinette and her circle.

However, the most enduring homage to the eighteenth century was Lanvin's *robe de style*, a sophisticated evening gown inspired by French gowns of the 1770–80s, which enjoyed huge popularity from 1918 to the 1940s. In 1938 Lanvin remarked, 'How can we neglect the fashions of the past? They represent all the work, art and thought of the centuries before us. … We need to adapt them to our modern taste and give a constantly new face to things that are eternally beautiful'.[18]

The *robe de style* was of a particularly fine and therefore clinging silk, often black, with a fitted bodice, dropped waist and full skirt that terminated either at the calves or ankles (fig.170). The defining feature of the style, however, was that it was worn over small or medium paniers, thereby recreating the silhouette of its late eighteenth-century inspiration. This revival of the panier, 'the venerable ancestor' of the crinoline as one fashion magazine put it in 1912, was consciously connected with Marie Antoinette – but what was once a symbol of the formality of court dress now brought a note of whimsy and, with the exposed lower legs and ankles, of sensuality.[19]

While Lanvin is credited with its invention, the *robe de style* was widely adopted by all the other couturiers, including Paul Poiret, Callot Soeurs, Paquin, Doeuillet, Lucile and Vionnet. Particularly notable is the *Bouquetière* design from the Boué Soeurs, which was available in rose pink, green and pale blue versions. A stunning tiered chiffon *robe de style* evening gown, it featured a panier silhouette, train and a large bow at the back, the gold lace skirt bearing a large stylized basket of flowers with the fashion house's signature festoons of appliquéd ribbon roses and detailed embroidery.[20] The sisters used a rose on their dress label, and their advertisements featured sketches of models in their transparent designs, known as 'lingerie frocks',

posing as Trianon-esque shepherdesses. The paniers are particularly exaggerated in another Boué Soeurs *robe de style* of peach-coloured lace and silk chiffon (fig.171).

A fashion plate by Barbier captures and acknowledges the *robe de style*'s debt to Marie Antoinette's court (fig.172). It depicts Cécile Sorel, an actress famed for her flirtatious roles, gazing at a bust of Marie Antoinette while dressed in a dramatic *robe de style*, which the title likens to a 'grand habit' (the formal dress of Marie Antoinette's court): 'Mademoiselle Sorel en grand habit'.

One of the most showstopping examples of all *robes de style* was that worn by Hollywood actress, Norma Shearer, in the 1929 MGM film *The Last of Mrs Cheyney*, which publicity stills show was a delicate rose-pink though this was not visible in the black-and-white film (fig.173). Designed by the celebrated costumier Adrian, this glittering moiré fabric evening gown was adorned with an oversized and stylized bow across the skirt and a long trailing bow across the back that descended from the shoulders, evoking the box pleats of a *robe à la française*. The skirt and bodice were embroidered with silver sequins in the shape of 'scallop-like' petals and Shearer carried a matching shell-pink fan, with leaves of sheer chiffon. The daring backless cut of the gown was perfectly suited to Shearer's character, a beautiful jewel thief who impersonates an heiress. Nine years later, Norma Shearer was again costumed by Adrian when she portrayed Marie Antoinette in the eponymous MGM classic of 1938.

The film was based on the 1932 biography by Austrian historian, Stefan Zweig (1881–1942), which was a watershed for the historiography and subsequent cultural perception of the queen. Zweig was the first biographer to strive for an accurate and dispassionate portrayal of Marie Antoinette, offering a fresh perspective on her life for a modern age. His use of solely uncontested correspondence and memoirs and his departure from the hagiographic approaches of his predecessors led to a more realistic and ultimately, compelling portrayal of the queen.

A follower of Sigmund Freud, Zweig used a pyschoanalytical approach to assess Marie Antoinette's character, which he asserted was but that 'of an average woman' in extraordinary times, his analysis reflecting the great societal shifts of his own time, in particular, advances in the rights and social status of women (suffrage was granted to Austrian and British women in 1918).[21] Perhaps most crucially, his biography allowed the queen a romantic and sexual life, bringing to wider knowledge the very recently deciphered letters between Marie Antoinette and the Swedish comte Fersen, which had revealed the long suspected love affair between them.[22]

As the reigning *grande dame* of Hollywood, married to a famous producer, Shearer's social status and reputation as a great film star gave her the required

GEORGE BARB

172. 'MADEMOISELLE SOREL EN GRAND HABIT',
1921
GEORGE BARBIER (1882–1932), HAND-
COLOURED POCHOIR PRINT FROM THE
LARGE-FORMAT ALBUM *LE BONHEUR DU JOUR,
OU LES GRACES A LA MODE*, ASSEMBLED AND
PUBLISHED BY JULES MEYNIAL, 1924. BRITISH
LIBRARY, LONDON: HS.74/1064

173. *THE LAST OF MRS CHEYNEY*, 1929
NORMA SHEARER, WEARING A *ROBE DE STYLE*
DRESS DESIGNED BY ADRIAN (1903–1959) FOR
THE MGM FILM

174. MARIE ANTOINETTE, 1938
NORMA SHEARER, WEARING A SILVER SILK
ORGANZA AND METALLIC SILVER LAMÉ COURT
GOWN DESIGNED BY ADRIAN (1903–1959).
PHOTOGRAPH BY LASZLO WILLINGER

175. MARIE ANTOINETTE, 1938
NORMA SHEARER AS MARIE ANTOINETTE,
FOR THE MGM FILM

clout to portray the famous queen while her reputation for playing flirtatious and assertive characters also gave her the necessary allure.[23] The film is considered a masterpiece of Art Deco cinema; even the defining author of the age, F. Scott Fitzgerald, was a contributor.[24]

Adrian created 1,200 costumes for the film, including 34 costumes and 18 wigs for Norma Shearer who appeared in almost every scene and set a new Hollywood record for her number of costume changes.[25] They were the most lavish and expensive costumes ever produced, all embroidered and beaded by hand, and Adrian carried out considerable research for the project, visiting Marie Antoinette's childhood residence of Schönbrunn, viewing her portraits in Paris and her letters in Vienna. 'I wished to absorb as much of the atmosphere of Marie Antoinette as possible', he said, 'and to saturate myself with her century'.[26]

And yet Adrian's genius was his ability to combine period detail with 1930s glamour, rendering Shearer part Hollywood siren, part sugarplum fairy. Nowhere is this more visible than in a captivating silk organza and metallic silver lamé court gown, which Shearer pairs with a transparent cape embroidered with silver shooting stars, her hair also wreathed in stars that catch the light like so many fizzing fireworks, in the scene where Marie Antoinette and Fersen meet and embrace for the first time, the gown a literal embodiment of their chemistry (fig.174).[27] This was Hollywood at its most magical and enchanting, resurrecting the apparitions of a vanished world.

MARIE ANTOINETTE AND SAPPHIC LOVE

Daniel Slater

On 28 August 2024, Donald J. Trump – 45th President of the United States and then candidate to be the 47th – reposted a message on social media. It featured pictures of the wife of the 42nd President and former Secretary of State (Hillary Clinton), and the Vice President and Trump's opponent in the election (Kamala Harris). The text: 'Funny how blowjobs impacted their careers differently'.

In this moment, Secretary Clinton and Vice President Harris shared something in common with Marie Antoinette. Deploying sexualization as a weapon against women draws on deep seams of tortured masculinity and torturous misogyny, mingling fear, desire, disgust and lust. Unpicking the social, psychological and ideological issues at work reveals a hugely complex web of conflicting forces, a whirling dance of lies, self-deception and hypocrisy. And never more complex than when the slander touches sapphic love, since lesbianism constitutes a triple provocation to heterosexual masculinity: at once an 'unnatural' outrage, a voyeuristic titillation ('look at what we are doing') and a challenge ('look at what we can do … without men').

Let us start with an obvious, but critical point. The depictions of Marie Antoinette as tribade (an eighteenth-century term for women who have sex with women)[1] are, first and foremost, the creations of the male mind. So much, despite their frequent anonymity, is obvious. Like most pornography, they are at pains to present themselves as if they captured the voyeur's peeping view. In the case of Plate 2 from *La journée amoureuse, ou les derniers plaisirs de Marie Antoinette*, the eighteenth-century viewer would have been presented with an image that is alarming even by today's standards. One woman bends over a chair, her full skirt lifted above her waist, exposing her lower body, bare save for her stockings. Another woman, fully dressed, stands behind her clasping a substitute phallus. As viewers, we confront these two women at the moment of penetration. One woman looks over her shoulder, either in a moment of shock, shame or tentative invitation. Her direct eye-contact actively engages us, making us [un]willing participants in the scene we behold. The closed curtain to the left of the couple creates an intimate atmosphere of secrecy, adding to the voyeuristic thrill – or repulsion – inspired in contemporary viewers. The explicit nature of this print increases exponentially when taking into account that this is a depiction of the Queen of France and her close friend and confidant the princesse de Lamballe. The substitute phallus – framed centrally within the composition – furthers the notion that satirical depictions of Marie Antoinette's rumoured sapphic affairs were a creation of the male, heteronormative, penis-centric mind. But this is not even the 'male gaze' – it is a projection of male fear and desire. We cannot approach it as if it told us anything at all about its ostensible subject. The light that it casts is on its creators, and its consumers.

176. ILLUSTRATION FROM *LES LIAISONS DANGEREUSES* (DETAIL OF FIG.179)

177. *'JE NE RESPIRE PLUS QUE POUR TOI... UN BAISER MON BEL ANGE!'* (I ONLY BREATHE FOR YOU... A KISS, MY BEAUTIFUL ANGEL!), FROM THE PLAY *LA DESTRUCTION DE L'ARISTOCRATISME*, 1789, ETCHING, 1790. MUSÉE CARNAVALET, PARIS: G.26420

178. ANONYMOUS, PLATE 2 FROM *LA JOURNÉE AMOUREUSE, OU LES DERNIERS PLAISIRS DE M** A********* COMÉDIE EN TROIS ACTES, EN PROSE, REPRÉSENTÉE POUR LA PREMIÈRE FOIS AU TEMPLE, LE 20 AOÛT 1792*** (THE AMOROUS DAY, OR THE LAST PLEASURES OF MARIE ANTOINETTE, COMEDY IN THREE ACTS, PERFORMED FOR THE FIRST TIME AT THE TEMPLE, 20 AUGUST 1792), ETCHING, PARIS, 1792. PRIVATE COLLECTION

Rumours that Marie Antoinette engaged in lesbian liaisons with various women – a commonly identified favourite was the duchesse de Polignac, depicted in a print with Marie Antoinette from the play, *La destruction de l'aristocratisme*, 1789 (fig.177), another the princesse de Lamballe – circulated at the end of the *ancien régime*, and became the subject of numerous pamphlets and satirical engravings.[2] Some of the themes of these works are simple enough for a modern audience to unpick: the hypocritical condemnation of vice as an occasion for pornography, still a familiar justification for many a tabloid revelation; the relentless stripping away, not just of nobility but of basic human dignity, which is inherent in the degree and type of exposure that works such as Plate 2 of *La journée amoureuse, ou les derniers plaisirs de Marie Antoinette* (fig.178) involve; and the absurd seaside-postcard ribaldry of a world in which the court is turned into a humming hive of nymphomania. Is the viewer of such works being invited to laugh, to curse, or to masturbate? Are we in the realm of satirical slander, or violence, or lust? We do not need much historical background to guess that the answer (as with similar modern satires and exposés) is that all of these factors are in play.

Je ne respire plus que pour toi... un baiser, mon bel Ange!

Deeper historical reflection, however, suggests that some of what is going on here involves a more complex shift in attitudes towards gender and sexuality. Viewed through this lens, the specific choice of lesbianism as the vehicle for satire carried a special charge.[3] In the course of the eighteenth century, homosexuality (and unconventional gender expression, with which it was closely associated) had come to be seen not simply as a (sinful) activity that people sometimes engaged in, but as a fundamental departure from the 'natural order'. So, by presenting Marie Antoinette as a lesbian, revolutionary pornographic satire was portraying her as a perverter of the natural order. As Elizabeth Colwill puts it, 'the depiction of Marie Antoinette as tribade during the revolution warned citoyens and citoyennes to police the "natural" boundaries of desire'.[4] It simultaneously reinforced propaganda juxtaposing the 'unnatural' activities and mores of the aristocratic court with the rationality of the revolutionary faith. On the one side, natural rights and reason – on the other, unnatural vice, a world turned upside down.[5]

The trope also drew on profound convictions about gender. On the one hand, behind the snicker, it is unmistakably misogynistic, violence directed against a woman. On the other, its targets included the king and male aristocrats, their virility called into question by 'their' women's preference for each other. In this way, too, the satire contrasted a 'natural order' – in which men were, literally and figuratively 'on top' – to an effete, effeminized, 'unnatural' and unreasonable courtly culture. Liberty versus the libertine.

What must be clear therefore is that this explicit satire is, to modern eyes, profoundly reactionary, that the assumptions about 'nature' and gender roles that it embodies are now highly contested. For in much of Europe and America, the twentieth century saw a huge shift in perspective towards sexuality. George Barbier's illustrations for a 1934 edition of *Les liaisons dangereuses* offer a more palatable, sugary-sweet depiction of sapphic love within the eighteenth-century French court, standing in stark contrast to the almost clinical depiction of sex in *La journée amoureuse*. In an illustration for Letter LXIII (fig.179), two women embrace, their faces obscured by an ornate wig, adding a sense of dignified anonymity. Rich textiles pool around the pair in a cocoon, blurring the boundary between where one body ends and the other begins. The viewer sneaks a glimpse of a bare breast and suggestively rouged knees and elbows. Like *La journée amoureuse*, one woman is in a state of undress whereas her partner remains fully clothed. It is almost as if, without the dominant presence of a man, a power dynamic needs to be established between the naked and vulnerable, and the protected and in-control. Also like the 1792 print, Barbier's illustrations for *Les liaisons dangereuses* are situated within the typically feminine domestic realm.

In the illustration for Letter LXIII, the women sit beneath a painting of Cupid. Perhaps their love has been ordained by the gods, and perhaps Barbier is offering a more lenient attitude to lesbianism than that of almost 150 years before. In another illustration from Letter LXIII (fig.180), the illusion of a *ménage à trois* is framed by powder-pink curtains. On the one hand, the yonic appearance of this drapery perhaps reminds the viewer of female pleasure, existing in a realm free of men. On the other, the curtains transform the intimate setting of the bedroom into a stage. Unlike *La journée amoureuse*, the lovers do not acknowledge or perceive their voyeurs, but the curtains still create a sense of performance for an unperceived audience. The [male] viewers penetrate this membrane through their gaze, depriving these women of privacy and intimacy. This furthers the archaic, yet still present, concept that depictions of sex between women is largely – or solely – for male gratification, which undermines lesbianism as a fundamental part of some women's identity. If we have inherited the eighteenth century's perception that sexual acts are not merely acts, but aspects of identity (so that homosexuality is not simply something people sometimes *do*, but something people fundamentally *are*), our public discourse decisively rejects – turns on its head – the assumptions of natural order on which these satires depended. For queer people, the liberating move has been the re-characterization of homosexuality as a 'natural' variation, so that it is homosexuality's repression that now stands accused of being an irrational perversion of the natural order. For women, the liberating move is the rejection of masculinity as a virtue, or as a claim to power.

Seen through that lens, Marie Antoinette becomes not an object lesson in sapphic vice, but an icon of sapphic virtue. It is not that we do not see, as the revolutionary satirists saw, a 'mixed up, muddled up, shook up world'.[6] But where they encouraged people to regard this with fascinated horror, we are tempted to look at it with compassion. On this reading (to be found in internet articles inviting readers to see Marie Antoinette as a lesbian icon), or in her deployment in drag or film (such as Benoit Jacquot's *Les adieux à la reine*, 2012), such a reworking reverses many of the assumptions of the satirists (fig.181). In place of the wicked woman whose private vices undermine public order, she becomes the victim of repressive public bigotry, ruthlessly exposed and stripped of her private dignity in a barbaric process which ends, of course, with the ultimate public horror: the cold rational steel of the guillotine.

As with so much about Marie Antoinette, however, such revisionist compassion seems every bit as much of a projection on to her as the violent satire that it challenges. The 'real' Marie Antoinette is no more clearly present. Rumours that were once used to incite hatred and ridicule become hints that are used to provoke sympathy. One propaganda objective becomes another. There appears to be no solid evidence, after all,

that Marie Antoinette's sexuality was ever more than an acutely targeted slander, and its transformation into a comforting myth brings us no closer to any sort of truth.

Perhaps we will do better if we turn our eyes away from what is depicted, and towards ourselves as we respond to those depictions, and to our eighteenth-century ghosts as they stand beside us. Let us not deceive ourselves, as we glance at an explicit depiction of aristocratic ladies wielding dildoes or fumbling under their elaborate petticoats. We, too, are voyeurs.

And, just as surely as the original creators of these works found justifications for their voyeurism ('Behold how vice subverts natural reason!'), we find our own ('Look where patriarchy and heteronormativity take you!'). But we might, perhaps, ask ourselves whether our own excuses are given in much better faith than theirs.

One might, confronted with this fear of complicity, simply shrug. Sex sells, human beings love gossip and the exposure of private secrets. But there seems to be more to it than that. Those who make use of Marie Antoinette's (rumoured, presumed, assumed) lesbian sexuality – whether they do so sympathetically or violently – have realized above all that by giving us access to something private, secret and intimate, they are giving us power over her. The 'revelation' of her sexuality to us puts her at our mercy. We are given the ability to know, and to judge. And it hardly matters how we judge, or whether what we are passing judgment on is true or false. The main thing is that, in that moment of revelation and judgment, she becomes public property – our property.

Understood like that, the depictions of Marie Antoinette as a lesbian have nothing much to do with Marie Antoinette, or with lesbianism. Any powerful person would do. Any sexual intimacy would do. These works are not so much, even as they appear to be, rallying cries to opposition, or support. They are about power: about taking power over the powerful by seeing things they want us not to see, and knowing things they want us not to know. As with Donald Trump's tweet, or revenge porn, or tabloid revelations, nothing is more potent than sexual secrets to achieve this end. But, ultimately, the aim and the dangerous attraction is the same, and the same in the eighteenth century as it is with today's gossip about royal families, billionaires, politicians or media stars. By learning their (real or imagined) secrets, we make them *ours*. By stripping them of their dignity, we strip them of their power.

For many people, famous momentarily or perhaps for a few decades, this happens, and then they lapse back to obscurity. But Marie Antoinette is, in this respect, the ultimate A-lister. The 'rumours' of her sexuality never become simply truths or untruths, facts of history. They remain perpetually rumours, stories, secrets to be 'uncovered' again and again, not so that we can fall under her spell, but so that she can fall under ours.

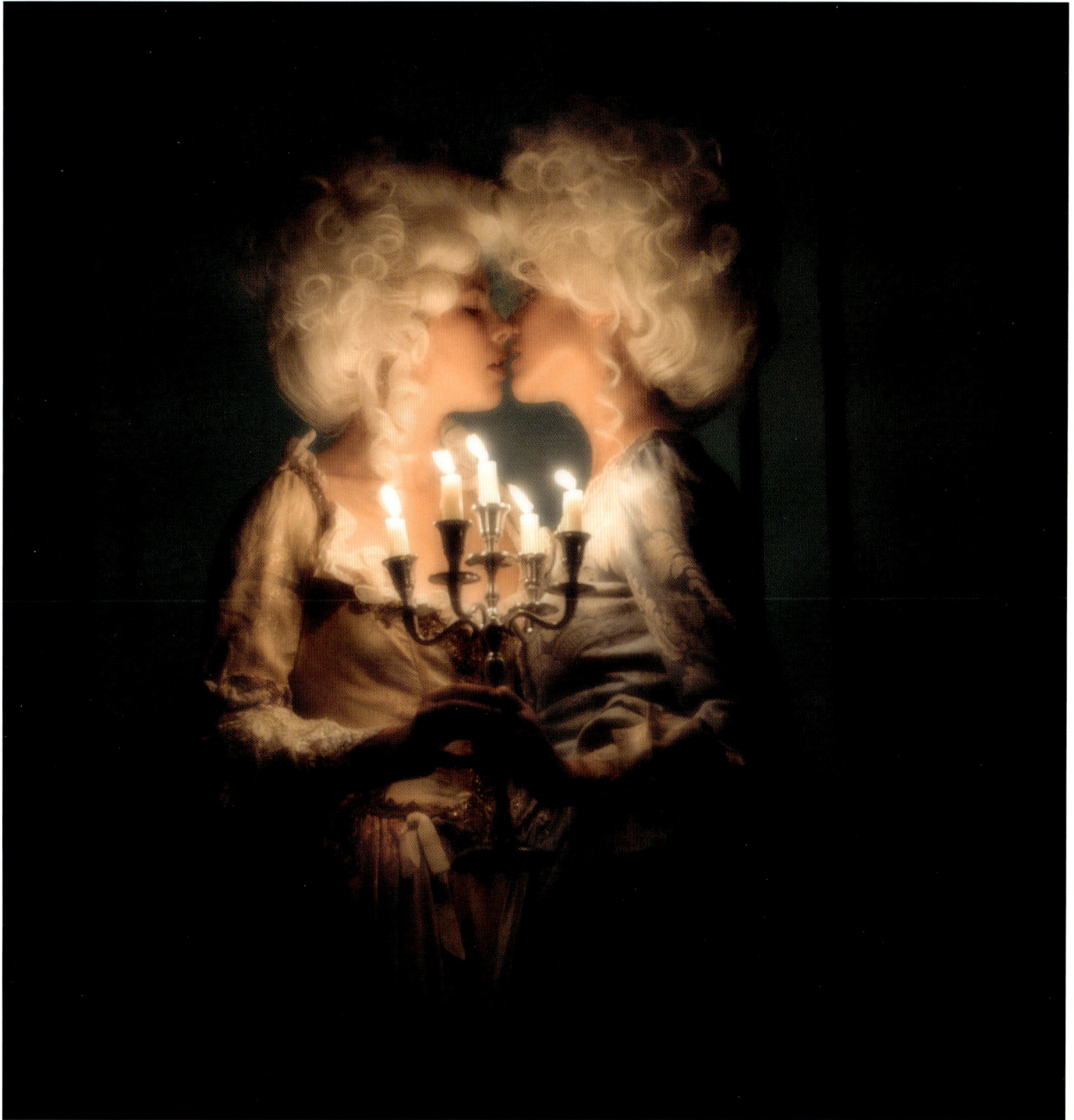

183. *AFFAIR OF THE DIAMOND NECKLACE*, 2015
TYLER SHIELDS, CHROMOGENIC PRINT

A QUEEN IN FASHION

Oriole Cullen

The myth of Marie Antoinette is one that is inseparable from the world of fashion. For over two centuries she has remained a symbol of the interplay between fashion and identity. As a young teenager, stripped of her clothing and her personal and national identity, before being symbolically remade in a new image through the donning of French attire, she swiftly grasped an understanding of the power of dress in the complex world of French court circles. It was her manipulation of fashion, encompassing changing styles in clothing, accessories, hair and make-up, which allowed her to assume a semblance of power in an aristocratic political environment where she was viewed as property of the court and for many years criticized as a foreign interloper who had failed to produce an heir. Marie Antoinette's method of doing so remains startlingly relevant today. In collaboration with her 'Minister of Fashion' Rose Bertin, a stylist-cum-designer figure, and her hairdresser Léonard Autié, she celebrated and disseminated her fashion choices through their own media platform – the *Journal des dames* fashion magazine. While she upended an established system of court and political life by reclaiming her body and visible identity through the manipulation of her appearance, her unparalleled success in doing so, ultimately hastened her demise, both within and outside of court circles.

Despite all we know of her life, as far as contemporary fashion references go, it is the imagined idea, the myth, rather than an accurate historical depiction of Marie Antoinette that persists to be translated in a myriad of ways. She is variously used as an indicator of luxury, frivolity, sensuality, sexuality, freedom, vanity and excess. This imagining of the young queen is intrinsically linked with the city of Paris, which, despite numerous revolutions and regime changes, has remained since Marie Antoinette's own time at the centre of the global fashion industry. So it is inevitable that Marie Antoinette, this emblem of French high life and all things fashion, is frequently a source of inspiration, a way to connect and comment in this heart of the industry.

From a mixture of images on a designer's mood board, to literary quotes, to performative interpretations, the very name Marie Antoinette can be a stimulant, encompassing multiple aspects of dress and appearance. A point of inspiration can lead to a design that closely resembles the source material or it can result in something that is a radical transposition of the original reference. As arguably the most recognized figure of fashion of the eighteenth century, Marie Antoinette frequently becomes an attribution for all things of the period, even where she herself is not in fact a direct point of origin. She is both a catalyst and a catch-all, which inevitably means that Marie Antoinette style within the fashion world is a shifting and mutable thing. Just as Marie Antoinette herself collaborated with various creatives and makers to perfect her own look, so today, in a complex fashion ecosystem, multiple players converge to crystallize, create and capture a fashion moment or confer its signifying message: from designers and stylists to photographers, make-up and hair artists, and fashion journalists.

When examining Marie Antoinette's enduring legacy as a touchstone for fashion designers in the late twentieth and early twenty-first century, it is interesting to recall that her own invention of dressing down and embracing comfort in her simple white cotton dress, the *chemise à la reine*, was viewed as much more radical in its time (see Banić and Harpley in this volume, p.113) than the imposing formal court dress of the *grand habit*, with its exaggerated panniered dresses coupled with the powdered and ornamented pouf hairstyles. Yet it is the latter with which she is most identified and which certainly allowed for the most excessive and sartorial statements. Of these two contrasting approaches to dress, it is the more lavish and ornamented incarnation that has more popularly continued to fuel the sartorial imagination, and offered rich grounds for sparking innovative interpretations, gaining momentum in the centuries following her untimely demise.

In 1989, as the bicentenary of the storming of the Bastille approached, *Vogue* noted that the Spring couture 'proves that the French haven't lost their taste for the royal treatment', singling out Emmanuel Ungaro for his jewel-bright silk dresses and coats in graphic floral patterns 'brazenly tongue-in-cheek references to Marie Antoinette herself'.[1] The 1980s was a decade that ushered in large, performative fashion shows, opening up the idea of fashion as major spectacle. Many designers began to create looks purely for the catwalk, allowing for evermore dramatic and impactful designs. Amid the varied and dynamic approaches taken by designers, the eighteenth century was one source of inspiration that was firmly back in vogue, with the work of top designers such as Christian Lacroix, Karl Lagerfeld, Jean Paul Gaultier, Vivienne Westwood and John Galliano regularly informed by their various and respective interests in the century of Enlightenment and Revolution. Fashion resonated with reinterpretations of panniered skirts, corsetry and sumptuous fabrics and even bewigged heads. In the wider sphere of popular culture, the 1988 Oscar-winning film *Dangerous Liaisons*, with costumes by James Acheson, inspired the fashion world; Vivienne Westwood created her 'DL' jacket in reference to title of the movie. There was also Madonna's celebrated 1990 MTV awards performance, when the singer chose Marie Antoinette – in a costume by Malene Stewart – to channel the extravagant fashion of New York's ballroom scene celebrated in her song 'Vogue'. In an age before social media it was a cultural event watched live by millions of viewers.

From the mid-1980s into the late 1990s, designer Vivienne Westwood's shows frequently included models with white painted faces, powdered hair and lavish ballgowns based on the sack-back dress. She famously recreated eighteenth-century stays as a corset for the late twentieth century[2] starting with her Spring/Summer 1986 collection *Mini-Crini*. Cut short on the waist with stretch panels and a low curved bodice enhancing the bust, paired with pearl chokers and voluminous hooped mini-skirts, the look was easy to wear and flattering. Adored by a generation of club kids and polite society alike, it underscored Westwood's self-professed fascination with the eighteenth century at this time. She drew inspiration from a wide range of sources, from literature to painting to furniture, embracing the social and sexual politics of the *ancien régime* and working them into her collections. Provocative and sensual, Westwood's work was not just about the look it conveyed but about the physical feeling it evoked in the wearers. Her clothes demanded a certain posture, a way of wearing and moving, which were viewed as empowering by many of her clients. Although frequently misunderstood by the British tabloids, with references to her work such as a 'cross between Marie Antoinette and Miss Jean Brodie on acid',[3] they translated the past into a new and contemporary way of dressing.

Westwood's fascination with the eighteenth century was more than matched by legendary designer Karl Lagerfeld, for many years creative director at the house of Chanel. Lagerfeld was also known for his extensive personal collection of eighteenth-century art and furniture. His own powdered hairstyle, with its low ponytail, channelled the powdered wigs of this historic period and for many years he also carried a fan as an accessory, stating that 'the eighteenth century is my Rosebud, I like the timeless quality...'.[4] Throughout his long career Lagerfeld often incorporated eighteenth-century design elements into his work. This came to an apex in 2012 when he chose Versailles as the location to show his Chanel Cruise 2013 collection (fig.185). Mixing the codes of Chanel, such as pastel tweeds and costume jewellery with ruffles, diamond chokers, and skirts and shorts that protruded from the hips in the style of panniered skirts, he played on the word rococo to theme the collection 'Coco Rock', after the name of the Chanel founder. Yet, when asked about his inspiration, while acknowledging Marie Antoinette, he conceded that she was really too specific a reference and he was drawing on numerous women associated with Versailles, including the duchesse de Polignac.[5] In particular, he emphasized his fascination with Madame du Barry, mistress of King Louis XV and arch-rival of Marie Antoinette, noting that 'she had exquisite taste'[6] and referencing the fact that she wore trousers – a tenuous link to Coco Chanel's own way of dressing. Underlining the interconnected nature of fashion, Chanel make-up director Peter Philips confirmed his own

references for this show had been Marie Antoinette and Manga. The press variously recorded the collection as 'Marie Antoinette-inspired designs',[7] 'a rock-inflected vision of Marie Antoinette',[8] and that it had 'a Marie Antoinette-inspired baroque mood'.[9]

Both Westwood and Lagerfeld revelled in references and inspirations drawn from the eighteenth century, but despite inferences drawn by the press they tended to avoid specifically referring to Marie Antoinette. For them, with their deep knowledge of the period, she was too obvious a source yet their work brought her name and style into the public arena. Conversely, one designer for whom Marie Antoinette would remain a definite and constant point of reference was John Galliano. He began his career with his 1984 graduate collection, which looked at the fashions of France's youthful post-Revolutionary reprobates *Les incroyables*, and the period remained an area of fascination for him.[10] While Galliano was known for drawing on and mixing up a multiplicity of sources in each of his collections, the figure of Marie Antoinette was recreated and referenced in much of his work for the house of Dior, suggesting parallels with the approach of Christian Dior himself who consistently referred back to eighteenth-century sources (see Banić and Harpley in this volume, p.125). However, although Galliano revelled in exploiting the silhouettes and embellishments associated with the queen's wardrobe, he also drew on the darker aspects of her personal life.

In Galliano's *Freud or Fetish* haute-couture collection of Autumn/Winter 2000–1, a doll-like Marie Antoinette figure made a memorable look, with a wind-up key and some straw stuffing protruding from her back, on her head a tall, powdered wig, and white make-up with a red cross on her neck (fig.186). She wore a richly embroidered panniered dress, the bodice emblazoned with a replica of the infamous necklace that had undermined the innocent queen's reputation. The dress was decorated with painted and embroidered floral motifs, bows, sheep and images of the queen surrounded by cupcakes. It also included more disturbing depictions of a *tricoteuse* knitting away by a bloodied guillotine, the severed head of a sheep and that of the queen herself. This stand-alone figure was part of the central 'nightmare scene' in the three-part show where Galliano aimed to 'symbolize what fetishism evokes in the psychology of clothing'.[11]

In 2007, the 60th anniversary of the house of Dior, Galliano created a celebratory collection based on how Christian Dior's work might have been represented by his favourite artists. Shown at the Palace of Versailles, the diamond necklace made another appearance, this time on an elaborate pink dress inspired by Fragonard and worn by the model Doutzen Kroes, her hair topped with a miniature *bergère*-style hat (fig.187). It was of course no surprise that a Versailles-based show might

187. JOHN GALLIANO FOR CHRISTIAN DIOR
PINK EVENING GOWN WITH A REPLICA OF THE
'AFFAIR OF THE DIAMOND NECKLACE' JEWEL,
HAUTE COUTURE COLLECTION AUTUMN/
WINTER 2007, WORN BY DOUTZEN KROES

188. JOHN GALLIANO FOR CHRISTIAN DIOR
EVENING GOWN WITH A PORTRAIT OF MARIE
ANTOINETTE, HAUTE COUTURE COLLECTION
SPRING/SUMMER 2006

feature references to Marie Antoinette, and Galliano's dress seemed to vie with the extravagances of the queen's most elaborate garments with its grand structured sleeves and vast asymmetric skirt, on one side a cascade of tumbling bows, on the other tiers of ruffles, all encased in an overlay of embroidered tulle. While the press noted that 'many of the clothes may have looked overpowering for mere mortals'[12] it represented Galliano's fantastical adventures in pushing the definition of fashion. Unlike Westwood, his catwalk garments were not necessarily designed to be worn by or recreated for clients, rather serving to convey the message and overall aesthetic of his collections.

Galliano presented a further, more disturbing reference to Marie Antoinette for his Dior haute-couture collection for Spring/Summer 2006 (fig.188). Based on the French Revolution, the show featured models with a deathly pallor to their faces, some with the date 1789 painted on their skin, wearing crucifixes around their necks and garments embroidered with the revolutionary slogans: Liberté, Egalité, Fraternité. Amid the voluminous cloaks and deconstructed corset dresses were leather garments and utility trousers worked with the quilted detail of eighteenth-century petticoats; many of the outfits had blood-drenched hems. The show notes included phrases such as 'Red is the new Libertine. Platinum is the new Marie Antoinette...'.[13] It was a dark and unnerving realization of the mayhem and chaos that accompanied the last years of the queen's life, unusual in its confrontational story, much closer to the experience of the real woman than the flamboyant depictions of court dress and pastel colours that one might expect from fashion.

Impending doom in the face of excess is the moralizing tale that is often associated with Marie Antoinette, and while the collection titled a 'Cautionary Tale' hints at this approach, London-based designers Meadham Kirchhoff were reflecting on 'luxuriating in beauty and wanting more of it'[14] when they looked to the eighteenth century to inspire their Spring/Summer 2013 collection (fig.189). Referred to in the press as representing a 'Marie Antoinette-style decadence',[15] they mixed classic references such as *bergère* hats, bows, stomachers and diamond jewellery with thigh-high boots and mini-skirts, while models walked the catwalk eating cake.

As referenced in many of these examples, Marie Antoinette style signifies a certain approach to dressing that involves complicated garments, layered accessories and dramatic hairstyles; however, some designers prefer the challenge of taking these references and translating them into a very different idiom. Japanese designer Rei Kawakubo has variously evoked the spirit of Marie Antoinette in her collections, always with an approach that defies the expected tropes. In 1998 she showed her Spring/Summer collection at the Conciergerie, where Marie Antoinette was

imprisoned and spent her final days before her execution. The collection explored a deconstructed approach to fashion through the use of mostly off-white raw-edged fabrics, asymmetric ruffles, full long skirts, simple chemise dresses and large, cascading, felted collars. Most notably the models wore headdresses made of lace or tulle gathered like unbalanced clouds and trailing as though a powdered wig had been knocked and pulled apart. The collection was haunting and beautiful, seeming to evoke the spirit of the condemned queen in an abstract way. Kawakubo would return to this source of inspiration in both her Autumn/Winter collection of 2016, inspired by punks in the eighteenth century, and in her Autumn/Winter 2024 collection with 'each model in some glossy, blackened Marie Antoinette-esque getup'.[16] It was a manifestation of intense feelings described by the designer as anger towards the world and herself.[17] The latter two collections incorporated towering wig-like headpieces and the monumental sculptural garments for which the designer has become known since 2014. Kawakubo's Marie Antoinette is an abstracted version of a voluminous eighteenth-century silhouette, her designs are radical expressions of freedom in how to adorn the body, extending the limits of what fashion can be through shape and form.

In 2016, performer and creative director Rihanna debuted a collection of her own Fenty fashion line with sportswear brand Puma and designer Melissa Battifarano (fig.190). Imaginatively titled 'Marie Antoinette at the gym', as one might expect from sportswear, it presented a relaxed and unrestricted style of clothing and did so not by evoking Marie Antoinette's simple cotton *chemise à la reine*, but through the lens of the lavish formal wear of Versailles, with non-gendered floral printed satins, corsetry, lace detailing and pearl and diamond necklaces. At the end of the show Rihanna took her bow waving a fan, wearing a pink zip-up top that evoked a present-day take on a mantua, with drawstring waist and a train cascading from the back to the floor, the petticoat replaced with tracksuit pants decorated in laser-cut floral motifs. While not the most practical of gymwear, this light-hearted experimental approach to fashion evoked a sensibility of the young queen while playfully pushing the boundaries.

Away from the catwalk, the creative processes of fashion give rise to multiple interpretations and reinterpretations of single ideas, which continue to evolve. The outfit worn in the finale of Galliano's Spring/Summer 1998 Dior collection – a tribute to the Italian heiress Marchesa Luisa Casati (1881–1957) – was an enormously skirted silk ballgown with voluminous hoop supports inspired by a Venetian masquerade costume worn by the marchesa in the early twentieth century. In 2006 the dress reappeared on the pages of *Vogue* in a shoot by photographer Mario Testino styled by Grace Coddington (fig.191). Here, the model Stella Tennant wore the dress with

191. 'NO-RULES BRITANNIA', AMERICAN
VOGUE, MAY 2006
FEATURING STELLA TENNANT (1970–2020)
WEARING JOHN GALLIANO FOR DIOR'S
SPRING/SUMMER 1998 HAUTE COUTURE
DRESS, STYLED BY GRACE CODDINGTON.
PHOTOGRAPH BY MARIO TESTINO

192. 'CHECKING OUT', AMERICAN *VOGUE*,
APRIL 2012
FEATURING KATE MOSS WEARING SARAH
BURTON FOR ALEXANDER MCQUEEN,
CORNFLOWER-BLUE SILK JACQUARD GOWN,
WITH LACE BUSTIER AND BOOTS, VAN CLEEF &
ARPELS DIAMOND NECKLACE, HEADPIECE BY
JULIEN D'YS. PHOTOGRAPH BY TIM WALKER

large, powdered wig, sprouting long white ostrich feathers, pale make-up and painted lips evoking the image of an eighteenth-century French courtier. No matter that the editorial is to celebrate a Costume Institute dedicated to Anglomania, this perfectly calibrated image sings of Marie Antoinette style. The dress would make another appearance in the exhibition *House Style* curated by Hamish Bowles at Chatsworth House in 2017. Evoking the spirit of the former chatelaine Georgiana, Duchess of Devonshire, the dress appeared alongside a portrait of the duchess, who had been a close friend of Marie Antoinette.

In 2006, Sofia Coppola's film *Marie Antoinette* revived the queen for another generation with an attempt to humanize her and show her as a young and joyful, albeit misguided, spirit. The distinct aesthetic of the film with its pastel hues, Manolo Blahnik shoes and Ladurée macarons would become the new reference point for years to come. In celebration of the film, *Vogue* commissioned an editorial and cover by photographer Annie Leibovitz (see fig.202). Actor Kirsten Dunst was pictured in various dramatic poses at the Palace of Versailles in a series of garments created especially for the photo shoot, each evoking a different designer or design house's take on the young queen. From Chanel's white-lace evening dress titled 'Petit Trianon', to a billowing Dior gown of foil and organza and a sophisticated chiné taffeta by Oscar de la Renta, each worn by Dunst with almost understated contemporary hair and make-up. This was a photo shoot of 'Marie Antoinette for today', the context provided by the actress, the setting of Versailles and the interspersed images of the cast in their film costumes designed by Milena Canonero. The editorial itself became a piece of fashion history, illustrating how garments commissioned from a designer for a specific themed photo shoot but never manufactured can in turn become a fashion reference.

Another commissioned editorial example of how new ideas emerge from the synthesis and reinterpretation of established concepts is demonstrated in a Tim Walker shoot from 2012 to commemorate the forthcoming renovation of the Paris Ritz hotel. In one image the model Kate Moss reclines in the pastel-coloured Louis XVI-style room of the Imperial Suite, surrounded by tiny chihuahua dogs. She wears a sumptuous Alexander McQueen dress of satin brocade, a tight bodice opening to reveal ruffles, a nod to the eighteenth-century stomacher, a flaring skirt featuring classical motifs. The dress itself is described as 'reminiscent of fifties couture' and certainly in its mid-calf skirt length and silhouette it recalls the eighteenth century as seen through the eyes of Christian Dior. On her feet she wears contemporary vertiginous lace platform heels. Yet the intent to evoke the eighteenth century is made explicit in the Julien d'Ys headpiece worn by Moss, created from blue and

193. JEREMY SCOTT FOR MOSCHINO
AUTUMN /WINTER 2020 COLLECTION

**194. ANDREA GROSSI, TOILE DE JOUY CULOTTE
MANTUA-STYLE GOWN FROM 2020 DEBUT
COLLECTION**
ALSO WORN BY LIL NAS X TO THE BLACK
ENTERTAINMENT TELEVISION AWARDS IN 2021

white fibre and ruffles, it echoes the stacked wigs of Marie Antoinette's hairdresser, Monsieur Léonard.[18] An entirely contemporary styling that avoids pastiche but instantly conveys its references.

Resurgences of Marie Antoinette style seem ever more frequent. In 2016 and in 2020 numerous designers incorporated eighteenth-century elements into their designs and TikTok popularized the 'coquette aesthetic', a feminine, romantic way of dressing that often referred to the queen as a source of inspiration. For Jeremy Scott, the infamous 'Let them eat cake' myth provided the inspiration for his Autumn/Winter 2020 collection for Moschino, a brand that revels in irreverence and whimsy (fig.193). Models in pouf-style wigs wore denim, leather and toile-de-Jouy panniered mini-dresses and sack-back dresses over jeans. The finale included five dresses styled like elaborate tiered iced cakes. Popular misconceptions persist because they are frequently more intriguing or scandalous than the truth and none more so, it seems, than the unfortunate cake quote.

As fashion had evolved away from set notions about gender, new and inventive interpretations of Marie Antoinette style widened her appeal. Designer Thom Browne created immaculate pastel versions of panniered skirts, trousers and coats in both his men's and womenswear collections of Spring/Summer 2020 and Andrea Grossi's 2020 *Welcome to DeusLand* collection created a dramatic toile-de-Jouy panniered trouser look, which was subsequently worn by musician Lil Nas X to the BET awards (fig.194). In June 2023, Simon Porte Jacquemus showed his Spring/Summer 2024 collection, *Le ChouChou*, at Versailles. Inspired by Princess Diana and Marie Antoinette, models wore transparent looks, long open robes, mini panniered skirts and panniered jackets over swagged satin knickers, recalling those designed by Vivienne Westwood and worn with her trademark corset in the *Cut, Slash and Pull* collection of Spring/Summer 1991. Such contemporary iterations demonstrate how the fashion vocabulary of Marie Antoinette continues to evolve and grow with every new creation.

Much like the court of Versailles in the late eighteenth century, fashion relies on artifice and novelty, a constant churn that demands renewal, engagement and excitement. The fashion world balances on a fulcrum of fantasy and commerce. As a known and celebrated reference, Marie Antoinette offers designers a point of identity from which to take flights of fancy. She opens a portal of imagination that runs the extremes, tipping from luxury and frivolity into a dark demise, allowing for experimentation and illusion far away from practical concerns. As during her lifetime, she continues to appear in new and surprising ways – an eternal life lived through the medium of fashion in which she herself found escape.

MARIE ANTOINETTE PERFORMED

Harriet Reed

'In the case of Madame Antoine, the enjoyment of music was from childhood central to her life.'
Antonia Fraser, *Marie Antoinette: The Journey* (2001)[1]

Performance was interwoven into Marie Antoinette's life and role at court. She was trained in music and dance, playing the flute, harp and harpsichord under the tutelage of composer Christoph Willibald Gluck.[2] She was a celebrated patron of the arts, and performed in concerts and plays in her own theatre, the Théâtre de la Reine at Versailles.[3] Marie Antoinette has also been credited as a composer herself, for setting the poetry of Jean-Pierre Claris de Florian to music:

If even without daring to say a word
His glance alone softens you
If without ever making you blush
His jollity always makes you smile

That's my friend
Give him back to me
I have his love
He has my word.[4]

These sentimental lines share the same wistfulness and romantic turmoil present in pop music of the twentieth and twenty-first centuries. And, just as Marie Antoinette may have sung them to express her power and talent, so too have a succession of modern performers sung their own compositions – while dressed as Marie Antoinette.

Performing as 'Marie Antoinette' has been a cultural touchpoint for decades. In music, from Madonna to Beyoncé, embodying the tragic young queen through videos and live performances has cemented a performer's status as a 'reigning queen' of the industry, or expressed their relationship to public scrutiny and wealth.

The performative nature of Marie Antoinette has also found relevance with the queer community. The perceived qualities embodied by her: vain, ostentatious, naïve, wealthy, powerful, tragic, beautiful and feminine, speak to the codes of drag performance. From fashion recreations to the emulation of courtly gestures and movement, the luxury of Marie Antoinette's court exemplifies Pepper LaBeija's quote in the 1990 documentary *Paris is Burning:* 'Opulence: you own everything'.[5]

In the worlds of film and television, portraying Marie Antoinette can be a landmark role for any actor, since it guarantees significant attention from the press,

195. *MARIE ANTOINETTE*, **1938**
NORMA SHEARER AS MARIE ANTOINETTE,
COSTUME AND HEADDRESS DESIGNED BY
ADRIAN (1903–1959)

196. *MARIE ANTOINETTE*, **1938**
NORMA SHEARER AS MARIE ANTOINETTE,
COSTUME AND HEADDRESS DESIGNED BY
ADRIAN (1903–1959)

analysis from historians, and an eye-catching wardrobe. From Norma Shearer's sympathetic monarch to Kirsten Dunst's troubled teen queen, the 'character' of Marie Antoinette continues to be open to different interpretations and characterizations, which define each decade.

When MGM's *Marie Antoinette* was released in 1938, the studio systems considered the casting of actresses as queens to be a savvy marketing move. As Elizabeth A. Ford and Deborah C. Mitchell explain: 'By casting its studio queens as real royals, Hollywood assured its own system of succession with an eternal stream of worshipping subjects and built a tight homology between reality and fantasy, between the private and public.'[6] Shearer's star vehicle, directed by W.S. Van Dyke, exemplified this strategy. The trailer boasted '4 years of preparation, 152 speaking parts, 5,500 extra players, 98 massive sets'.[7] The production involved extensive research across Europe, including the collecting of antiques, garments, accessories and jewels from the period. Under costume designer Adrian (Adrian Adolph Greenburg), a staggering 1,200 costumes were made (figs 195 and 196). Costumes were dyed to match eighteenth-century portraits and Shearer's eye colour, despite a later economical decision to shoot in black and white.[8] Comparisons were frequently made to exaggerate the expense, claiming 'Not even history's real Marie Antoinette had been dressed with a more lavish hand!'[9]

Based on Stefan Zweig's biography of the queen, first published in 1932 and subtitled 'Portrait of an Average Woman', Shearer influenced a more complex story of a 'tragic heroine', developing the romantic storyline with comte Fersen and integrating political events. Despite this, the film underperformed at the box office.

> Positioned in relation to the rise of the National Socialists in Germany, the decline of production oversight under [MGM Studio Head] Louis B. Mayer in the USA, and the eclipse of the 1920s–1930s contract actress on the MGM lot, [Shearer's] creative efforts can be viewed as having personal and professional resonance that involve issues of sexuality, gender, celebrity, proprietorship, and legacy.[10]

The film was out of step with American audiences who identified more with a message of 'liberté, égalité and fraternité'.

Marie Antoinette was again extravagantly recreated in the film *To Catch a Thief* (1955), directed by Alfred Hitchcock. Costume designer Edith Head combined both eighteenth-century and 1950s styles to create the looks of the climactic masquerade ball (figs 197 and 198). 'Hitchcock instructed Edith to dress Grace [Kelly] as a

198. GRACE KELLY IN *TO CATCH A THIEF*, 1955
COSTUME BY EDITH HEAD (1897–1981),
STRAPLESS GOLD LAMÉ SWEETHEART
NECKLINE AND PANNIERED EVENING GOWN,
EMBELLISHED WITH BUTTERFLIES/STYLIZED
BIRD WINGS, WITH FAN, FULL-LENGTH
EVENING GLOVES AND MASK (NOT PICTURED)

"fairy princess" for the ball. Edith created a ball gown with a huge skirt of gold mesh adorned with fabric birds and accessorized with a golden mask, and topped Grace's head with a golden wig.'[11] Inspired by the court of Marie Antoinette, the scene embraced the theme of ostentatiousness and folly as a jewel thief preys on oblivious wealthy guests. As with Shearer's star vehicle, the expense of costuming the eighteenth century inspires creative excellence, and *To Catch a Thief* is the crowning achievement of Head's collaboration with Grace Kelly.

Pop queens of the twenty-first century have also melded Hollywood, fashion and historical references while performing as Marie Antoinette. At the time of writing, artists have included Katy Perry, Lil Nas X, Beyoncé, Rihanna, Taylor Swift, Dua Lipa, Laverne Cox, Selena Gomez, Charli XCX and Chappell Roan, all of whom have used the imagery to communicate their own fairytale rise to celebrity, status, spectacle and power.

For the promotional film of the 'Mrs Carter World Tour' in 2013, Beyoncé wore a vintage Thierry Mugler gold corset (Spring/Summer 1997) with an Alexander McQueen coat and gold panier-style skirt, styled by Ty Hunter. With sceptre, crown, medals (reading 'Justice' and 'Philanthropy'), a jewelled miniature of Jay-Z and star initialled 'B.R.' (perhaps Beyoncé Regina), the outfit harks to both Marie Antoinette and Queen Elizabeth I.

The styling followed an impeccably strategized year of self-promotion. In 2013, Beyoncé sang the American national anthem at Barack Obama's presidential inauguration, headlined a critically acclaimed Super Bowl XLVII Halftime Show, and released the documentary *Life is but a Dream* on HBO. Halfway through the tour, she surprise-released her self-titled album to critical and commercial success. Although she had already been nicknamed 'Queen B' and 'Queen Bey' over the previous decade, online petitions in 2011 determined her fanbase as the 'BeyHive', and her title 'Queen Bey'.[12] This magisterial imagery marked her full embrace of the title, and the beginning of her ascent to cultural icon.[13]

Queer performance has also used the iconography of Marie Antoinette to explore power and visibility, from the use of her name in the eighteenth and nineteenth centuries as a secret sapphic code, to the drag ballroom culture of the twentieth century.

'In the same way that Marie Antoinette's enormous "pouf sentimental" hairdo was a symbol of wealth and power… queer opulence offers a site for the transformative power of performance through the material signifiers of "success" to a community previously denied this kind of indulgence or visibility.'[14] Pop artists such as Lil Nas X (wearing an ostentatious blue wig in the music video for 'Montero'; fig.199)

202. THE CAST OF *MARIE ANTOINETTE*, DIRECTED BY SOFIA COPPOLA, AMERICAN *VOGUE*, SEPTEMBER 2006
WITH COSUMES BY MILENA CANONERO, SHOES BY MANOLO BLAHNIK AND JEWELS BY FRED LEIGHTON. PHOTOGRAPH BY ANNIE LEIBOVITZ

stated that 'Marie was into fashion so we wanted the film to feel fashionable'.[20]
Manolo Blahnik designed 25 pairs of heels for the film, Fred Leighton supplied $4
million worth of diamond jewellery and K.K. Barrett designed the sets, including a
detailed recreation of Marie Antoinette's bedroom.[21] With references crossing the
historical and contemporary, costume and set design worked together 'to capture the
essence of the period, to suggest mood, to reinforce and comment on character, to
project the state of mind of its heroine, and to visualize the director's concerns'.[22]

Fiona Handyside writes that the film showcases 'friendship, girlness, fashionable
clothes and beautiful homes.'[23] In her screenplay, Coppola describes the film as
a 'gold-plated Versailles hangover of the memory of a lost girl, leaving childhood
behind, to the final dignity of a woman'.[24] Her aim was

> not to make a historical epic … I really wanted to focus on trying to make
> more an impressionistic telling of her point of view … Because so many of
> the stories we know of Marie Antoinette are people's perceptions of her, and
> the more I learned about her and what she went through I imagined more
> the personal side.[25]

Coppola's vision, of a young, rebellious, melancholy and disenchanted young
princess, brought her story to a young audience which was primed for its
idiosyncrasies and postmodern aesthetic.

The film has had a long-lasting cultural legacy on music, advertising, fashion, film
and television. '[*Marie Antoinette*] has left the most enduring dent in the world of
female-centred fashion and lifestyle, spawning fashion editorials and collections in
the years after the film's release, but steadily coming back into circulation whenever
the late queen is referenced.'[26] Now almost 20 years old, it has aged with a generation
who can draw links between Marie Antoinette's self-reflective and image-obsessed
society and today's social-media-driven world.

One television series which has been compared to *Marie Antoinette* is *The Great*,
'an occasionally true story' of Catherine the Great, Empress of Russia. The wit
and ahistorical approach of creator and writer Tony McNamara was shared by its
costumes, designed by Sharon Long for Seasons 2 and 3. *W* magazine wrote that
the costumes 'could have been plucked from the set of Sofia Coppola's Marie
Antoinette' for their whimsical, flirtatious and pastel look.[27] Long drew from both
period research and contemporary fashion, using shapes and materials which
crossed eighteenth-century portraiture and the designs of Comme des Garçons
and Molly Goddard.

Character detail was also embedded into Long's creative process, including a notable costume for Catherine (played by Elle Fanning) from Series 3, episode 3 (fig.203). Constructed from a bespoke toile de Jouy, co-designed with Benjamin Thapa, it tells the story of the series through its print.[28] This irreverent, high-fashion lens has been replicated across period film and television, including recent adaptations of *Emma* (2020), *The Pursuit of Love* (2021) and *Bridgerton* (from 2020), which features a soundtrack of classical instrumental covers in a similar way to *Marie Antoinette*.

Pop culture's vision of Marie Antoinette is colourful, youthful and primed for consumption, and often reflects times of struggle and self-reflection. 'People tend to gravitate to her myth when times are turbulent, society is insecure, and therefore, the idea of a happy, pleasurable domain on the cusp of extinction has the greatest appeal.'[29] It is a strong argument for why designers choose to use Marie Antoinette as a receptacle for their messages, and how the modern culture of celebrity has made the queen a blank screen for the projection of public fantasies.

LET THEM EAT CAKE

Colin Jones

Louis XIV probably never said 'L'état, c'est moi' ('I am the state'), any more than Machiavelli opined that 'the end justifies the means', that British Prime Minister Harold Macmillan informed voters that they 'had never had it so good', or indeed that Humphrey Bogart's Rick, in the film *Casablanca*, ever instructed his pianist to 'Play it again, Sam'. Marie Antoinette's strangely defining signature quotation, 'qu'ils mangent de la brioche' – 'let them eat cake' – joins this excellent company in being completely apocryphal.

Despite absence of substantiation, the quotation has been an albatross around the neck of the image of Louis XVI's ill-starred queen ever since its first attribution to her. This was in the middle of the nineteenth century, a full 50 years after her death by guillotine in October 1793. Yet once used, the words have stuck.[1]

The expression and the idea behind it were certainly, however, in existence in France in her life-time. In his *Confessions*, the famous philosopher Jean-Jacques Rousseau related with amused contempt the callous insouciance shown by a 'great princess' who on being told that the peasants could not afford bread at a time of dearth remarked 'qu'ils mangent de la brioche'.[2] The *Confessions* were published in 1782, but had largely been written in the 1760s, when Marie Antoinette was a mere child, living at the Viennese court of her mother, Holy Roman Empress Maria Theresa. As an adult, Marie Antoinette proved something of a Rousseau fan, although we do not know if she read the *Confessions*. Yet, even if she had, such was the heavy sarcasm with which Rousseau told the story that it seems highly unlikely that she would have let the phrase pass her lips. She would have realized, moreover, that had she done so, she might have been accused of having 'made a brioche'.[3] The expression, *faire une brioche*, derived from the practice of musicians in the Paris Opera from the late seventeenth century of imposing a fine on their fellows who committed an error in their playing – the proceeds would be spent on a large brioche to be consumed in common. The practice passed into general usage, so that a 'brioche' became synonymous with a blunder, or a *faux-pas*.

Is the brioche a cake or a pastry? In twenty-first-century America it is definitely the former, judging by the gloriously stylish confections on display, for example, in Sofia Coppola's 2006 film, *Marie Antoinette*. The eighteenth century was more divided: *espèce de gateau* and *espèce de pâtisserie* both figure in the period's dictionaries. Whichever (or both), brioches were certainly far out of the reach of most of the French population, for they required expensive white flour and butter. Wheat was adjudged a perquisite of the social elite, and the dark, dense bread that the lower classes consumed as their staple food and main dietary item was made of rye, buckwheat or some other inferior grain and baked in large loaves – the *baguette* was an effete nineteenth-century Parisian invention. Adults might eat up to a kilo of this unappetizing fare each day, sometimes made more palatable through soup, gruel or a scrap of butter.

A bread-based diet meant that most of the population was sensitive to bread's affordability. Bad harvests caused by climatic volatility in both 1787 and 1788 caused the price of bread to shoot up, and it was at its highest in the mid-1789 just prior to the harvest, as the population used up remaining stocks from the previous year.

If grain shortages and high bread prices caused hunger, they also triggered anger. Across the century, there was a growing suspicion that dearth and famine were man-made: greedy individuals were thought to be stocking up and then waiting for prices to rise higher still before releasing them on the market, making fortunes in the process. This so-called 'Famine Plot' was attributed mainly to financiers and capitalists, but from the middle of the century suspicion spread that these inhumane machinations could be traced back to the royal court. Rousseau was in fact reflecting this widespread 'Famine Plot' belief by retailing his 'great princess' story and the inhumane suggestion that the hungry poor should gorge on brioches.[4]

'Famine Plot' fears do not explain why the famous phrase should be attached to Marie Antoinette as opposed to any other princess or courtier. The queen was in fact noted at Louis XVI's court for her acts of charity. She made gifts to families in need, provided dowries for poor brides, made a sizeable donation to a fund to provide new Parisian hospitals in the 1770s and from 1788 was patron-president of the newly founded Society of Maternal Charity (*Société de charité maternelle*), which supported poor mothers.[5] In the 1789 crisis, far from heartlessly recommending brioches to the poor, she made over a tidy sum to Paris' municipal pawnshop (*mont-de-piété*) instructing its director to use it to allow the most needy to redeem articles placed in hock.

Yet any praise the queen might have garnered for her philanthropy was more than offset by the tidal waves of criticism which came her way before as well as during the Revolution. Much of this (but not all) was undeserved. From her first entry into the royal court following her marriage to Louis XVI in 1770 she was a target for attacks by envious, resentful and vicious courtiers. Brought up at the Austrian court in Vienna, she found it difficult to adapt to the tediously punctilious protocols of Versailles. She put her trust in a small number of favourites, making it difficult to break into the charmed circle around her. Resentment was amped up by a concern that she was influencing her husband to follow pro-Austrian policies that were bad for France. It was usually royal mistresses – such as Mesdames de Pompadour and du Barry under Louis XV – who were hated as 'wicked counsellors'. Louis XVI's uxorious monogamy

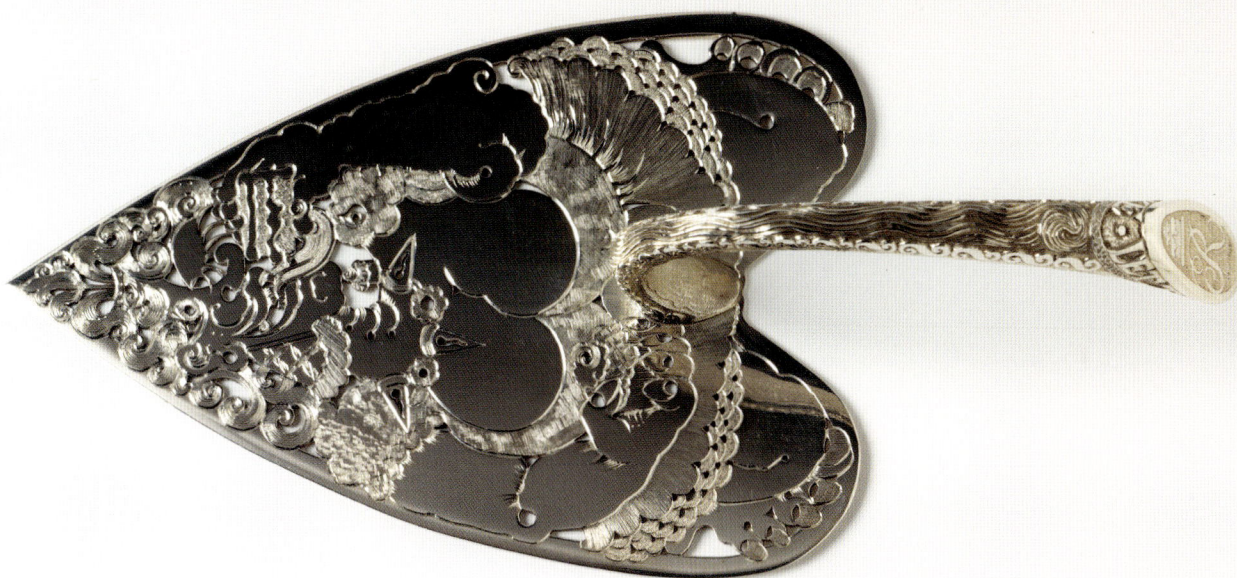

ensured that it was his queen who took the flak. The early period of her time in Versailles, in which Louis failed to have procreative sex with her, produced industrial quantities of tittle-tattle: it was she, it was said, who was failing in a French queen's prime duty – to produce male heirs – by cheating on the king with sundry lovers. The reputation for infidelity stayed with her even after the marriage's consummation and the birth of two boys.[6]

Prior to 1789, most of this gossipy unpleasantness was confined to the royal court at Versailles. Trying to spread rumours more widely risked imprisonment in the Bastille. The freedom of the press introduced in the 1789 Declaration of the Rights of Man allowed such stories much wider circulation. In the process, attacks were magnified. Accusations of infidelity now morphed into a belief that the queen was a modern-day

Messalina. In addition, after 1792, when France went to war with Austria and most of Europe, her pro-Austrian sympathies were interpreted as outright treason.

Yet the most vehement charges against the queen during the Revolution focused on behaviour at which no courtier had turned a hair prior to 1789: namely, her financial profligacy. Grumbles in the public sphere about her love of stylish luxury had surfaced in the 1780s, as evidenced in particular by her expenditure on jewels, precious metals, high-end accessories, building projects and (especially) fashion. To some extent this was not out of line with queenly behaviour in the past, but it was put in a different complexion by the financial crisis of the French Crown which triggered the political revolution of 1789. 'Madame Déficit' took the rap for the state's spiralling bankruptcy, even though her own spending was overwhelming outweighed by Louis XVI and his predecessors' massive and continual overspending on warfare. Yet the record of continued spending by 'Madame Déficit' on luxuries at a time when the wider population faced hunger, job losses and higher taxes was not a good look.

Perhaps the most jarring example of this disjunction was her costly devotion to the Trianon complex at Versailles, in particular the little hamlet (*hameau*) she constructed there from 1783, which reproduced the picturesque peasant cottages found in the pastoral paintings of the day.[7] Leisure pursuits included engaging in the everyday activities of a farmer's wife. Marie Antoinette left Versailles for good in 1789, but stories circulated during the Revolution that she had effectively played the peasant while real-life peasants faced starvation. This added fuel to the fires of outrage at her alleged behaviour.

The service rooms attached to the cottage in the *hameau* designated for the queen's personal use contained an oven that was built in the style of local peasant homes. We will probably never know whether the queen baked her own bread in it (and even her own brioches?). Probably not, one imagines. Yet even so, it was doubtless the heartless insouciance attributed to her in the *hameau* that, more than anything else, laid the basis for the posthumous 'qu'ils mangent de la brioche' attribution. It seemed to suggest that, even if there is no proof positive, this is the kind of thing she would have said and felt.

Louis Capet

de Lamballe

veuve Capet

du Barry.

Foulon

citoyenne Roland

MADAME TUSSAUDS AND MARIE ANTOINETTE NOIR

Zoe Louca-Richards

The atrocities of the French Revolution saw Anna Maria Grosholtz (1761–1850) – better known today as Marie Tussaud, founder of Madame Tussauds London[1]– reportedly taking the posthumous likenesses of some of its most prominent participants and unfortunate victims. As her grandson John Theodore Tussaud would later recount, 'she was compelled to reproduce the lineaments of Louis XVI, Marie Antoinette, Hébert, Danton, Robespierre, Carrier, Fouquier-Tinville – the best and fairest, and also the worst and vilest'.[2]

As numerous biographical sources of both Marie Antoinette and Marie Tussaud document, shortly following the queen's execution on 16 October 1793, Tussaud was escorted to the Madeleine cemetery, tasked secretly by the National Assembly to cast a death mask directly from Marie Antoinette's severed head. A few months earlier she had been compelled to undertake the same task following Louis XVI's execution. Marie Tussaud and a few select generals were the only ones aware of their creation, and the masks were ordered never to be displayed. What is fascinating about the story of Marie Antoinette's death mask is its absence from Marie Tussaud's own memoirs.[3] In the 1838 text, edited by Francis Hervé, Tussaud discusses extensively taking the death masks of a number of prominent individuals on both sides of the political divide. She gives a detailed description of Marie Antoinette's exceptional character, and her tragic demise, and recalls her time living at Versailles alongside the royal family as tutor to Louis XVI's sister, a story we now believe to be an embellishment of the truth.[4] An omission of such an important role following the queen's death therefore seems peculiar, considering the emphasis she placed on her connection to the French royal family and Marie Antoinette, and on her work taking death masks. It is not until 43 years following her death, in the 1893 Madame Tussauds London exhibition catalogue, that we see the first claim of Tussaud having undertaken this gruesome, yet significant, duty.

The prevalence of this fascinating, yet questionable story has engendered a tied mythology between Marie Antoinette, Marie Tussaud and Madame Tussauds London, that remains to this day. The quintessentially gothic image of the young wax sculptress sorting through corpses to find the severed head of one of history's most iconic women is a compelling one, popular with nineteenth-century and modern audiences alike. It satiates our very human curiosity about the darker side of humanity. It is an image that Marie Tussaud's sons and grandsons, who managed the attraction following her death, recognized the value of, and were keen to capitalize on.

The social landscape of Britain changed dramatically in the nineteenth century. Advances in science and technology were challenging well-established norms in religion and politics, and greater social mobility engendered by industrialization fuelled

207. DRAWING OF SEVERED HEADS OF
ROYAL FAMILY AND REVOLUTIONARIES ON
PIKES, INCLUDING KING LOUIS XVI, MARIE
ANTOINETTE, MADAME DU BARRY, THE
PRINCESSE DE LAMBALLE, ROBESPIERRE,
DANTON, SAINT-JUST, CAMILLE DESMOULINS
AND MADAME ROLAND, 1910
EDMUND JOSEPH SULLIVAN (1869–1933),
ILLUSTRATION FOR 1910 EDITION OF THOMAS
CARLYLE'S *THE FRENCH REVOLUTION*. PRIVATE
COLLECTION

208. 'FIN TRAGIQUE DE MARIE ANTOINETTE
D'AUTRICHE. REINE DE FRANCE, EXÉCUTÉE LE
16. OCTOBRE 1793', 1793
FRANCE, PRINT SHOWING THE EXECUTION
OF MARIE ANTOINETTE AND EXECUTIONER
HOLDING HER HEAD ALOFT, ETCHING AND
AQUATINT. BRITISH MUSEUM: 1861.1012.151

209. *MADAME TUSSAUD'S RELICS OF THE
FRENCH REVOLUTION* POSTER, c.1914
DESIGNED BY JOHN HASSALL, ADVERTISING
THE LONDON WAXWORKS MUSEUM, COLOUR
LITHOGRAPH. V&A: E.586–1915

*Fin tragique de Marie Antoinette d'Autriche
Reine de France, exécutée le 16. Octobre 1793.*

increased class conflict. The spectacle of the French Revolution across the Channel
had in no small way exacerbated social unease, and demonstrated the potential for
indiscriminate brutality in the name of progress. Simultaneously, wider circulation of
newspapers increased public awareness and anxiety surrounding crime and murder;
with sensationalist reporting intensifying the Victorians' growing fascination with
death. While gothic literature and penny papers provided a means to continue safely

MADAME TUSSAUD'S

RELICS
OF THE
FRENCH REVOLUTION

BRUTON & Cº PRINTERS, BUNHILL ROW, LONDON.

210. PHOTOGRAPHS OF THE WAX BUST OF MARIE ANTOINETTE'S SEVERED HEAD, SUPPOSEDLY FROM HER DEATH
PHOTOGRAPHS TAKEN AT MADAME TUSSAUDS, LONDON, 1907. BIBLIOTHÈQUE NATIONALE DE FRANCE, PARIS: RESERVE FT 4-QB-370 (42)

211. REIGN OF TERROR GUILLOTINE BLADE, c.1793
FORMERLY DISPLAYED IN THE CHAMBER OF HORRORS AT MADAME TUSSAUDS, LONDON

exploring these fears and anxieties through literature, Madame Tussauds London offered a uniquely physical space in which to experience them, through the development of the popular Chamber of Horrors. From the mid-nineteenth century onwards, significant attention was placed on the development of this space.

During Marie Tussaud's management of the attraction emphasis was placed on Marie Antoinette's virtuosity, her full figure featuring exclusively in the main attraction among the other historical greats and contemporary celebrities. However, shifting interest in Marie Antoinette's complex character was clearly reflected in the development of her display in the second half of the nineteenth century. Unlike any other individual in the attraction, Marie Antoinette uniquely embodied every type of fame that Tussauds sought to represent: royalty, celebrity, victim and villain. While Marie Tussaud had sought to emphasize a connection to the French queen's life, both through the display of her figure and in her memoirs, her descendants, and later managers of the attraction, sought instead to capitalize on a connection to her death. For their nineteenth-century audience Marie Antoinette epitomized the 'gothic' identity of the Chamber of Horrors, representing both innocent heroine and tyrannical monster.

In the mid-nineteenth century, two significant items were added to the Chamber of Horrors that demonstrate this shift in representation: Marie Antoinette's wax Death Head[5] added in 1865, and a French Revolution guillotine blade added around 1856. Initially the catalogue description for the effigy of Marie Antoinette's disembodied head did not mention it being cast directly from a death mask taken by Tussaud. However, by 1893, the catalogue description read: 'HEAD OF MARIE ANTOINETTE. Guillotined 16 October 1793. (Taken immediately after her execution by order of the National Assembly of France by Marie Tussaud)'.[6] There is no record before this of Marie Tussaud taking the death mask of Marie Antoinette, but this description of the death heads has remained in some form ever since, and it is from this point that we see the popular story of Marie Tussaud taking the queen's death mask emerge.

A decade before, Marie Tussaud's sons, Frank and Joseph Tussaud, had travelled to Paris to acquire a French Revolution guillotine blade and lunette from Henry-Clément Sanson, grandson of Charles-Henri Sanson, High Executioner during the Revolution (fig.211). The 1856 catalogue entry reads: 'The Most Extraordinary relic in the world being a melancholy recollection of the first French Revolution. The original Knife and lunette, the identical instrument that decapitated the unfortunate Louis XVI and Marie Antoinette ... and the best and worst blood of France.'[7] The blade remained on display in the Chamber of Horrors for over a century. By the late twentieth century its description had changed to: 'This Guillotine blade is the

5745

212. *MARIE ANTOINETTE HEAD*, 2019
SIMON FUJIWARA, WAX, HAIR AND
METAL ROD, 42 × 21 × 21 CM

213. KATY PERRY AS MARIE ANTOINETTE,
EXECUTION SCENE FROM 'HEY HEY HEY'
MUSIC VIDEO, 2017

one that beheaded Marie Antoinette in 1793'. The authenticity of the Tussaud Blade has repeatedly come into question. While there is no way of knowing whether it was indeed the exact blade that beheaded Marie Antoinette, its provenance seems to indicate that it is authentic to the Reign of Terror, and therefore undoubtedly brought an end to a number of revolutionary lives.[8]

Both of these objects have continued to influence representations of Marie Antoinette beyond Madame Tussauds London. The blade featured in the creation of artist Cornelia Parker's 1998 work *Shared Fate (Oliver)*, where it was used to cut a small Oliver Twist doll in half, creating an artificial 'shared fate' between the French queen and the Dickensian character. More recently, the artist Simon Fujiwara explicitly cited Madame Tussauds London and the death-mask story as the influence for *Marie Antoinette Head* (2019), a wax portrait head of Marie Antoinette, trunkless, with positioning spike intact, which featured as part of his exhibition *The Antoinette Effect* (2019), a commentary on the continued commodification of the French queen (fig.212).[9]

Establishing the authenticity of these objects is not integral to our understanding of Madame Tussauds' role in facilitating the public's continued fascination with

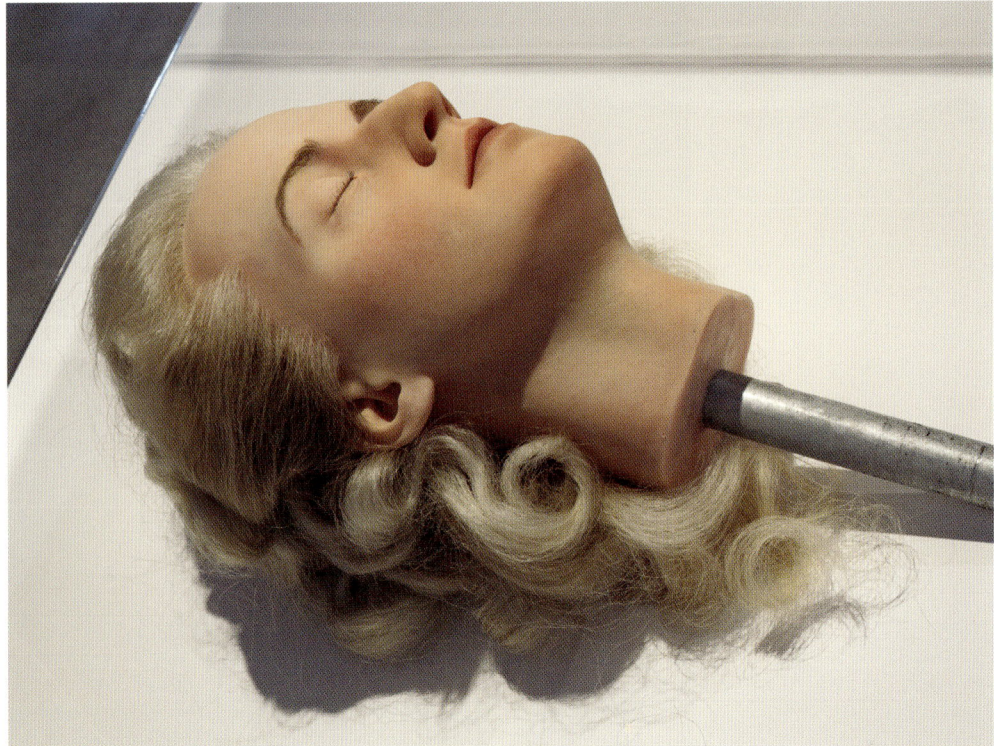

Marie Antoinette's death. In fact, a deliberate embellishment of their provenance to position them as 'authentic' signifies astute awareness of the particular marketability of the image of the decapitated queen. Marie Tussaud wished the attraction to be as educational as it was entertaining, and as a result initiated a tradition that continues to this day of acquiring authentic 'relics' to display alongside her 'replica' wax figures. The perceived authenticity of the objects shifts the visitor experience from cheap spectacle of death, to a deeply affecting encounter with historical human brutality.

But why this emphasis on Marie Antoinette's story in particular? At its core, Madame Tussauds trades in the commodification of celebrity, through the medium of wax. Since Marie Tussaud first arrived in England in 1802 the company has continued to pride itself on providing a true representation of who's who in popular culture, not according to the media, but according to its visitors. Marie Antoinette was arguably the first celebrity, widely recognized, deified, vilified and commodified, in life and in death. Celebrities have come and gone from its cast with relative frequency over its two-century history. That Marie Antoinette is one of only a handful of individuals who has remained continuously represented within the walls of Madame Tussauds London is indicative of the continued public interest in her. The changing nature of her display, from main attraction to the Chamber of Horrors, is a reflection on how her complex and contradictory character has rendered her broadly relatable across generations.

The image of Marie Antoinette's decapitated head is one that continues to permeate our contemporary visual culture, a testament that our continued fascination with the French queen lies not only in the glamour and extravagances of her life, but in the violence of her death. For Madame Tussauds London, the guillotine blade remains the most notorious artefact in its collection, and the tale of the death mask is still widely circulated.

NOTES

INTRODUCTION: MARIE ANTOINETTE STYLE
Sarah Grant

1 Letter from Maria Theresa to Marie Antoinette, Vienna, 21 April 1770. 'Tous les yeux seront fixés sur vous, ne donnez donc point de scandale.' Arneth and Geffroy 1874–5, vol.1, p.2.
2 See, for example, William Doyle (ed.), *Old Regime France: 1648–1788* (Oxford 2001) and Hardman 2020.
3 Letter from the duchesse de Polignac to Georgiana, Duchess of Devonshire, Versailles 9 June 1784, Chatsworth Archive (CS5/616).
4 See Olivette Otele, *African Europeans: An Untold History* (London 2020) and Anne Lafont, *L'art et la race: L'Africain (tout) contre l'œil des Lumières* (Dijon 2019).
5 Christy Pichichero, 'Race, Revolution, and Celebrity: The Case of Joseph Bologne, Chevalier de Saint-George', in David A. Bell and Colin Jones (eds), *French Revolutionary Lives* (Cham 2024), pp.13–28.
6 I am grateful to Dr David McCallam, Reader in French Eighteenth-Century Studies at the University of Sheffield, for allowing me to read an advance copy of his essay: David McCallam, 'A Male "Ourika"? Jean Amilcar, Marie-Antoinette's Adopted Black Boy', in Charles Forsdick and Mark Towsey (eds), *Essays in Memory of Kate Marsh* (Liverpool 2025, forthcoming). Miranda Spieler, 'Ourika and the Chevalier de Boufflers', in Bell and Jones 2024 (cited note 5), pp.29–47.
7 See Versailles (MV5718 and MV9082). Both portraits date from about 1783; it is not clear whether it is the same individual in both portraits; neither figure has yet been identified.
8 Ribeiro 1988, p.122.
9 'Elle parut avec éclat dans une cour qui commençoit à vieillir; et son mariage qui faisoit espérer de voir bientôt les petits fils du monarque avoir des compagnes jeunes et aimables, faisoit plaisir aux Français, pour qui la cour alors étoit un spectacle où ils aimoient à voir des personnages brillans', Elisabeth Guénard, *Mémoires de la Princesse de Lamballe* (Paris 1801) vol.3, p.84.
10 Rachel Syme, 'Crème de la Crème. Sofia Coppola's Path to Filming Gilded Adolescence', *The New Yorker* (29 January 2024), pp.24–35. See also Keaton Bell, '"It was like Hosting the Ultimate Party": An Oral History of Sofia Coppola's *Marie Antoinette*', British *Vogue* (30 October 2021); 'Style Secrets of Marie Antoinette: Kirsten Dunst as the Teen Queen who Rocked Versailles', American *Vogue* (September 2006); Coppola 2023.
11 Fraser 2001, p.200. G.-A.-H. de Reiset, *Modes et usages au temps de Marie-Antoinette. Livre-journal de Madame Eloffe* (Paris 1885), p.473.
12 *Mercure de France* (June 1770), p.158.
13 'Royal Jewels from the Bourbon Parma Family' sale, Sotheby's Geneva, 14 November 2018, lots 91–100.
14 'Magnificent Jewels' sale, Christie's Geneva, 9 November 2021, lot 12.
15 'Exceptional' sale, Christie's Paris, 22 November 2022.
16 'Collection Hubert Guerrand-Hermès' sale, Sotheby's Paris, 13 December 2023, lot 7.
17 See Pierre Saint-Amand, trans. Jennifer C. Gage, 'Terrorizing Marie Antoinette', in Goodman and Kaiser 2003, pp.253–72 and Melissa Hyde and Jennifer Milam (eds), *Women, Art and the Politics of Identity in Eighteenth-Century Europe* (Abingdon 2003).

THE QUEEN'S PRIVATE APARTMENTS AND THE PETIT TRIANON
Hélène Delalex

1 Charles-Félix, comte d'Hézecques, *Souvenirs d'un page à la cour de Louis XVI* (Paris 1873), p.154.
2 'At the first word she spoke to the king about the Petit Trianon, he replied with genuine eagerness that this pleasure house belonged to the queen and he was delighted to give it to her', confirms a letter from Mercy-Argenteau to Maria Theresa of Austria, 7 June 1774, in Arneth and Geffroy 1874–5, vol.2, pp.159–63.
3 Sold during the French Revolution, it is now preserved at the Metropolitan Museum of Art in New York.
4 Château de Versailles (V 6206).
5 This was probably confused with the 'diamond' set created under the previous reign for the theatre at Fontainebleau or with the set for *Zémire et Azor* shown at the queen's little theatre at Trianon.

COCOONED: MARIE ANTOINETTE IN SILK
Lesley Ellis Miller

Acknowledgements: I am extremely grateful to colleagues in Austria and Switzerland for their guidance on Austrian sources and their help with translations from German: Birgitt Borkopp (University of Bern), Anna Jolly (Abegg-Stiftung, Riggisberg), Katja Schmidt-Von Ledebur (Kunstkammer, Vienna), Lara Steinhäußer (MAK, Vienna). As ever, I am indebted to Clare Browne for her knowledgeable response to my text. All translations from French are my own, unless otherwise stated.

1 Campan 1988, vol.1, Chapter 3, p.55.
2 Weber 2007, p.254.
3 Ibid., pp.268–9 and no.100.
4 Ibid., pp.280–1.
5 Elfriede Iby, 'L'enfance d'une princesse à la cour de Vienne', in *Marie-Antoinette* 2008, pp.26–69.
6 Weber 2007, p.29. On court dress and etiquette, see *Fastes de cour* 2009 and Chrisman-Campbell 2015, pp.20–31 and 70–147.
7 Pascale Gorguet Ballesteros, 'Marie-Antoinette et la mode', in *Marie-Antoinette* 2008, pp.258–61; p.258.
8 Missing petition from M. Vial, syndic du Bureau, presented to the king on 29 December 1774. 'Considérations sur le luxe national des étoffes de Lyon', recorded in the inventory of the Grande Fabrique and cited in Justin Godart, *L'ouvrier en soie* (Geneva 1976, facsimile of first print 1899), p.211.
9 Cited in Godart 1899 (cited note 8), p.48.

10 At the French court, the *dame d'atours* was responsible for the queen's wardrobe and jewellery and supervised the dressing of the queen and the chamber staff of *femmes du chambre*. Anne Kraatz, 'La gazette des atours de Marie-Antoinette', in *Les atours de la reine. Art et commerce au service de Marie-Antoinette* (Paris 2001), pp.25–37; James-Sarazin and Lapasin 2023.
11 Kimberly Chrisman-Campbell, 'Fit for a Queen: A Fragment of Court Dress Belonging to Marie-Antoinette', *Text: For the Study of Textile Art, Design and History*, vol.31 (2003–4), pp.30–3 and Chrisman-Campbell 2015, pp.289–91.
12 Wrigley 2002, Chapter 1, especially pp.20–5.
13 Arizzoli and Coural in *Soieries de Lyon. Commandes royales au XVIIIe siècle, 1730–1800*, exh. cat., Musée historique des Tissus (Lyon 1988), cats 11, 24, 29, 30 bis, 34, 35, 45, 47, 49, 50, 51, 52, 55.
14 Gorguet Ballesteros 2008 (cited note 7), pp.258–60.
15 Dagmar Schäfer, Giorgio Riello and Luca Molà (eds), *Threads of Global Desire. Silk in the Pre-Modern World* (Suffolk 2018), Introduction.
16 Moriz Dreger, *Beginn und Blüte der Wiener Seidenweberei* (Vienna 1915), p.20.
17 Helene Deutsch, *Die Entwicklung der Seidenindustrie in Osterreich (1660–1840)* (Vienna 1909); Franz Bujatti, *Die Geschichte der Seiden-Industrie Osterreichs* (Vienna 1893); Dreger 1915, pp.7–25; Katja Schmidt-von Ledebur, *Gottes Lob. Kirchliche Textilien aus der Zeit Maria Theresias*, exh. cat., Kaiserliche Schatzkammer (Vienna 2016), pp.19–20.
18 Michael Yonan, *Empress Maria Theresa and the Politics of Habsburg Imperial Art* (Pennsylvania 2011), p.10.
19 Godart 1899 (cited note 8), pp.390, 441, 'Mémoire concernant la manufacture des étoffes d'or, d'argent et de soye de la ville de Lyon envoyé à M. de Gournay qui demandait à la connaître'.
20 Jean Cordey (ed.), *Inventaire des biens de Madame de Pompadour, rédigé après son décès* (Paris 1939), pp.54ff; Bibliothèque nationale de France (Ms Fr 8157).
21 I use the term figured here to refer to any silk with woven patterning, rather than brocaded, which refers to a particular technique of woven patterning. Plain is used to describe unpatterned silks in simple weaves. Banić in L.E. Miller, A. Cabrera Lafuente and C. Allen-Johnstone (eds), *Silk: Fibre, Fabric and Fashion* (London 2021), pp.106–15; Lesley Ellis Miller, *Selling Silks: A Merchant's Sample Book 1764* (London 2014), Chapter 1.
22 *Statuts et règlements pour la Communauté des maîtres marchands et maîtres ouvriers à façon en étoffes d'or, d'argent et de soie et autres mêlées de soie, laine poil, fil et coton, de la ville et fauxbourgs de Lyon, et pour la fabrique desdites étoffes* (Lyon 1744); *Lettres patentes du roi concernant les manufactures* (Marly 1779).
23 Godart 1899 (cited note 8), p.26.
24 Miller, Cabrera Lafuente and Allen-Johnstone 2021 (cited note 21), pp.68–72; Miller 2014 (cited note 21), pp.20–6. On consumption of silks across the century, see Roche 2008, Chapter 6; Annik Pardailhé-Galabrun, *La naissance de l'intime. 3000 foyers parisiens XVIIe–XVIIIe siècles* (Paris 1988), Chapter 10, especially pp.366–75.

25 Élisabeth Vigée Le Brun, *Marie Thérèse, Madame Royale and her brother the Dauphin Louis-Joseph*, 1784, Château de Versailles (MV 3907).

26 Jean Paulet, *L'art du fabricant des etoffes de soie* (Paris 1779), vol.IX, p.665 and ANF F12 765 *Mémoire et lettre du 29 juin 1779*.

27 Jacques Savary des Bruslons, *Dictionnaire universel de commerce* (Paris 1723–30), vol.2, p.996.

28 Jacques Savary des Bruslons, *Dictionnaire universel de commerce* (Geneva 1762), vol.3, pp.914–16. For a fuller technical description of all these fabrics and techniques, see the CIETA vocabularies, https://cieta.fr/cieta-vocabulaire/.

29 Godart 1899 (cited note 8), pp.409–10; Carolyn Sargentson, *Merchants and Luxury Markets: The Marchands Merciers of Eighteenth-Century Paris* (London 1996), Chapter 5; Lesley Ellis Miller, 'Material Marketing. How Lyonnais Silk Manufacturers Sold Silks, 1660–1789', in B. Blondé and J. Stobart (eds), *Selling Textiles in the Long Eighteenth Century: Comparative Perspectives from Western Europe* (London 2014), pp.85–98.

30 Arizzoli and Coural 1988 (cited note 13), pp.51–2; Chantal Coural, 'Quelques remarques sur le décor textile du Versailles de Louis XIV', in *Furnishing Textiles. Studies in Seventeenth- and Eighteenth-Century Interior Decoration* (Riggisberg 2009), pp.10, 11, 15, 19.

31 See Peter Thornton, *Baroque and Rococo Silks* (London 1965); Natalie Rothstein, *Silk Designs of the Eighteenth Century in the Collection of the Victoria and Albert Museum, London* (London 1990).

32 Paulet 1779 (cited note 26), pp.659–77.

33 BnF Ms Fr 8157 *Comptes de Madame du Barry*, 10 October 1783, from the royal mercer Lenormand et cie., BnF, Ms Fr 8157 *Comptes de Madame du Barry*, 1769–92, especially silks supplied by Buffault, 1769–71, Lenormand Prosper, Leduc et cie. 1771–3 and Lenormand et cie. 1774–87.

34 Arizzoli and Coural 1988 (cited note 13), pp.49 and 118, cat.29; Durand in *Le génie de la fabrique*, exh. cat., Musée des Tissus (Lyon 2016), pp.70–2. For further discussion of these styles, see Anna Jolly, *Seidengewebe des 18. Jahrhunderts II, Naturalismus* (Riggisberg 2002) and Adam Geczy, *Fashion and Orientalism: Dress, Textiles and Cultures from the 17th to the 21st Century* (London 2013), pp.41–84.

35 Banić in Miller, Cabrera Lafuente and Allen-Johnstone 2021 (cited note 21), p.323.

36 Da Vinha 2018, transcription of wardrobe, pp.68–85; Arizzoli and Coural 1988 (cited note 13), p.122, cat.47.

37 AML HH139 *Mémoire pour les Sieurs Saint Michel, Dany et cie. contre les Sieurs Thevillon et Vingtain* 2.03.1761, ff. IV.–2; AML Imprimé 450.183 *Mémoire de Thevillon et Vingtain contre Saint-Michel, Dany et cie.*, Paris 1762.

38 Antoine-Nicolas Joubert de l'Hiberderie, *Le dessinateur pour les fabriques les étoffes d'or, d'argent et de soie* (Paris 1765), Chapter VIII.

39 Tabitha Baker, 'The Embroidery Trade in Eighteenth-Century Paris and Lyon', unpubl. PhD thesis (University of Warwick 2019), pp.247–52; Moïra Dato and Pascale Gorguet Ballesteros, 'Lyonnais silks "ad uttimo gusto": The Trade in Fashionable Waistcoats between France and Italy in the Second Half of the 18th Century', in Giampiero Nigro (ed.), *Datini Studies in Economic History: Fashion as an Economic Engine: Process and Product Innovation, Commercial Strategies,*

Consumer Behavior (Florence 2022), pp.173–200; Olwen Hufton, 'Women and the Family Economy in Eighteenth-Century France', *French Historical Studies*, vol.9, no.1 (Spring 1975), pp.1–22.

40 Marie Antoinette to Maria Theresa, 12 July 1770, Bernier 1986, p.40.

41 *Almanach général du commerce, des marchands, négociants, armateurs etc et des autres parties du monde* (Paris 1788), pp.346–7.

42 Roberta Orsi Landini, *The Velvets in the Costume Collection of the Costume Gallery in Florence* (Florence and Riggisberg 2016), pp.15–24 and 265–73.

43 Da Vinha 2018, p.73.

44 Musée national des châteaux de Versailles et de Trianon (MV 8061).

45 Élisabeth Vigée Le Brun, *Marie Antoinette and Her Children*, 1787, Musée national des châteaux de Versailles et de Trianon; Jean-Marc Nattier, *Marie Leczinska*, 1748, Musée national des châteaux de Versailles et de Trianon (MV 5672).

46 Arizzoli and Coural 1988 (cited note 13), pp.65–76.

47 Ibid., p.67 and cat.49.

48 Ibid., p.119, cats 34 and 35; Durand 2016 (cited note 34), pp.67–9 and 105–29.

49 Moïra Dato, 'Habiller les demeures de la Couronne. Les soieries lyonnaises et le Garde-Meuble au XVIIIe siècle', in Muriel Barbier et al. (eds), *Arts en cour: les Garde-Meubles en Europe (XVIe–XXIe siècles)* (Paris 2023), pp.403–17; Jean Coural and Chantal Gastinel-Coural, 'La fabrique lyonnaise au XVIIe siècle: la commande royale de 1730', *Revue de l'Art* (1984), no.62, pp.49–64; and Arizzoli and Coural 1988 (cited note 13), pp.51–2, cats 1–5.

50 Ibid., p.74.

51 Banić in Miller, Cabrera Lafuente and Allen-Johnstone 2021 (cited note 21), pp.486–7.

52 Weber 2007, p.281.

MARIE ANTOINETTE'S WARDROBE
Sarah Grant

1 'J'y vis la reine dans la plus grande parure, couverte de diamans, et, comme un magnifique soleil l'éclairait, elle me parut vraiment éblouissante', Élisabeth Vigée Le Brun, *Souvenirs de Madame Vigée Le Brun* (Paris 1835–7), vol.1, p.70.

2 A gown of *drap d'Argent*, also known as silver cloth or silver tissue. *Wiener Zeitung* (21 April 1770), p.6.

3 There is considerable confusion among historians about the gown Marie Antoinette wore for her Versailles wedding service. The convention, however, was that the gown worn at the proxy service be reworn for the second service. This was the case for her sister-in-law, the comtesse d'Artois, and for other foreign royal brides at European courts.

4 Journal of the duc de Crŏy, quoted in *Marie Antoinette* 2008, p.79.

5 James Greig (ed.), *The Diaries of a Duchess: Extracts from the Diaries of the First Duchess of Northumberland (1716–1776)* (London 1926), p.112.

6 Ibid.

7 Henriette Lucie (Dillon) de La Tour du Pin, *Memoirs of Madame de La Tour du Pin*, trans. Felice Harcourt (New York 1971), p.69.

8 Maurice Boutry, *Le Mariage de Marie-Antoinette* (Paris 1904), p.43.

9 On the fashions of Marie Antoinette's court, see Chrisman-Campbell 2015 and Trey 2014.

10 Pernilla Rasmussen, 'Four *Robes de Cour* Worn at the Swedish Court: Tradition and Change in Tailoring and Significance', in Frank M. Kammel and Johannes Pietsch (eds), *Structuring Fashion: Foundation Garments through History* (Munich 2020), pp.84–99, p.88.

11 Ibid.

12 Claude-Louis Desrais was known for his meticulously observed crowd scenes. See *Marie-Antoinette* 2008, p.79, cat.43.

13 Françoise Tétart-Vittu, 'Grandes robes d'étiquette à la cour de Marie-Antoinette. Contribution de la famille Saint-Aubin aux métiers de la mode', *Versalia. Revue de la Société des Amis de Versailles*, no.9 (2006), pp.142–55. Pascale Gorguet Ballesteros, 'Petite étude du grand habit à travers les mémoires quittances de la comtesse d'Artois (1773–1780)', *Apparence(s). Histoire et culture du paraître*, vol.6 (2015), pp.197–212, doi.org/10.4000/apparences.1325 (accessed 30 September 2024).

14 'Passion for Fashion' sale, Kerry Taylor London, 17 June 2019, lot 28.

15 See Versailles portraits (MV 8061, 3892 & 4519).

16 Count Hampus Mörner to Gustav III, quoted in Rasmussen 2020 (cited note 10), p.88.

17 Like her three predecessors, Marie Antoinette was not crowned and took no part in the ceremony. Hervé Pinoteau, 'Le roi et la reine de France en majesté', in *Fastes de cours* 2009, pp.110–21, 116.

18 Fraser 2001, pp.158–9.

19 *Décoration du sacre de Louis XVI à Reims le 11 juin 1775*, 1775, pen and ink drawing; the print made after the drawing and published in 1779 specifies 'Dessiné d'après Nature et gravé par J.M. Moreau le Jeune' (Château de Versailles, INV.DESS 889 and INV.GRAV 6936).

20 'J'ai pensé, si vous vouliez m'envoyer une bonne mesure, vous faire faire ici des corps ou corsettes. On dit que ceux de Paris sont trop forts; je vous les enverrai par courrier.' Letter from Maria Theresa to Marie Antoinette, Schönbrunn, 1 November 1770, Arneth and Geffroy 1874–5, vol.1, p.85.

21 AN K 506., no.25, pièce 4.

22 Jeanne L.H. Campan, *Mémoires sur la vie privée de Marie-Antoinette, reine de France et de Navarre*, 2nd edn, 3 vols (Paris 1823), vol.1, pp.223 and 317.

23 Results from XRF analysis of the spangles, undertaken by Maria Ecenarro, Conservation Scientist at the V&A, in April 2025 showed they are made of gilded silver while the metal thread is made of almost pure silver. Kimberly Chrisman-Campbell, 'Fit for a Queen: A Fragment of Court Dress Belonging to Marie-Antoinette', *Text: For the Study of Textile Art, Design and History*, vol.31 (2003–4), pp.30–3. The fragments were given to the museum by a descendant of a Monsieur Bésnard who claimed to have been part of Marie Antoinette's *garde-robe*, though no-one of this name appears in the *Almanach royal* or in the records of the Gardrobe. I thank Beatrice Behlen and Kate Riggs at the London Museum.

24 W.S. Lewis (ed.), *The Yale Edition of Horace Walpole's Correspondence*, 48 volumes (New Haven 1937–83): Horace Walpole to Lady Ossory, 23 August 1775, Paris, vol.32, p.253.

25 Denis Pierre Jean Papillon de La Ferté, *Journal de Papillon de La Ferté, intendant et contrôleur de l'argenterie, menus-plaisirs et affaires de la chambre du roi (1756–1780)* (Paris 1887), pp.415, 378 and 379.

26 Letter from the princesse de Lamballe to her cousin the Landgräfin de Hesse-Rothembourg, 26 June 1784, C. Schmidt (ed.), 'Lettres inédites de La Princesse de Lamballe', *Société de l'histoire de la Révolution française*, vol.39 (1900), pp.271–7, 272.

27 Papillon de La Ferté 1887 (cited note 24), p.416.

28 'où l'on va non pour danser, mais pour jouir du Spectacle sans être connu', *Gallerie des Modes*, pl.86.

29 Jean-Michel Moreau le Jeune, *Le bal masqué. Fête donnée au Roi et à la Reine par la ville de Paris le 23 janvier 1782 à l'occasion de la naissance de Monseigneur le Dauphin*, 1782, etching, published Paris. Château de Versailles (INV.GRAV 6936).

30 'On voulait à l'instant avoir la même parure que la reine', Campan 1823 (cited note 21), vol.1, p.95.

31 Janet Arnold, *Patterns of Fashion 6: The Content, Cut, Construction and Context of Women's European Dress c.1695–1795* (London 2021), pp.101–9 and Kendra Van Cleave and Brooke Welborn, '"Very Much the Taste and Various are the Makes": Reconsidering the Late Eighteenth-Century Robe à la Polonaise', *Dress: The Journal of the Costume Society of America*, vol.39, no.1 (2013), pp.1–24.

32 This has been well traversed in the literature. See Pascale Gorguet Ballesteros, 'De la robe chemise à la robe droite. Variations picturales autour du blanc', in *À la mode* 2021–2, pp.218–43; Jane G. Ashelford, '"Colonial Livery" and the *chemise à la reine*, 1779–1784', *Costume*, vol.52, no.2 (2018), pp.217–39; and Chrisman-Campbell 2015, pp.172–99.

33 I thank Dr Susan North for this identification. This gown has been variously identified as both a *robe à la française* and a *robe à l'anglaise* and it is regrettable that the portrait is only half-length and does not reveal the full silhouette. The inverted 'V' front opening and the differently coloured bodice underneath are clearly visible, especially in the earlier version of the portrait. The small triangle of fabric that is visible behind Marie Antoinette's back precludes the close-fitting *robe à l'anglaise*, which would not leave a visible excess of fabric, nor does it suggest the box pleats of the *robe à la française* which, even if very narrow, as they became later in the period, would not fall in this way and would to some degree be visible descending from the back of the neck, as they are in the 1788 portrait of Madame Victoire by Adélaïde Labille Guiard (Château de Versailles). This small triangle of fabric resembles the gape that occurred in a *robe à la polonaise*, which was not fitted to the back of the waist and is worn here long/unbustled. This can be seen in fashion plates of the time and it was popular to wear the Polonaise in this way during this period – see Van Cleave and Welborn 2013 (cited note 30). The date is too late for Marie Antoinette to be wearing a *robe à la française*, the only other example from this period being the portrait of Madame Victoire, Louis XVI's aunt, who at 55 years old was considered elderly and therefore wore the fashions of a previous generation. The visible collar of Marie Antoinette's gown would also preclude box pleats. It is worth noting the colour discrepancy between the two versions of this portrait. In the Versailles version the gown appears steel blue, whereas in the private collection version it appears pearl grey.

34 Chrisman-Campbell 2003–4 (cited note 22).

35 Result from XRF analysis of 15 spangles from the fragments, undertaken by Maria Ecenarro, Conservation Scientist at the V&A in September

36 Marguerite Jallut, *Les peintres et les portraits de Marie-Antoinette* (Paris 1936), p.42.

37 AN K 506., no.25, pièce 2.

38 Kendra Van Cleave, 'Contextualizing Wertmüller's 1785 Portrait of Marie-Antoinette through Dress', *Costume*, vol.54, no.1 (March 2020), pp.56–80.

39 'cette entreprise qui fixera les yeux et la critique de tout Paris', letter from Madame Campan to Wertmüller quoted in ibid.

40 AN K 506., no.25, pièces 1, 11, 3.

41 G.-A.-H. de Reiset (ed.), *Modes et usages au temps de Marie-Antoinette. Livre-journal de Madame Eloffe* (Paris 1885), pp.38; 431.

42 *Souvenirs du baron de Frénilly, pair de France (1768–1828)* (Paris 1909).

43 AN K 506., no.25, pièce 3.

44 Juliette Trey, *Madame Elisabeth. Une princesse au destin tragique 1764–1794* (Milan 2013), p.52.

45 Da Vinha 2018, pp.38, 98, 99.

46 Author's translation, Cradock's journal (1896) quoted in ibid., p.39.

47 Ibid., p.38.

48 Ibid., p.36.

49 James-Sarazin and Lapasin 2023, p.16.

50 Letter from Mercy to Maria Theresa, 29 February 1772, Paris, Arneth and Geffroy 1874–5, vol.1, p.277.

51 James-Sarazin and Lapasin 2023, p.16.

52 Campan 1823 (cited note 21), vol.1, p.223.

53 Archives Nationales, *Louis XVI, Marie-Antoinette et la Révolution. La famille royale aux Tuileries (1789–1792)* (Paris 2023), p.83.

54 Chrisman-Campbell 2015, p.3.

55 'pierrots de percale, rose et blanc, bleu et blanc: un pierrot de toile de Jouy'. La Morinerie, 'Papiers du Temple (1792–1794)', *La nouvelle revue*, vol.27 (1 April 1884), pp.587–625, p.594.

QUEEN OF SPARKLE: DIAMONDS, FASHION AND POLITICS
Vincent Meylan

1 *Livre de compte, de correspondance et journal d'Aubert*, Archives nationales, Paris (Cote T/299).

2 The English equivalent is sometimes given as a milliner.

3 Austrian State Archives, Vienna (Cote AT-OeStA/HHStA StAbt Frankreich Diplomatische Korrespondenz 149-1).

4 The *dame d'atours*, literally the 'lady of finery', was the senior lady-in-waiting responsible for the queen's wardrobe and jewels.

5 Austrian State Archives, Vienna (Cote AT-OeStA/HHStA UR FUK 2054b).

6 Ibid.

7 Germain Bapst, *Inventaire de Marie-Josèphe de Saxe, dauphine de France. Portrait de la cour* (Paris 1883), pp.182–7.

8 *Livre de compte, de correspondance et journal d'Aubert*, Archives nationales, Paris (Cote T/299.)

9 *Journal de Louis XVI, tome II, contenant les dépenses et gratifications particulières sur sa cassette* (AE/I: Armoire de fer; Carton no.6 : Louis XVI. -- AE/I/4/2 --).

10 *Livre de compte, de correspondance et journal d'Aubert*, Archives nationales, Paris (Cote T/299).

11 Ibid.

12 *Protokoll über die im Beisein von Erzherzog Karl Ludwig vorgenommene Öffnung eines, den Schmuck der Königin Marie Antoinette von Frankreich enthaltenden Behältnisses* (AT-OeStA/HHStA HausA Handarchiv Kaiser Franz 20-3-3).

13 *Livre de compte, de correspondance et journal d'Aubert*, Archives nationales, Paris (Cote T/299).

14 Ibid.

15 Ibid.

16 *Journal de Louis XVI, tome II, contenant les dépenses et gratifications particulières sur sa cassette* (AE/I: Armoire de fer; Carton no.6: Louis XVI. -- AE/I/4/2 --).

17 Germain Bapst, *Histoire des joyaux de la couronne de France d'après des documents inédits* (Paris 1889), p.440.

18 *Pièces Justificatives pour Monsieur le cardinal de Rohan, Déclaration authentiques suivant la forme anglaise*, 1786.

19 *Protokoll über die im Beisein von Erzherzog Karl Ludwig vorgenommene Öffnung eines, den Schmuck der Königin Marie Antoinette von Frankreich enthaltenden Behältnisses* (AT-OeStA/HHStA HausA Handarchiv Kaiser Franz 20-3-3).

20 Ibid.

TOILES DE JOUY: MARIE ANTOINETTE AND COTTAGECORE
Silvija Banić & Jessica Harpley

1 Pascale Gorguet Ballesteros, 'De la robe chemise à la robe droite. Variations picturales autour du blanc', in *À la mode* 2021–2, pp.218–43; Jane G. Ashelford, '"Colonial Livery" and the *chemise à la reine*, 1779–1784', *Costume*, vol.52, no.2 (2018), pp.217–39; and Chrisman Campbell 2015, pp.172–99.

2 Henri Clouzot, *Painted and Printed Fabrics: The History of the Manufactory at Jouy and other Ateliers in France, 1760–1815* (New York 1927), p.14.

3 One unusual example is preserved in the V&A, a man's dressing gown of toile de Nantes, c.1830. Made to be worn in private, the garment's print has the suitably masculine subject of war, depicting French soldiers within its vignettes (V&A: T.377-2009).

4 In 1907, *Vogue* notes original toiles 'have usually faded but slightly, the original colourings of that period being very delicate in nuance, especially good in pastel pink': 'Paris (From our own Correspondent)', American *Vogue*, vol.29, no.21 (23 May 1907), p.847.

5 'Paris (From our own Correspondent)', American *Vogue*, vol.30, no.12 (19 September 1907), p.333; 'Paris (From our own Correspondent)', American *Vogue*, vol.29, no.21 (23 May 1907), p.847.

6 Ibid.

7 Christian Dior, *Dior by Dior* (London 2007), p.21.

8 See for example the Lanvin 1946–7 toile-skirted dress in the collection of the Museum of the City of New York (72.34.4AB.ALT3), and the Pauline Trigère toile dress pictured in American *Harper's Bazaar* (May 1949), p.19.

9 An advert for Tanner of North Carolina by Dorothy Cox, appearing in American *Vogue*, vol.137, no.2 (15 January 1961), depicts a model in the countryside wearing a toile sundress and sunhat, cradling a basket of flowers. The text underscores the sentimental messaging, claiming the dress 'Harks back: The good old days as they never were, recaptured in cotton Toile de Jouy printed in our own colors for the better days ahead. Voilet, blue, black. About $28.'

10 In 2021, leading cottagecore fashion brand Batsheva collaborated with Laura Ashley on a line of clothing drawing on the Laura Ashley archive of prints to complement their typically flouncy, feminine designs.

11 Fashion collections featuring iterations of toile are too numerous to mention, but include: Cacharel Spring/Summer 2001; Dior Couture Autumn/Winter 2001–2; Balmain Couture Autumn/Winter 2001–2; Erdem Spring/Summer 2009 and Spring/Summer 2021; Valentino Couture Spring/Summer 2012; Carven Spring/Summer 2013; Christian Dior Resort 2019; Acne Studios Spring/Summer 2019; Oscar de la Renta Resort 2019; Andrea Grossi's 2020 *Welcome to DeusLand* collection; Libertine Spring/Summer 2021; Stella McCartney Spring/Summer 2022; Philosophy di Lorenzo Serafini Spring/Summer 2023; Thom Browne Pre-Fall 2023; Carolina Herrera Spring/Summer 2024; Levi's Spring/Summer 2024 *Western Toile* collection; Tanner Fletcher Spring/Summer 2025; and Shinyakozuka Spring/Summer 2025.

12 For other examples, see *Not in Arcadia* by English Eccentrics (V&A: T.303–1988); *Insult to Injury* by Jake and Dinos Chapman (V&A: E.180–2010).

13 See *Glasgow* toile by Timorous Beasties (V&A: T.53–2018); *London* toile by Timorous Beasties (V&A: T.4–2014); Toile-de-Jouy tracksuit by Sibling (V&A: T.86:1, 2–2015).

14 See Renée Green, *Commemorative Toile* (V&A: E.2320–1997).

15 Sheila Bridges, *Harlem Toile*, date unknown, https://www.sheilabridges.com/product-category/harlem-toile/ (accessed 11 September 2024).

THE PERFUMED PALACE: MARIE ANTOINETTE AND SCENT
Sarah Grant

1 *Mercure de France* quoted in De Feydeau 2013, p.11.

2 Memoirs of the baronne d'Oberkirch quoted in ibid., p.29.

3 William Ritchey Newton, *Vivre à Versailles. Derrière la façade, la vie quotidienne au château* (2nd edn Paris 2014), p.13. Falling to 188 apartments in 1781. William Ritchey Newton, *L'espace du roi: La Cour de France au château de Versailles 1682–1789* (Paris 2000), p.26

4 'a prodigious Mixture of Magnificence and Negligence, with every kind of Elegance except that of Cleanliness'. Letter from Benjamin Franklin to Mary Stevenson, 14 September 1767, Paris, https://founders.archives.gov/documents/Franklin/01-14-02-0152 (accessed 30 September 2024).

5 Newton 2014 (cited note 3), pp.179, 188, 197.

6 Ibid.

7 It was common practice for the court to vacate Versailles for several weeks every year when the cesspits needed to be emptied, so intolerable were the odours: ibid., p.197.

8 Alice Camus, 'L'apparat olfactif du courtisan', in *Séduction et Pouvoir. L'art de s'apprêter à la cour aux XVIIe et XVIIIe siècles*, exh. cat., Musée du Domaine Royal de Marly (Paris 2023), pp.38–49.

9 *Magasin des modes nouvelles, françaises et anglaises*, Paris (30 November 1787), p.15.

10 Jean-Louis Fargeon, *L'art du parfumeur* (Paris 1801).

11 'Au Signe Des Parfums. Rue du Roulle'. This

bill dated January 1780 records Fargeon as Paris perfumer to the 'king and court' and seller of scented gloves, pomade, purging powders and 'Nérola' (neroli) powder to the duchesse de Villeroy (AN. T//129/5).

12 AN K 506., no.25, pièces 4 & 5.

13 'Catalogue des marchandises qui se vendent chez M. Savoye, rue Thérèse, au coin de celle Sainte-Anne' (AN. T//165/16). Eugénie Briot, 'Jean-Louis Fargeon, fournisseur de la cour de France: art et techniques d'un parfumeur du XVIIIe siècle', *Artefact*, vol.1 (2014), https://doi.org/10.4000/artefact.1123 (accessed 30 September 2024).

14 Camus 2023 (cited note 8), p.40.

15 As recalled by Madame Campan, quoted in De Feydeau 2013, p.53.

16 A bill for this purchase made ahead of the queen's attempted flight to Varennes survived in the early 20th century in the then archives of Houbigant. Jean-François Houbigant, 'A la Corbeille de Fleurs', 19 rue du Faubourg Saint-Honoré, June 1791. 'An Historical Document of Tragic Fragrance', American *Vogue*, vol.60, no.10 (15 November 1922), p.62.

17 Stéphanie-Félicité du Crest, Madame de Genlis, 'Parfum', in *Dictionnaire critique et raisonné des étiquettes de la cour* (Paris 1818), vol.2, p.39.

18 Letter from the comte de Chalon to the Duchess of Devonshire, 4 March 1780, Versailles (Chatsworth Archives, CS5 268).

19 Trade card of Dulac, marchand gantier-parfumeur et bijoutier, late 18th century (AN T//315/3).

20 French safflower mixed with Briançon chalk and oil, which was boiled for 24 hours. Bibliothèque de l'Académie nationale de médecine, Paris (SRM 100 dossier 27, nos 2–3). The ingredients for this rouge were sourced within France but other cosmetics might contain ingredients coming from Brazil, Asia or Mexico and Central America thereby linking them to the triangular trade that included enslaved people, see Oliver Wunsch, 'Making up Race: Whiteness, Pinkness, and Pompadour', in A. Cassandra Albinson (ed.), *Madame de Pompadour: Painted Pink*, (New Haven and London 2022) pp.74–85.

21 This was a ruse and part of the plan for the flight to Varennes. Jeanne L.H. Campan, *Mémoires sur la vie privée de Marie-Antoinette, reine de France et de Navarre*, 2nd edn, 3 vols (Paris 1823), vol.2, p.141.

22 See Campan on Marie Antoinette's bathing and toilette rituals: ibid., vol.1, p.104. M. Déjean [Antoine Hornot], *Traité des odeurs, suite du traité de la distillation*, 2nd edn (Paris 1777), p.467.

23 F.J.B. Watson, *The Wrightsman Collection Volumes I and II: Furniture, Gilt Bronze and Mounted Porcelain, Carpets* (New York 1966), pp.578, 590.

24 'cassolette' and 'cassolette, parfum', in *Encyclopédie ou dictionnaire raisonné des sciences, des arts et des métiers*, vol.6 (1781), p.483. See for instance, Charles Leclercq's portraits of the comtesse d'Artois and Madame Élisabeth (Versailles, MV 8572 and MV 8965). Juliette Trey has noted that this appears to have been Leclercq's hallmark, Juliette Trey, *Madame Élisabeth. Une princesse au destin tragique 1764–1794* (Milan 2013), p.46.

25 Vincent Cochet and Alexia Lebeurre, *Le boudoir turc de Marie-Antoinette et Joséphine à Fontainebleau* (Paris 2023), p.68.

26 G. Lenotre (pseud. Louis L.T. Gosselin), *The Last Days of Marie Antoinette* (London 1907), p.86.

27 Ibid.

THE UNIVERSE AT HER FEET: MARIE ANTOINETTE'S SHOES
Helena Cox

1 Vigée Le Brun 1869, p.253.

2 A 10-year-old Marie Antoinette, garlanded with flowers for her role as Flora, dances with her siblings in the ballet *The Triumph of Love*, wearing a pointed satin shoe with a round silver buckle in Johann-Georg Weikert's 1765 painting (Château de Versailles, MV 3945). Other paintings with glimpsed shoes: in Gautier-Dagoty's 1775 ceremonial portrait of the recently made queen (Château de Versailles, MV 8061), she wears a blue *grand habit*, a single silvery-blue pointed slipper peeps out from under her dress. Another blue silk slipper is visible in Josef Hauzinger's 1778 portrait of Marie Antoinette, Louis XVI and archduke Maximilian (Kunsthistorisches Museum, Vienna, Gemäldegalerie). Equestrian portraits of Marie Antoinette show her either donning riding boots (Château de Versailles, MV 5718), or riding side-saddle wearing black, heeled, pointed riding boots with a large bow (Château de Versailles, MV 9082). In Wertmüller's 1785 portrait of Marie Antoinette and her children in the Petit Trianon gardens (Nationalmuseum, Stockholm), her oyster-taupe pointed heel matches the *soie changeante* of her dress. Finally, in Dumont's miniature of the queen (Louvre, Paris, RF 28719, Recto), vibrant pointed blue slippers with a tiny heel peek out from beneath her white belted *cheruque* dress.

3 Sylvie Le Bras-Chauvot, *Marie-Antoinette l'affranchie. Portrait Inédit d'une icône de mode* (Paris 2020), p.105.

4 The polarities of the well-heeled versus the down-trodden clog-wearing poor became metaphors of the class divide with sartorial conflict explored in rhetoric and satire between *le soulier* and *le sabot*.

5 John Adams, *A Biography in his own Words: Volume 2, The Founding Fathers* (New York 1973), p.296.

6 Élisabeth Vigée Le Brun, *Memoirs of a Painter: An Extraordinary Life Before, During and After the French Revolution* (Coventry 2009), p.93.

7 Arneth and Geffroy 1874–5, vol.1, p.277.

8 Joseph-Alphonse, abbé de Veri, *Journal de l'abbé de Véri*, vol.2, ed. baron Jehan de Witte (Paris 1928), p.429.

9 AN K 506., no.25, pièces 4, 5.

10 Such as the *polonaise* and certain *robe à l'anglaise retroussée* designs.

11 Such as pattens and gentrified clogs to protect finery.

12 Arneth and Geffroy 1874–5, vol.1, p.106.

13 Judith Chazin-Bennahum, *The Lure of Perfection: Fashion and Ballet, 1780–1830* (New York 2005), p.21.

14 Fraser 2001, p.92.

15 Ibid., p.103.

16 La Tour du Pin 1913, p.9.

17 V.-M.V. Vaublanc, *Mémoires de M. le comte de Vaublanc* (Paris 1857), p.136.

18 Inscribed garters likewise allowed for flirtatious conceits. An embroidered silk pair reputedly belonging to Marie Antoinette is inscribed: 'Je peins une beauté fidèle; Je forme un ensemble parfait; Et quand je trace ce portrait, Vous seule en êtes le modèle'. Garters, Snowshill Wade Costume Collection, Gloucestershire, National Trust (NT 1350074).

19 *Horace Walpole's Correspondence* 2023, p.324, https://libsvcs-1.its.yale.edu/hwcorrespondence/page.asp?vol=20&seq=348&type=b (accessed 5 August 2024).

20 A plate from a 1793 illustrated edition of *Dangerous Liaisons* depicts a *cordonnier* kneeling at Cécile's feet, in the act of measuring her foot with an early foot-measuring instrument.

21 C. Valfons, *Dix-huitième siècle. Souvenirs du marquis de Valfons* (Paris 1860), p.416.

22 Other surviving shoes: a pair of green silk embroidered low-heeled mules with silver thread and floral motifs. Versailles, Musée Lambinet (inv.79); a dark-brown leather and Gros de Tours silk shoe, 1792, Musée des arts décoratifs, Paris (inv. Louvre BJ 143); a black silk single shoe by Fraysee & Associés, 12 June 2013.

23 De Goncourt 1879, p.419.

24 Striped green and pink low-heeled beribboned silk slippers, 'Souvenirs Historiques Familles Royales – Militaria' sale, Drouot, 17 October 2012, lot 20, sold for €50,000. Ecru-coloured pointed shoe in silk and kidskin leather with delicate pleated ribbons, 'La Royauté à Versailles' sale, Osenat, 15 November 2020, lot 48, sold for €43,750. A pair of mules, silk with tricolour ribbon, 'Collection of Paul Rousseau' sale, Toulon, 24 March 2012, lot 68, sold for €43,225.

25 'La Royauté à Versailles' sale, Osenat, 15 November 2020, lot 48.

26 Simon Schama, *Citizens: A Chronicle of the French Revolution* (London 2004), p.373.

27 Ribeiro 1988, p.56.

28 G.-A.-H. de Reiset, *Modes et usages au temps de Marie-Antoinette. Livre-journal de Madame Eloffe* (Paris 1885), p.337.

29 This draws upon Monsieur d'Aubier's (gentleman-in-ordinary to the king) first-hand witness, referenced in a letter, December 1794. The transcript can be found in A.F. de Molleville's *Histoire de la Révolution de France. Partie 2*, vol.9 (Paris 1801–3), p.449. Likewise drawn upon by the Goncourt brothers (De Goncourt 1879, p.318).

30 De Reiset 1885 (cited note 27), french: 'serin en violet' – 'bleus en blanc' – 'taffeta gros-vert'– 'taffeta violet' – 'satin bleue' – 'satin rose' – 'galou gris' – 'puce' – 'nacarat' – 'puce en comète' – 'comète grise', pp.507–9.

31 Ibid., p.61.

32 Ibid., p.390.

33 Gérard Walter, *Le procès de Marie-Antoinette. 23–25 vendémiaire an II, 14–16 octobre 1793* (Brussels 1993), p.89.

34 The slippers were exhibited in the 1927 exhibition *La Reine Marie-Antoinette et sa Cour* at Versailles (cat.321; formerly in the collection of Austrian collector Anna Porgès who was fascinated by the French queen).

35 G. Lenotre (pseud. Louis L.T. Gosselin), *The Last Days of Marie Antoinette* (London 1907), p.137.

36 Lamorlière 1897, p.11.

37 Ibid.

38 Ibid., p.19.

39 Le Bras-Chauvot 2020 (cited note 3), p.310.

40 Musée des Beaux-Arts de Caen (800.111).

41 It was allegedly picked up when the queen lost it and immediately purchased by Monsieur the Count of Guernon-Ranville.

42 Adolphe Thiers, *The History of the French Revolution*, vol.3 (Princeton 1881), p.232.

43 Rouy l'aîné, 'Le Magicien Républicain', *La Quotidienne ou La Gazette universelle*, no. 396 (Paris [1793]).

44 Archibald Alison, *Histoire de l'Europe durant la Révolution et les Guerres de la République de 1789 à 1797*, vols 4–6 (Brussels 1860), p.157.

45 See Bibliothèque nationale de France (De Vinck, 5490. 1793. RESERVE QB-370 (33)-FT 4)

46 Gisèle d'Assailly, *Ages of Elegance: Five Thousand Years of Fashion and Frivolity* (Paris 1968), p.150.

47 G.-A.-H. de Reiset (ed.), *Lettres inédites de Marie-Antoinette et de Marie-Clotilde de France (soeur de Louis XVI), reine de Sardaigne* (Paris 1876), p.189.

NEVER WITHOUT A FAN
Helena Cox

1 Edith A. Standen, 'Instruments for Agitating the Air', *The Metropolitan Museum of Art Bulletin*, vol.3, no.7 (March 1965) p.243.

2 Denis Diderot, *Encyclopédie, ou Dictionnaire raisonné des sciences, des arts et des métier* (Briasson 1765), 'servir de countenance', p.139.

3 Philippe Mesmer, *Fan Tales* (New York 2002), p.39.

4 *Fans in Fashion: Selections from the Fine Arts Museums of San Francisco* (San Francisco 1981), p.12.

5 George Woolliscroft Rhead, *History of the Fan* (London 1910), p.114.

6 Joseph Addison, *The Spectator*, no. 102 (June 1711).

7 See British Museum, London (1891,0713.125 and 1891,0713.508).

8 Arneth and Geffroy 1874–5, vol.1, p.191.

9 Chéry in Volmert and Bucher 2019, p.97.

10 De Goncourt 1879, p.24.

11 Sotheby, Wilkinson & Hodge, *Catalogue of the Cabinet of Old Fans, the Property of Mr. Robert Walker of Uffington, Berkshire* (London 1882), lot 380, p.30. This fan is probably still in private hands. A garlanded shield is inscribed with her monogram, themes of auspicious fortune and love continue with the Three Graces weaving garlands of roses, Cupid banishing Midas and Miscordia. The reverse depicts the happy royal couple guided by blind love into a wood.

12 Fraser 2001, p.178.

13 D'Oberkirch 1853–4, vol.1, pp.86–7.

14 Ibid.

15 Jeanne L.H. Campan, *Mémoires sur la vie privée de Marie-Antoinette, reine de France et de Navarre*, 2nd edn, 3 vols (Paris 1823), vol.1, p.91.

16 Ibid.

17 Ibid.

18 Rose Bertin, *Mémoires de Mademoiselle Bertin sur la reine Marie-Antoinette, avec des notes et des éclaircissements* (Paris 1824), p.261.

19 D'Oberkirch 1853–4, vol.1, pp.217–18.

20 Sophie von La Roche, *Journal d'un voyage à travers la France, 1785* (Saint-Quentin-de-Baron 2012), p.284.

21 Fans from Marie Antoinette's collection:
• Probably still in a private collection, sold Sotheby, Wilkinson & Hodge, *Catalogue of the Cabinet of Old Fans, the Property of Mr. Robert Walker of Uffington, Berkshire* (London 1882), lot 381. A fan of Louis XVI and Marie Antoinette renewing their vows at the altar of Hymen, marking the birth of the Dauphin.
• Royal Collection, 'Marie Antoinette's fan', acquired for Queen Victoria in Paris by her aunt, Queen Louise (RCIN 25092).
• Bâtonnier, Paris. A musical-themed fan was allegedly given by Marie Antoinette to her lawyer Chauveau-Lagarde to thank him during her trial.
• Private collection. An ivory 20-leaf fan depicting the interview between Alexander the Great and defeated Indian King Porus, presented by the town of Dieppe to Marie Antoinette after the birth of the Dauphin (1785), sold by Sotheby's in 2019, initially passing from the queen to Madame du Crey (the keeper of the queen's laces).
• Ickworth, Suffolk, National Trust (NT 852846).
• Greys Court, Oxfordshire, National Trust (NT 195548).

22 De Nolhac 1929, p.16.

23 G.-A.-H. de Reiset (ed.), *Modes et usages au temps de Marie-Antoinette. Livre-journal de Madame Eloffe* (Paris 1885), p.520. AN K 506., no.25, pièce 4: La Dame Berthelot à Paris pour les blondes et evantails [sic]. In 1781 she spent 350 *livres* on fans.

24 Fraser 2001, p.99.

25 Arneth and Geffroy 1874–5, vol.1, p.64.

26 See Fan Museum, London ('Scandal of the necklace' fan, HA Collection 1624) and Carnavalet (EV166).

27 H.-L. de La Tour du Pin, *Escape from Terror: The Journal of Madame de la Tour du Pin*, ed. and trans Felice Harcourt (New York 1979), p.99.

28 De Reiset 1885 (cited note 23), p.87.

29 Simon Schama, *Citizens: A Chronicle of the French Revolution* (London 2004), p.351.

30 See Fan Museum, London, *Le Miroir Magique*, c.1795 (HA1421).

31 See Musée Carnavalet, Paris, 'C'est incroyable' fan, c.1795 (EV205).

32 See Musée des arts décoratifs, Paris, royalist fan with the profiles of Louis XVI and Marie Antoinette in the contours of an urn; profiles of their children hidden in the tree.

33 See British Museum, London, royalist fan with concealed royal silhouettes within the central sequin motifs, inscribed 'vive Le Roy', c.1793 (1891,0713.149).

34 *Journal de la justice civile, criminelle, commerciale et militaire* (Paris, 1 July 1796), pp.168–70.

35 Ibid.

36 Louis-Sébastien Mercier, *Le nouveau Paris*, vol.3 (Paris 1797), p.23.

37 Ibid., pp.26–7.

IN HER OWN WORDS: MARIE ANTOINETTE'S LETTERS
Catriona Seth

1 Archives nationales, Paris (AE/1/7-8/pièce 3), illustrated and transcribed in *Marie-Antoinette* 2008, p.374, cat.285.

2 See Catriona Seth, 'D'Antoine à Marie Antoinette: (re)lire les lettres de l'archiduchesse', in *Relire la lettre*, ed. Philippe De Vita and Bénédicte Obitz-Lumbroso (forthcoming, 2025).

3 The full text of the note reads as follows: 'Auspice Deo!/Les bontés de Votre Majesté sont au-dessus de tous remerciements je ne puis douter de son souvenir pour l'avenir, que ne puis la mériter aussi bien par ma conduite que par la vive et respectueuse reconnaissance dont mon cœur est pénétré, que Votre Majesté mette le comble à ses bontés par ses avis maternels cette précieuse leçon tous les jours présente à mon esprit, sera mon plus grand secours dans l'éloignement, et l'unique consolation qui puisse adoucir les regrets de la très humble et soumise fille/ Antoine/ le 16 mars 1770', in Seth 2006a, p.3.

4 François Dumont, *Marie Antoinette Seated at her Desk Writing a Letter*, c.1777, miniature, watercolour on ivory, 109 × 90mm (private collection).

5   Marie Antoinette to Maria Theresa, 13 June 1776: 'Il est affligeant pour moi que ma chère maman croyait à mon désavantage des rapports souvent faux et presque toujours exagérés', in Seth 2006a, p.60.

6   Marie Antoinette to Maria Theresa, October 1777: 'Permet-elle donc que je finisse par l'embrasser tendrement et l'assurer que personne au monde ne lui est plus tendrement et plus respectueusement attachée et ne désire plus vivement de continuer à mériter ses bontés que moi?', in Seth 2006a, p.76.

7   Marie Antoinette to Count Rosenberg [1775], Stefan Zweig collection vol.CLXXI, British Library (Zweig MSS 171).

8   Silver and ebony 'cachet' seal/stamp with Marie Antoinette's cypher/monogram from the queen's nécessaire, 1787–8, Musée du Louvre, Paris.

9   Marie Antoinette to Yolande de Polastron, duchesse de Polignac, 16 July 1789: 'Adieu, la plus tendre des amies. Ce mot est affreux, mais il le faut. Voilà l'ordre pour les chevaux; je n'ai que la force de vous embrasser', in Evelyne Lever (ed.), Marie Antoinette, Correspondance 1770–1793 (Paris 2005), p.486.

10 Marie Antoinette to Mercy, 16 August 1791: 'On nous dit, et les frères du Roi mandent chaque jour, qu'il faut tout refuser, et que nous serons soutenus. Par qui? Il me semble que les Puissances étrangères ne font pas de grands efforts pour venir à notre secours', in Seth 2019, p.215.

11 Marie Antoinette to Mercy, 4 July 1792: 'Je me plais à croire que je partage le sentiment qui vous attachait à ma mère. Voilà le moment de m'en donner une grande preuve en sauvant moi et les miens, moi s'il en est temps', in Seth 2019, p.260.

12 See: https://www.sciences-patrimoine.org/projet/rex-2-Marie-Antoinette/

13 'Adieu, ma princesse. Ils m'ont tout ôté, hors mon cœur, qui me restera toujours pour vous aimer, n'en doutez jamais; c'est le seul malheur que je ne pourrais supporter', in Lever 2005 (cited note 9), p.851.

14 Félix-Sébastien Feuillet de Conches (1798–1887) was a diplomat and autograph collector. He was accused of stealing a Montaigne letter from the Bibliothèque nationale. He owned numerous authentic and counterfeit historical documents and is believed to have been behind the creation of fakes, including letters purportedly by Marie Antoinette.

15 Alfred von Arneth (ed.), Maria Theresia und Marie Antoinette, ihr Briefwechsel (Paris and Vienna 1865), and Arneth and Geffroy 1874–5.

16 Stefan Zweig, Marie Antoinette. Bildnis eines mittleren Charakters (Leipzig 1932). First translation Zweig 1933.

17 On the question of the authenticity of the letters, which has sometimes been debated, see Ariane Ducrot, 'Histoire de faux? Une lettre de Marie Antoinette à la princesse de Lamballe', in Histoires d'archives. Recueil d'articles offert à Lucie Favier par ses collègues et amis (Paris 1987), pp.277–89.

18 See the collaborative 'Lettres de Marie Antoinette' (LMA) project hosted by the Centre de recherche du château de Versailles: https://chateauversailles-recherche.fr.

EMPRESS EUGÉNIE'S FASCINATION WITH QUEEN MARIE ANTOINETTE

Alison McQueen

Research for this essay has been supported by a grant from the Social Sciences and Humanities Research Council of Canada. All translations are my own.

1   Pierre Josserand (ed.), Mémoires du comte Horace de Viel-Castel sur le règne de Napoléon III, 1851–1864, 2 vols (Brussels 1942), vol.1, p.172.

2   I have intentionally avoided characterizing Eugénie's interest in Marie Antoinette as a 'cult' as that was deployed as a pejorative descriptor by contemporary detractors, including Princess Mathilde (recorded by the Goncourt brothers) and Austrian diplomat Hübner. Edmond and Jules de Goncourt, Journales. Mémoires de la vie littéraire, ed. Robert Ricatte, 3 vols (Paris 1989), vol.1, p.232; Comte de Hübner, Neuf ans de souvenirs d'un ambassadeur d'Autriche à Paris sous le second empire, 1851–1859 (Paris 1904), pp.320–1, 441.

3   This tapestry, the second produced, was ordered to be sent to Saint-Cloud on 25 April 1856. Maurice Fenaille, État général des tapisseries de la manufacture des Gobelins depuis son origine jusqu'à nos jours 1600–1900 (Paris 1922), p.400. Henri Clouzot documented it in Eugénie's cabinet de travail while Arnaud Denis indicates it hung in the grand salle à manger. Henri Clouzot, Des Tuileries à Saint-Cloud. L'art décoratif du second empire (Paris 1925), p.200. Emmanuelle Le Bail et al., Les derniers feux du palais de Saint-Cloud (Saint-Cloud 2019), p.133.

4   The position and context are visible in a photograph by Pierre-Ambroise Richebourg, Salon of 1857, view of a room, Musée d'Orsay, Paris (PHO 2000 13 6).

5   Bibliothèque historique de la ville de Paris, Schneider papers, fols 210 and 238. In 1866, Eugénie left the portrait in this room when she transferred other works to a venue in Paris (Archives nationales [AN] 20144790/107). After the end of the Second Empire, the painting was moved to the Louvre (21 September 1870; AN 20150044/148). It was restituted to Eugénie in 1881 (AN 20150162, dossier 1, 19 January 1881, n.230). After her death, it was sold by descendants in 1927, owned by Seligman et Cie and donated to the Metropolitan Museum in 1978 (Christie's, 1 July 1927, cat.99). See also Catherine Granger, L'Empereur et les arts. La liste civile de Napoléon III (Paris 2005), pp.701–2.

6   An article published in the early 20th century created narratives for the 18th-century styles as: 'en Costume Watteau', 'en Robe Louis XVI', and 'en Marie-Antoinette'. Hélène Avry, 'Les travestis de l'Impératrice Eugénie', Femina, vol.15, no.242 (February 1911), pp.84–5. Eugénie's long-time family friend, writer Prosper Mérimée, did not approve of her dressing in the late queen's style. Prosper Mérimée to Edward Childe Fils, 11 February 1866. Prosper Mérimée, Correspondance générale, ed. Maurice Parturier with P. Josserand and J. Mallion, 16 vols (Paris 1953–64), vol.13, pp.34–5.

7   F. de Villars, 'Décoration des appartements de l'impératrice aux Tuileries', Revue universelle des arts, vol.10 (1859), p.235.

8   Hélène Demoriane, 'Le Louis XVI qu'aimait Eugénie', Connaissance des arts, no.116 (October 1961), p.76.

9   The desk, estimated at 60,000 francs, was part of the collection of the prince de Beauvau sold at Hôtel Drouot in April 1865. Courrier artistique (30 April 1865), p.192. The Journal of the Society of Arts recorded Eugénie as the buyer (26 May 1865), p.469. The purchase was later recorded as 68,000 francs from her private funds. Clouzot 1925 (cited note 3), p.115. On the history of the desk see Pierre Verlet, Le mobilier royal français. I, meubles de la couronne conservés en France (Paris 1990), pp.30–1.

10 Mathieu Caron, 'Les apartements de l'impératrice Eugénie aux Tuileries: le XVIIIe siècle retrouvé?', Bulletin du Centre de recherche du château de Versailles (2015), pp.4–5.

11 I thank Frédérine Pradier and Marion Falaise for facilitating my research at the Musée des Tissus in Lyon.

12 Élisabeth Claude, 'La Chambre de Marie-Antoinette au Petit Trianon, L'Esprit de 1867 et des années revival', in Versailles Revival, ed. Laurent Salomé and Claire Bonnotte (Paris 2019), pp.46–7, 49.

13 Armand Schneider, Papiers d'Armand Schneider, régisseur du palais de Saint-Cloud (Bibliothèque historique de la ville de Paris), manuscript folio 197.

14 De Lescure 1867, cats 32, 36, 44, 47, 52, 54, 56, 58, 59, 64 and 77 (two items). See also Christophe Pincemaille, 'L'impératrice Eugénie et Marie-Antoinette, autour de l'exposition des souvenirs de la reine au Petit Trianon en 1867', Versalia, vol.6 (2003), pp.124–34; and Allison Unruh, 'Rococo in Second Empire France', Doctoral Dissertation (New York University, 2008), pp.253–61. On Léopold Double, who helped organize the exhibition and contributed loans, see Tom Stammers, The Purchase of the Past: Collecting Culture in Post-Revolutionary Paris, c.1790–1890 (Cambridge 2020), pp.225–36, 240. Eugénie arranged for an exhibition dedicated to Empress Joséphine to take place simultaneously at the château de Malmaison.

15 The bow was originally part of a belt crafted in 1855 by François Kramer. It became an independent piece in 1864 when the five pendants forming a fringe (pampilles) were added, most likely by Alfred Bapst. See Anne Dion-Tenenbaum, 'L'Impératrice Eugénie et les diamants de la couronne', in Eugénie, Impératrice des français. Actes du colloque du centenaire de la disparition d'Eugénie de Montijo, ed. Maxime Michelet (Paris 2024), pp.105, 108–9; Marc Bascou, 'Grand nœud de corsage de l'impératrice Eugénie', in Dion-Tenenbaum 2023, pp.238–42; and Marc Bascou and Anne Dion-Tenenbaum, 'Le joaillier Kramer et les diamants de la couronne sous le second empire', La revue des musées de France/Revue du Louvre, no.4 (2018), pp.80–92.

MARIE ANTOINETTE AND THE *BAL POUDRÉ* IN VICTORIAN FANCY DRESS

Susan North

1   Benjamin Wild, Carnival to Catwalk: Global Reflections on Fancy Dress Costume (London 2020), DOI: 10.5040/9781350015029.ch-001, pp.1–32.

2   Rebecca N. Mitchell, 'The Victorian Fancy Dress Ball, 1870–1900', Fashion Theory, vol.21, no.3 (2016), pp.291–315, p.293.

3   Benjamin L. Wild, 'Romantic Recreations: Remembering Stuart Monarchy in Nineteenth-

Century Fancy Dress Entertainments', in *Remembering Queens and Kings of Early Modern England and France: Reputation, Reinterpretation and Reincarnation*, ed. Estelle Paranque (Cham 2019), pp.179–96, p.189.

4 *The Morning Herald* (15 May 1842), p.5.

5 *Gloucestershire Chronicle* (2 January 1869), p.2.

6 *The Queen* (26 April 1873), p.339.

7 Mitchell 2016 (cited note 2), p.298.

8 Aileen Ribeiro, *Facing Beauty: Painted Women and Cosmetic Art* (New Haven and London 2011), pp.251–3.

9 *The Queen* (13 February 1869), p.92.

10 *Huddersfield Daily Examiner* (20 December 1886), p.2.

11 *The Queen* (9 February 1895), p.238.

12 Ibid.

13 Many thanks to Sarah Grant for making this connection. None of the newspaper descriptions of the Duchess of Devonshire's ball mentions the costume of Lady Isobel or Lady Alexandra.

14 *The Queen* (20 February 1869), p.113. In fact, moiré or watered silk long predated the 18th century, and 'blonde' or lace made with silk yarn was fashionable in the early 1700s.

15 *The Queen* (5 June 1869), p.351.

16 *The Queen* (27 January 1872), p.55.

17 *The Queen* (10 February 1872), p.91.

18 *The Queen* (25 June 1870), p.404.

19 *The Queen* (10 July 1897), p.73.

20 Many thanks to Sarah Grant for spotting this source.

21 Sophia Murphy, *The Duchess of Devonshire's Ball* (London 1984), p.50; https://collections.vam.ac.uk/item/O1274207/fancy-dress-costume-worth/.

22 Diana de Marly, *Worth: Father of Couture* (London 1980), pp.171–86.

23 *The Queen* (10 July 1897), pp.75–6.

24 *The Queen* (5 June 1869), p.351.

25 Holt 1887, p.254.

26 *The Queen* (5 June 1869), p.351.

27 *The Queen* (27 March 1869), p.195.

28 *The Daily Packet* (28 March 1846), p.3.

29 *The Queen* (2 February 1895), p.194.

30 *The Queen* (14 March 1903), p.100.

31 *The Sketch* (18 March 1903), p.321; *The Queen* (14 March 1903), p.100.

32 *The Hendon and Finchley Times* (17 February 1911), p.8.

33 Celia Marshik, *At the Mercy of their Clothes: Modernism, the Middlebrow and British Garment Culture* (New York 2017), pp.103–7.

MARIE ANTOINETTE, ENCHANTMENT AND ILLUSION 1910–40
Sarah Grant

1 'Nous avons fait un beau rêve, voilà tout', Letter from Marie Antoinette to the chevalier de Jarjayes, Temple prison, Paris, February/March 1793. Maxime de La Rocheterie and Gaston du Fresne de Beaucourt (eds), *Lettres de Marie-Antoinette: recueil des lettres authentiques de la reine*, 2 vols (Paris 1895–6), vol.2, p.433, letter CCCLXXX.

2 Lucy Moore, *Anything Goes: A Biography of the Roaring Twenties* (London 2009), p.71.

3 On the revival of Versailles see Salomé and Bonnotte 2019. Pierre de Nolhac: *La reine Marie-Antoinette* (1889); *Les consignes de Marie-Antoinette au Petit Trianon* (1890); *Marie-Antoinette à Trianon*

(1893); *Le Château de Versailles au temps de Marie-Antoinette* (1889); *La dauphine Marie-Antoinette* (1896); *Le Trianon de Marie-Antoinette* (1924); *Autour de la reine* (1929).

4 Cecil Beaton, *The Book of Beauty* (London 1930), p.9.

5 See Horst P. Horst's photographs of a model wearing Cartier diamonds, Charlotte Benton, Tim Benton and Ghislaine Wood (eds), *Art Deco 1910–1939* (London 2002), pp.278–9.

6 *Harper's Bazaar* (January 1920), p.38.

7 *La Femme chic à Paris* (1 November 1921), p.8.

8 See for example, Edmund Dulac's Fairy Godmother in *Cinderella* and also illustrations for *Sleeping Beauty* in Arthur Quiller-Couch's *The Sleeping Beauty and Other Fairy Tales* (London 1910); Kay Nielsen's illustrations for *The Twelve Dancing Princesses* in Arthur Quiller-Couch's, *In Powder and Crinoline* (London 1913), Félix Lorioux's illustrations for *Cinderella* in Charles Perrault's *Les contes de Perrault* (Paris 1927), and Aubrey Beardsley's illustrations for *The Rape of the Lock* (London 1897).

9 On Barbier see Clara Terreaux, 'Le Paradis Perdu de George Barbier', in Salomé and Bonnotte 2019, pp.392–5 and Barbara Martorelli (ed.), *George Barbier: The Birth of Art Deco* (Venice 2008).

10 The facade of the main palace of Versailles is visible in 'Cortège', the Belvedere appears in 'Mandoline'.

11 It is also possible that the sphinx theme was suggested by the playful pair of marble sphinxes by Jacques Houzeau and Louis Lerambert in the château gardens. The firedogs are in Versailles collections: Inv. V 4838.2.

12 Listed under 'L' in the manuscript catalogue of her library in the main château at Versailles. *Catalogue des livres de la Reine*, 1781, p.70 (Bibliothèque Nationale, NAF 3209) and in the 1792 catalogue (BN, NAF 2512), p.21.

13 Barbara Martorelli, 'George Barbier/ 1882–1932', in Martorelli 2008 (cited note 9), pp.14–53, p.35.

14 'The Mode of Marie Antoinette and Louis XVI', American *Vogue* (1 July 1925), p.65.

15 Boué Soeurs advertisement for 'Lingerie Frocks', 15 April 1916.

16 'un petit cachet ancien tout à fait authentique'. 'La Mode de Demain', *La Femme chic à Paris* (1 May 1921), p.7.

17 Julia Westerman, 'The Theatrical Wonders of Jeanne Paquin's Belle Epoque Parisienne', *Art Herstory* (4 August 2020), https://artherstory.net/jeanne-paquins-belle-epoque-parisienne/ (accessed 7 September 2024).

18 Quoted in Pierre Toromanoff and Agata Toromanoff, *Jeanne Lanvin: Fashion Pioneer* (Augsburg 2023), p.148.

19 'voici que le panier revient sur l'eau'; 'le panier en question est celui que nos couturiers vont tenter de renouver pour agrémenter la toilette féminine', Marcel Nadaud, 'Les Robes a Paniers – Leur Histoire', *La Femme chic à Paris* (1 April 1912), np.

20 'A rare Boué Soeurs pale-pink silk-taffeta Robe de Style, model "Bouquetière", 1927–28', Kerry Taylor, Vintage Fashion, Antique Costume and Textiles, 25 October 2021, lot 221. Philippe Montégut, 'Boué Soeurs: The First Haute-Couture Establishment in America', *Dress*, vol.15, no.1 (January 1989), pp.79–86. See also Waleria Dorogova, 'Boué Sœurs, "Compelled by the War"', in Maude Bass-Krueger, Hayley Edwards-Dujardin and Sophie

Kurkdijan (eds), *Fashion, Society and the First World War: International Perspectives* (London 2021), pp.29–45.

21 Stefan Zweig, *Marie Antoinette*, trans. Eden and Cedar Paul (London 2010; first published 1932), p.589.

22 Alma Söderhjelm, *Fersen et Marie-Antoinette. Correspondance et journal intime inédits du comte Axel de Fersen* (Paris 1930).

23 See David M. Lugowski, 'Norma Shearer and Joan Crawford: Rivals at the Glamour Factory', in Adrienne L. McLean (ed.), *Glamour in a Golden Age: Movie Stars of the 1930s* (New Brunswick NJ 2011) and Larkin 2019.

24 Mary Jo Tate, *Critical Companion to F. Scott Fitzgerald: A Literary Reference to His Life and Work* (New York 2007), p.146.

25 'Adrian Designs for Norma Shearer', American *Vogue* (1 May 1938), p.83.

26 Leonard Stanley and Mark A. Vieira, *Adrian: A Lifetime of Movie Glamour, Art and High Fashion* (New York 2019), p.69.

27 The gown is now in the collection of LACMA, Gift of Bob Carlton (M.86.237a-h).

MARIE ANTOINETTE AND SAPPHIC LOVE
Daniel Slater

1 See Elizabeth Colwill, 'Pass as a Woman, Act Like a Man: Marie Antoinette as Tribade in the Pornography of the French Revolution', in Goodman and Kaiser 2003, pp.139–69.

2 See Annie Duprat, 'Une reine traînée dans la boue', in *Marie-Antoinette 2020*, pp.77–82.

3 See Thomas 1999.

4 Elizabeth Colwill, 'Pass as a Woman, Act Like a Man', in Jeffrey Merrick and Bryant T. Ragan (eds) *Homosexuality in Modern France* (Oxford 1996), p.63.

5 Ibid.

6 Ray Davies, 'Lola' (1970).

A QUEEN IN FASHION
Oriole Cullen

1 'Fashion: Couture Report: The Paris Revue', American *Vogue*, vol.179, no.4 (April 1989), p.368.

2 A version of the corset first appeared in Spring/Summer 1986 *Mini-Crini* collection and resolved into its popular form in the following Autumn/Winter collection of 1987–8 *Harris Tweed*. Dubbed the 'Stature of Liberty' corset it first appeared in its most famous version in the *Portrait* collection of Autumn/Winter 1990–1 featuring gold foil straps and a print of François Boucher's 1743 painting *Daphnis and Chloe*.

3 Damon Syson, 'Life Darling, is that Really You?', *The Express* (2 March 1998), p.27.

4 American *Vogue* (1 March 1995), p.425.

5 'Le défilé Chanel croisière 2013 à Versailles', https://www.youtube.com/watch?v=49SiSYi5YWg (accessed 2 October 2024).

6 André Leon Talley, 'Flash: Life With André Garden State', American *Vogue*, vol.202, no.8 (1 August 2012), p.94.

7 Derek C. Blasberg, 'Very Versailles: Chanel Cruise 2013 Debuts', *Harper's Bazaar* (14 May 2012), Chanel Cruise 2013 – Chanel Resort Cruise 2013 (harpersbazaar.com) (accessed 9 September 2024).

8 'Fashion: Chanel Cruises into Versailles', *Elle* (15 May 2012), https://www.elle.com/uk/fashion/news/g7004/chanel-cruises-into-versailles/ (accessed 9 September 2024).

9 'SHOWS|Oddities|Chanel Cruise 2012/13', *Vogue Italia*, Marie Antoinette-inspired baroque mood, Chanel Cruise 2012/13 - Vogue.it (accessed 10 September 2024).

10 John Galliano would directly reference *Les incroyables* once again in his *Margiela Artisanal* Autumn/Winter 2016 collection.

11 Alexander Fury and Adela Sabatini, *Dior Catwalk: The Complete Collections* (London 2017).

12 Cathy Horyn, 'Fashion Review, At Versailles: Let Them Wear Cake', *New York Times* (5 July 2007).

13 Fury and Sabatini 2017 (cited note 11).

14 https://www.vogue.com/fashion-shows/spring-2013-ready-to-wear/meadham-kirchhoff (accessed 19 September 2024).

15 Lauren Cochrane, 'Why Meadham Kirchhoff Bewitched the Critics at London Fashion Week', *Guardian* (19 September 2012), https://www.theguardian.com/fashion/fashion-blog/2012/sep/19/meadham-kirchhoff-london-fashion-week (accessed 10 September 2024).

16 Miles Socha, 'Comme des Garçons Fall 2024 Ready to Wear: Anger Management Meets Avant Garde Fashion', *Women's Wear Daily* (3 March 2024), Comme des Garçons Fall 2024 Ready-to-Wear Runway, Fashion Show & Collection Review (wwd.com) (accessed 10 September 2024).

17 Ibid.

18 Julien d'Ys, who also works closely with Rei Kawakubo of Comme des Garçons, is noted for his signature candy-floss style wigs which often evoke a deconstructed 18th-century pouf.

MARIE ANTOINETTE PERFORMED
Harriet Reed

1 Fraser 2001, p.19.

2 James 2021, p.6.

3 Ibid., p.7.

4 'C'est mon ami', by Queen Marie Antoinette, https://oxfordsong.org (accessed 19 August 2024). Translated from the French by Katherine Astbury: 'Si même n'osant rien vous dire / Son regard sait vous attendrir; / Si sans jamais faire rougir, / Sa gaieté fait toujours sourire, / C'est encore lui, / rendez le moi, / J'ai son amour, / il a ma foi.'

5 Jennie Livingston (dir.), *Paris is Burning* (1990).

6 Elizabeth A. Ford and Deborah C. Mitchell, *Royal Portraits in Hollywood: Filming the Lives of Queens* (Lexington 2009), p.135.

7 *Marie Antoinette* (1938) official trailer, https://www.youtube.com (accessed 22 August 2024).

8 Larkin 2019, p.225.

9 Tino Balio, *Grand Design: Hollywood as a Modern Business Enterprise, 1930–1939* (Los Angeles 1995), pp.93–4.

10 Larkin 2019, p.20.

11 Jay Jorgensen, *Edith Head: The Fifty-Year Career of Hollywood's Greatest Costume Designer* (New York 2010), p.217.

12 https://web.archive.org/web/20120503015331/http://www.beyonceonline.com/us/news/video-premiere-i-was-here-live-roseland (accessed 21 August 2024).

13 Constance Grady, 'How Beyonce turned herself into a pop god', *Vox* (15 August 2022), http://www.vox.com (accessed 21 August 2024).

14 'Queer Opulence: How Marie Antoinette Became a Gay Icon', *Sunstroke Magazine* (accessed 27 August 2024).

15 Keaton Bell, '"It Was Like Hosting The Ultimate Party": An Oral History of Sofia Coppola's "Marie Antoinette"', British *Vogue* (30 October 2021), http://www.vogue.co.uk (accessed 25 August 2024).

16 'The Making of Marie Antoinette pt.1/2 (Kirsten Dunst, Jason Schwartzman, Judy Davis, Rose Byrne', https://www.youtube.com (accessed 20 August 2024).

17 https://www.youtube.com/watch?v=tliM2wXKcnI (accessed 23 August 2024).

18 https://www.brightwalldarkroom.com/2021/02/15/notes-on-marie-antoinette-or-the-mtv-sensibilities-of-sofia-coppola/ (accessed 19 August 2024).

19 Naaman Wood and Christopher Booth, *A Critical Companion to Sofia Coppola* (London 2022), p.5.

20 Bell 2021 (cited note 15).

21 Ibid.

22 Pam Cook, 'Portrait of a Lady: Sofia Coppola and Marie Antoinette', *Sight and Sound* (November 2006), republished BFI (accessed 22 August 2024).

23 Stephanie Russo, *The Anachronistic Turn: Historical Fiction, Drama, Film and Television* (London 2023), p.137.

24 Sofia Coppola, *Marie Antoinette: From Screenplay to Film* (New York 2006).

25 'The Making of Marie Antoinette' (cited note 16).

26 Kira Schneider, *Reclaiming Girlishness: Images of Young Women in Contemporary American Cinema* (Berlin 2018), p.4.

27 Carolyn Twersky Winkler, 'The Great's Costume Designer on Dressing Modern Characters in an 18th-Century Setting', *W* magazine (20 February 2024), https://www.wmagazine.com (accessed 26 August 2024).

28 Emma Fraser 'How "The Great" Costume Designer Captures Power and Whimsy', https://backstage.com (accessed 26 August 2024).

29 Seth 2006b, p.37.

LET THEM EAT CAKE
Colin Jones

1 See the excellent survey of Véronique Campion-Vincent and Christine Shojaei Kawan, 'Marie-Antoinette et son célèbre dire', *Annales historiques de la Révolution française*, no.327 (2002), pp.29–56. See p.38 for the first attribution (in 1843). See too the biographies of Marie Antoinette, especially by Antonia Fraser, John Hardman and Evelyne Lever.

2 Jean-Jacques Rousseau, *Les Confessions* (London 1786), vol.2, p.296, as cited in Michael Sonenscher, *Sans-Culottes: An Eighteenth-Century Emblem in the French Revolution* (Princeton 2008), p.23.

3 The variety of definitions of the term 'brioche' may be followed in the historical dictionaries available online at the 'Dictionnaires d'autrefois' site, https://artfl-project.uchicago.edu/content/dictionnaires-dautrefois.

4 Steven L. Kaplan, 'The Famine Plot Persuasion in Eighteenth-Century France', *Transactions of the American Philosophical Society*, vol.72, pt.3 (Philadelphia 1982).

5 Stuart Woolf, 'The *Société de charité maternelle, 1788–1815*', in Jonathan Barry and Colin Jones (eds), *Medicine and Charity before the Welfare State* (London 1991), pp.98–112.

6 See Goodman and Kaiser 2003; and Lynn Hunt (ed.), *Eroticism and the Body Politic* (Baltimore 1991), especially her own essay, 'The Many Bodies of Marie-Antoinette: Political Pornography and the Problem of the Feminine in the French Revolution', pp.108–30.

7 Meredith Martin, *Dairy Queens: The Politics of Pastoral Architecture from Catherine de' Medici to Marie-Antoinette* (Cambridge, MA 2011); and Patrice Higonnet, *La gloire et l'échafaud. Vie et destin de l'architecte de Marie-Antoinette* (Paris 2011), especially pp.83–126.

MADAME TUSSAUDS AND MARIE ANTOINETTE NOIR
Zoe Louca-Richards

1 Known today as Madame Tussauds London, during the late 19th century the attraction was known by the name Madame Tussaud's & Sons.

2 John Theodore Tussaud, *The Romance of Madame Tussaud's* (London 1920), pp.87–8.

3 Marie Tussaud, *Madame Tussaud's Memoirs and Reminiscences of France, forming an Abridged History of the French Revolution*, ed. Francis Hervé (London 1838).

4 For more on the dispelling of the Versailles myth, see Pamela Pilbeam, *Madame Tussaud and the History of Waxworks* (London 2006).

5 The 'death head' of Louis XVI was added at the same time.

6 George Augustus Sala, *Madame Tussaud & Sons Exhibition Catalogue* (London 1893).

7 *Madame Tussaud & Sons Exhibition Catalogue* (London 1853).

8 Historic metals cannot be tested using analytical methods to establish a reliable date of manufacture. Metal was an expensive commodity; when an object reached the end of its lifespan it would be melted, with other similar materials, to form a billet. This new billet would be worked to produce new materials. Unlike modern alloys there would not be a consistent mix of various materials e.g. steel and carbon, foundries would have their own recipes for producing metals with different working properties but it was not an exact science. This mix of metals from various sources along with the slightly different alloys gives too many variables to accurately provide a date. Provenance records are the most reliable source in dating metals of this kind. With thanks to Katrina Redman, Senior Conservator of Metals at the V&A for this information and for sharing her expertise.

9 Sasha Rossman, 'The Antoinette Effect: An Interview with Simon Fujiwara', *Journal18* (December 2019), https://www.journal18.org/4492 (accessed 17 October 2024).

SELECT BIBLIOGRAPHY

À la mode 2021–2
À la mode. L'art de paraître au 18 siècle, exh. cat., Musée d'arts de Nantes (Nantes 2021–2)

Arneth and Geffroy 1874–5
Alfred Ritter von Arneth and Auguste Geffroy (eds), *Correspondance secrète entre Marie-Thérèse et le comte de Mercy-Argenteau: avec les lettres de Marie-Thérèse et de Marie-Antoinette*, 3 vols (Paris 1874–5)

Arnold 2018
Janet Arnold, *Patterns of Fashion 5: The Content, Cut, Construction and Context of Bodies, Stays, Hoops and Rumps, c.1595–1795* (London 2018)

Barbier 2022
Patrick Barbier, *Marie-Antoinette et la musique* (Paris 2022)

Berly 2013
Cécile Berly and Catherine Pégard, *Le Versailles de Marie-Antoinette* (Paris 2013)

Bernier 1986
Olivier Bernier, *Imperial Mother, Royal Daughter: The Correspondence of Marie Antoinette and Maria Theresa* (London 1986)

Blahnik 2015
Manolo Blahnik, *Fleeting Gestures and Obsessions* (New York 2015)

Campan 1988
Jeanne L.H. Campan, *Mémoires de Madame Campan, première femme de chambre de Marie-Antoinette* (Paris 1988, originally published 1822)

Chapman 2007
Martin Chapman, *Marie-Antoinette and the Petit Trianon at Versailles*, exh. cat., Legion of Honor (San Francisco 2007)

Chrisman-Campbell 2015
Kimberly Chrisman-Campbell, *Fashion Victims: Dress at the Court of Louis XVI and Marie-Antoinette* (New Haven and London 2015)

Comment m'habillerai-je? 2024
Comment m'habillerai-je? Se vêtir sous la Révolution française, 1789–1804, exh. cat., Musée de la Révolution française et la Bibliothèque nationale de France (Ghent 2024)

Coppola 2023
Sofia Coppola, *Sofia Coppola Archive, 1999–2023* (London 2023)

Da Vinha 2018
Mathieu da Vinha, *Dans la garde-robe de Marie-Antoinette* (Paris 2018)

De Feydeau 2013
Elisabeth de Feydeau, *From Marie-Antoinette's Garden: An Eighteenth-Century Horticultural Album* (Paris 2013)

De Goncourt 1879
Edmond and Jules de Goncourt, *Histoire de Marie-Antoinette* (Paris 1879)

Delalex 2015
Hélène Delalex, *Un jour avec Marie-Antoinette* (Paris 2015)

Delalex et al. 2016
Hélène Delalex Alexandre Maral and Nicolas Milovanovic, *Marie-Antoinette* (Los Angeles 2016)

Delalex 2021
Hélène Delalex, *Marie-Antoinette. La légèreté et la constance* (Paris 2021)

De Lescure 1867
Mathurin de Lescure, *Les palais de Trianon. Histoire, description, catalogue des objets exposés sous les auspices de Sa Majesté l'Impératrice* (Paris 1867)

Delpierre 1996
Madeleine Delpierre, *Se vêtir au XVIIIe siècle* (Paris 1996)

De Nolhac 1889
Pierre de Nolhac, *La reine Marie-Antoinette* (Paris 1889)

De Nolhac 1929
Pierre de Nolhac, *Autour de la reine* (Paris 1929)

Dion-Tenenbaum 2023
Anne Dion-Tenenbaum (ed.), *Les diamants de la couronne et joyaux des souverains français* (Paris 2023)

D'Oberkirch 1853–4
Henriette d'Oberkirch, *Mémoires de la baronne d'Oberkirch, publiés par le Comte de Montbrison son petit-fils*, 2 vols (Brussels 1853–4)

Fastes de cour 2009
Fastes de cour et cérémonies royales. Le costume de cour en Europe, 1650–1800, exh. cat., Château de Versailles (Paris 2009)

Firmin et al. 2016
Gwenola Firmin, Frédéric Lacaille and Béatrice Sarrazin, *Le Goût de la parure. Portraits du château de Versailles* (Paris 2016)

Ford and Mitchell 2009
Elizabeth A. Ford and Deborah C. Mitchell, *Royal Portraits in Hollywood: Filming the Lives of Queens* (Lexington 2009)

Fraser 2001
Antonia Fraser, *Marie Antoinette: The Journey* (London 2001)

Goetz 2005
Adrien Goetz, *Marie-Antoinette Style* (New York, 2005)

Goodman and Kaiser 2003
Dena Goodman and Thomas E. Kaiser (eds), *Marie-Antoinette: Writings on the Body of a Queen* (London 2003)

Grant 2010
Sarah Grant, *Toiles de Jouy: French Printed Cottons, 1760–1830* (London 2010)

Grant 2019
Sarah Grant, *Female Portraiture and Patronage in Marie Antoinette's Court: The Princesse de Lamballe* (New York 2019)

Gril-Mariotte 2015
Aziza Gril-Mariotte, *Les toiles de Jouy: histoire d'un art décoratif, 1760–1821* (Rennes 2015)

Hardman 2019
John Hardman, *Marie-Antoinette: The Making of a French Queen* (New Haven and London 2019)

Holt 1887
Ardern Holt, *Fancy Dresses Described; or, What to Wear at Fancy Balls* (London 1887)

James 2021
Barrington James, *The Musical World of Marie-Antoinette: Opera and Ballet in 18th-Century Paris and Versailles* (Jefferson 2021)

James-Sarazin and Lapasin 2023
Ariane James-Sarazin and Régis Lapasin, *Gazette des atours de Marie-Antoinette. Garde-robe des atours de la reine. Gazette pour l'année 1782* (Paris 2023)

Jones 2003
Colin Jones, *The Great Nation: France from Louis XV to Napoleon* (London 2003)

Lamorlière 1897
Rosalie Lamorlière, *La dernière prison de Marie-Antoinette* (Paris 1897)

Larkin 2019
T. Lawrence Larkin, *In Search of Marie-Antoinette in the 1930s: Stefan Zweig, Irving Thalberg, and Norma Shearer* (London 2019)

La Tour du Pin 1913
Henriette-Lucy de La Tour du Pin, *Journal d'une femme de cinquante ans, 1778–1815* (Paris 1913)

Le Bras-Chauvot 2020
Sylvie Le Bras-Chauvot, *Marie-Antoinette l'affranchie. Portrait inédit d'une icône de mode* (Paris 2020)

Le coton et la mode 2000
Le coton et la mode. 1000 ans d'aventures, exh. cat., Palais Galliera (Paris 2000)

Marie-Antoinette 2008
Marie-Antoinette. Album de l'exposition, exh. cat., Grand Palais (Paris 2008)

Marie-Antoinette 2020
Marie-Antoinette. Métamorphoses d'une image, exh. cat., Conciergerie (Paris 2020)

Modes et révolutions 1989
Modes et révolutions, 1780–1804, exh. cat., Palais Galliera
(Paris 1989)

North 2018
Susan North, *18th-Century Fashion in Detail*
(London 2018)

Revolution in Fashion 1989
Revolution in Fashion, 1715–1815, exh. cat., Kyoto
Costume Institute (Kyoto 1989)

Ribeiro 1988
Aileen Ribeiro, *Fashion in the French Revolution*
(London 1988)

Roche 2008
Daniel Roche, *The Culture of Clothing: Dress and Fashion
in the Ancien Régime* (Cambridge 2008, revised edition)

Salomé and Bonnotte 2019
Laurent Salomé and Claire Bonnotte (eds), *Versailles
Revival, 1867–1937*, exh. cat., Château de Versailles
(Paris 2019)

Séduction et Pouvoir 2023
*Séduction et Pouvoir. L'art de s'apprêter à la cour aux
XVIIe et XVIIIe siècles*, exh. cat., Musée du Domaine
Royal de Marly (Paris 2023)

Seth 2006a
Catriona Seth, *Marie-Antoinette. Anthologie et
dictionnaire* (Paris 2006)

Seth 2006b
Catriona Seth, *Marie-Antoinette. Femme réelle, femme
mythique* (Paris 2006)

Seth 2019
Catriona Seth (ed.), *Marie-Antoinette. Lettres inédites*
(Paris 2019)

Söderhjelm 1930
Alma Söderhjelm, *Fersen et Marie-Antoinette.
Correspondance et journal intime inédits du comte Axel de
Fersen* (Paris 1930)

Thomas 1999
Chantal Thomas, *The Wicked Queen: The Origins of the
Myth of Marie-Antoinette* (New York 1999)

Trey 2014
Juliette Trey, *La mode à la cour de Marie-Antoinette*
(Paris 2014)

Van Cleave 2023
Kendra Van Cleave, *Dressing à la Turque: Ottoman
Influence on French Fashion, 1670–1800* (Kent 2023)

Vigée Le Brun 1869
Élisabeth Vigée Le Brun, *Souvenirs de Madame Vigée Le
Brun* (Paris 1869)

Volmert and Bucher 2019
Miriam Volmert and Danijela Bucher (eds), *European
Fans in the 17th and 18th Centuries: Images, Accessories,
and Instruments of Gesture* (Berlin and Boston 2019)

Weber 2007
Caroline Weber, *Queen of Fashion: What Marie Antoinette
Wore to the Revolution* (London 2007)

Wrigley 2002
Richard Wrigley, *The Politics of Appearances:
Representations of Dress in Revolutionary France*
(Oxford 2002)

Zweig 1933
Stefan Zweig, *Marie Antoinette: The Portrait of an
Average Woman*, trans. Eden and Cedar Paul
(New York 1933)

PICTURE CREDITS

ACKNOWLEDGEMENTS

The idea for this exhibition first arose in 2017 and with its development over such an extended period there are many people to thank. I begin by thanking Helena Cox, Exhibition Research Assistant for *Marie Antoinette Style*, my wonderful colleague whose enthusiasm for all things Marie Antoinette matches my own and who has given so much to this project. I thank Daniel Slater for his guidance and expertise and for believing in the exhibition.

Across the V&A, many colleagues have been instrumental in bringing both the exhibition and publication to life. Heartfelt thanks in particular go of course to the Exhibitions team: Vanessa North for her wisdom and experience, and similarly to Sarah Scott, Anna Fletcher, Briony Smith, Isabella Eggert and Belén Lasheras Díaz. In the Art, Architecture, Photography and Design department, special thanks go to Christopher Turner for his advice, support and expertise. I also thank Jenny Gaschke, Martin Barnes, Marta Weiss, Juliet Ceresole and Ruth Hibbard. In the Performance, Furniture, Textiles and Fashion department, sincere thanks go to Susan North for her collegial generosity and scholarly contributions. As a great expert in this field her input has been invaluable and I am very grateful to her. Warm thanks also go to Oriole Cullen for her insights and support. More widely in the Performance, Furniture, Textiles and Fashion department I thank Christopher Wilk, Jenny Lister and Jenny Saunt; in Decorative Art and Sculpture I warmly thank Alice Minter for according us the benefit of her considerable expertise. Thanks also go to James Robinson, Reino Liefkes, Simon Spier and Helen Molesworth; Anna Jackson; Evonne Mackenzie; Catherine Yvard and Joanna Norman; Muriel Bryans, Rachel Flaxman and Emilie Foyer; Jane Lawson, Katie Bruce, Bethan Korausch and Beatrice Fenton; Hannah Kingwell and Holly Hyams; Callum Walker and Shannon Nash; Melissa Buron and Clare Inglis. Special thanks also go to Antonia Boström, Linda Lloyd-Jones and Julius Bryant for their support in the early stages of the project.

The work of colleagues in the Conservation department has naturally been integral to this project and special thanks go to: Sophie Croft and Louise Egan; Textile Conservation: Lara Flecker, Hannah Sutherland, Lauren Quinn, Elizabeth-Anne Haldane, Jessica Abel and Pedro Gaspar; Paper and Book Conservation: Susan Catcher, Jackie Coppen and Barbara Borghese; Science: María Ecénarro and Lucia Burgio; Metal: Katrina Redman; Furniture: Zoe Allen; Paintings: Nina Jimenez Gray; Frames: Yuki Barrow; Sculpture: Kasia Weglowska; Ceramics: Johanna Puisto; Preventative Conservation: Sarah VanSnick.

I am indebted to the vision and expertise of the Publishing team: Tom Windross, Coralie Hepburn, Emma Woodiwiss and Andrew Tullis. I owe a special debt of thanks to the brilliant Kirstin Beattie, with whom it has been a joy to collaborate. The book's beautiful design is thanks to Daniela Rocha. Grateful thanks go to the contributing authors: Lesley Ellis Miller, Vincent Meylan, Silvija Banić, Jessica Harpley, Catriona Seth, Alison McQueen, Harriet Reed, Colin Jones and Zoe Louca-Richards. Thanks to Lindsay Porter, who translated two of the essays in this publication. And for his beautiful photography thanks also goes to Kieron Boyle.

For their many talents in exhibition design, graphics and lighting, I acknowledge OMMX: Hikaru Nissanke and Zeena Ismail; Kellenberger–White: Sebastian White, Eva Kellenberger and Sohee Kim; Flemming Associates: SorLan Tan and Keith Flemming.

I am extremely grateful to the many institutions, private collectors, artists and fashion houses whose generous loans have made this exhibition possible. First and foremost, I thank colleagues at the Musée national des châteaux de Versailles et de Trianon for their profound generosity and support. I warmly thank: Laurent Salomé, Frédéric Lacaille, Hélène Delalex, Bertrand Rondot, Olivier Delahaye, Violaine Solari, Paul Chaine, Morgane Bertho, Florence Caillieret and Erwan Longo.

Special thanks also go to: Lady Antonia Fraser, Sofia Coppola, Bumble Ward, Lisa Antonecchia, Beth Katleman, Tim Walker, Robert Polidori, Victor Glemaud, Richard Mansell-Jones and to Olivier Bihel at Le Bristol, Paris, Oetker Collection.

Thanks go to all other lenders: Hélène Alexander and Mary Kitson at the Fan Museum; Lieve Beumer at the Flowers Gallery; Hugo Chapman at the British Museum; Eleanor Summers at the Bath Fashion Museum; Beatrice Behlen, Flora Ryles and Kate Riggs at the London Museum; Rachel Whitworth at the Bowes Museum; Lauren Porter, Emma Stuart, and Kathryn Jones at the Royal Collection; Dr Xavier Bray at the Wallace Collection; Matthew Winterbottom at the Ashmolean; Catherine Angerson at the British Library; Fiona Campbell at the Lady Lever Gallery; Alec Cobbe, Hatchlands Park, Cobbe Collection; Charlotte McReynolds at the National Museums Northern Ireland; Kirsten Toftegaard at the Designmuseum Danmark; Sofia Nestor at the Livrustkammaren, Stockholm; Aaron Wile at National Gallery of Art, Washington; Clarissa M. Esguerra at LACMA; Dr Rolf H. Johannsen and Dr Alena Volk at the Heidi Horten Collection; Pascale Gorguet Ballesteros at Galliera, Paris; Anne Zazzo at Musée Carnavalet, Paris; Pierre Gandil at the Bibliothèque municipale de Châlons-en-Champagne; Viviane Mesqui at Sèvres – Manufacture et Musée nationaux; Nathalie Coilly at the Bibliothèque nationale de France; Anne Forray-Carlier and Anne Dion at the Musée du Louvre; Camille Moreau at the Musée de la Toile de Jouy; Pierre Jugie at the Archives nationales de France, Paris.

I am enormously grateful to Manolo Blahnik – Mr Blahnik, Kristina Blahnik, Jodie Blake, Chris Massingham, Charlotte Moss and Holly Roberts; The One Costumes – Alessandra Cinti; Milena Canonero; Fred Leighton – Rebecca Selva; Chanel – Sarah Piettre and Odile Premel; Andrea Grossi; Erdem – Erdem Moralioglu; Valentino – Alessandro Michele and Violante Valdettaro; Meadham Kirchhoff – Edward Meadham; Dior – Perrine Scherrer; Vivienne Westwood – Andreas Kronthaler and Eleanor Boyce; Moschino – Adrian Appiolaza, Theo Katsaros and Sugar Ansari; Fenty – Rihanna and Jennifer O. Hill; Marmalade, Oliver Williams; Sharon Long; Zita Brack; Kristen Kuroski; Khadija Brockington.

Finally, I am deeply grateful to the specialists in their respective fields who have so generously shared their knowledge: Andres White Correal, Emily Barber and Clarisse Mariotti at Sotheby's; Adrian Hume-Sayer, Benedict Winter and Keith Gill at Christie's; Alexandre de La Forest Divonne at Coutau-Bégarie. And to my own little Versaillaise, Adelaide Elizabeth Flora Haigh.

INDEX

Illustrations are indicated by *italic* page numbers.
MA refers to Marie Antoinette.